LAND OF SHA1

Judy Vowles

With thanks to my wonderful husband, John, who slipped away to be with his Lord before this book was completed.

I thank our Lord who gave me the opportunity to share John's life and his love for his beloved Zimbabwe, its people and its wildlife. For the insight I gained and the truths I learned about the spiritual life in this beautiful country, and for the guidance, teaching and protection of the Holy Spirit. It is my prayer that those who read this book, for whatever reason, will see something of themselves in its pages and in some small way be helped by it.

In the context of this book, 'African' refers to those amongst whom we lived, worked and knew. It does not mean that the beliefs, customs and attitudes described relate to everyone in Africa!

LAND OF SHADOWS

PROLOGUE

The cockerel's crow cut through the pre-dawn blackness of a Devon February morning, wringing a truly negative remark from my slumbering husband. Our little old mobile home perched insignificantly on top of a Dartmoor hill, and was dwarfed by the big Dutch barn in the lea of which it nestled and from which the cockerel crowed. Its thin walls were neither water nor sound proof, and the constant drip of rain seeping through the roof and plopping into the many bowls and buckets had kept sleep to that shallow level that leaves one a little more tired each day until the sleep of exhaustion takes over. It had rained it seemed, for weeks. But at least it was calm now, and the hurricanes which had threatened to tear our home up by its wired down roots and fling us into the valley had gone to wreak havoc in some other part of England.

We had just finished lambing our two hundred ewes, and it was a truly desolate affair. We had been on our farm for just over a year. John and I had married ten years earlier, when he had sadly left his native Africa to start a new life in England. Our resolution then had been to own, one day, a piece of land to farm and from day one we had worked towards our dream. A year ago it had happened. Forty four acres of gently sloping pasture land with breathtaking, panoramic views over Dartmoor and out to Exmoor had become ours. It was the most beautiful, beautiful place with the loveliest of neighbours and everything we had ever wanted. It had no house, of course, but that was a detail. With the blessing of the locals we moved our ramshackle old caravan for its last time, wired it down securely against wind and weather and put down our roots alongside. We had found our dream.

Our sheep had lambed soon after we moved onto the place, and their lambs did fairly well but not brilliantly. We knew our husbandry was good and after introducing a system of small pastures, moving the sheep quickly over the ground, the ewes blossomed. Then this terrible weather had hit us and everything had gone wrong. Our sheep had lost condition rapidly and one or two had died. We followed our veterinary advice to the letter, but still they died. In their weakened condition, heavily in lamb, they fell before the icy rain and 100 m.p.h winds which swept the open hillsides. Then someone in the village ventured an opinion. The ground had previously been rented to a dealer, they told us, and this unworthy and unscrupulous man had packed over a thousand sheep onto the place. Many had died, there had been little supervision, the ewe subsidy and the wool clip had been collected and the survivors sold on. Our farm was totally sheep sick. We had talked to the vets and they had agreed, the answer was to keep sheep off the ground for at least seven or eight years. Our dream had crumbled.

Now the cockerel, like some deafening repeater alarm that you couldn't switch off, made staying in bed only marginally better than getting up, and I pushed my feet wearily onto the cold, damp floor to face another day.

I loved lambing, but this year was heartbreaking. Those lambs born alive were weak and their mothers rejected them. Those born strong had taken a toll on their mothers and the ewes had no milk. It was like a battleground and there was nothing anyone could do about it. I made us a cup of tea each and went back for a few brief moments under the cosy duvet, putting off the discovery of the new disasters which assailed us daily. Later that morning, my heart full, my direction gone, I wandered down to the gate to our post-box, to collect the usual array of brown window envelopes. Range upon range of hills stretched out on all sides of me, some lost in the winter mist, but I knew they were there. I stopped and gazed for a while. Our beautiful dream had become a hideous nightmare and I didn't understand why.

When John and I had married I had a real dream, which I had always believed had been sent by God. In that dream we stood together looking out across a heaving mass of a dark city to beyond, where stood a sheer cliff. At the top of the cliff we could see a beautiful place, trees, mountains, blue skies, green grass - and peace. It called us. Together we went to the base of the cliff. At one end were steps, but they were behind a gate which was barred and locked, impossible to pass. The only way was to climb. The cliff was sheer, but we climbed. At times I was in front, at times John was pulling me, and a few times we both slid but held on. Eventually we were hanging, fingers gripping the edge, exhausted, looking over at this new land. And then, out of nowhere, came a mighty push that took us up over the edge and we were there. My interpretation had been that if we stuck together and helped each other with one goal in mind we would, with God's help, get there. I believed it utterly, and it had been our strength during our long search for our farm. Now we were in a beautiful place, at the top of a very high hill and we had helped each other over a tough and difficult ten year journey. And now!

I opened the box and scooped up the mail. There, like a bright blue flower amongst the brown autumn leaves lay an Airmail letter, postmarked Zimbabwe. Turning it over and over in my hand I walked slowly back to the caravan. There we made some coffee, stoked up the little, smoky wood burner against the cold, and opened our mystery letter. It was from one of John's old friends, who was very successfully running a tobacco farm in the centre of Zimbabwe, and it was an invitation to join him.

"....As you know (he wrote) with our relatively small acreage (1350 acres) the main crop is and, as far as one can foresee, will remain tobacco. However with our water resources there are various other enterprises worth investigating. The first one is cattle and sheep based on irrigated pastures. At present we have 50 cows with first calves - quite nice stock - and a few scraggy sheep. The enterprise needs someone to decide upon a proper programme and then to take control of it. I would propose that to begin with there would be a salary together with accommodation, lights, water, two domestic workers, medical aid and a petrol allowance. A bonus will be payable which should be considerable. There will be a house ready for you by the end of August...."

We looked at each other in silence for a long time. Then John said quietly,

"I think we go, don't you?"

Later that day I took a new look at my dream. Maybe this hadn't been the top of the cliff. Maybe this terrible winter was the push God was giving us. I knew that John was terribly homesick for Zimbabwe, although he had always denied it, so maybe if we were to find peace it would be where his heart really was, in Africa.

Six months later we landed in Harare. .

CHEGUTU

1990 - 1992

"He who believes and is baptized will be saved" *(Matthew 16 v 16)*

"I will never leave you nor forsake you" *(Hebrews 13 v 5)*

CHAPTER ONE

Orbit stood at the gate of the night kraal, his ex-army boot lodged firmly against the bottom of the wire mesh gate, the gate slightly ajar. The boots fitted snugly and were buckled up past his ankles, but beneath the strong uppers his pink toes peeped shyly out. The flock of Dorper sheep, anxious to go out to pasture after their night in the barren, sandy enclosure, jostled each other towards the gap, glancing first at the open gate and then up at Orbit. The African's expression was one of deep concentration below the pink cotton rim of his crownless hat, and as he leaned on the gate one long arm moved rhythmically back and forth touching each sheep on the head as it passed through, his lips counting soundlessly. It was part of the daily routine, but some still resented his touch and dashed through almost on their bellies to avoid it. Others lingered, sniffing the outstretched hand, then wandered past and came round to stand by me, rubbing their heads against my bare legs, hoping to get their ears scratched as I stood back counting too. Harrison waited in the background for the final figure, for he would be responsible for them during the day, as Orbit the night guard had been from 6:00 the previous evening. The Chinese lantern tree outside the pen, decked with the delicate pink and yellow blossoms that gave it its name, was festooned with graceful, white cattle egrets. They had quickly adapted to becoming sheep egrets, accompanying the flock as it moved out over the wide green pastures, snatching at the insects disturbed by the passing hooves. The last of the group were hanging back, and Orbit opened the gate wider, tempting them to dash through, but they still got an accelerated pat in passing, for Orbit's reasoning was simple - if he had touched it, it was there.

"One-twenty-one," said Orbit, in a tone which denied argument.

I nodded, one-twenty-one it was. The first ones out were already streaming away Indian file along the narrow sandy trail that meandered through the rough brown star grass, burned by the sun and yet to spring into life. The rains were still to come. Beyond, a wide succulent green strip of kikuyu grass marked the line of irrigation from the great river that bordered the farm, and it was on this that Harrison herded them during the day. Fences would eventually take his place but meanwhile labour was plentiful. The sheep grazed where they pleased selecting the best grasses, their chosen plants and browsing the lower branches of the bush trees. When the sun reached its height they migrated back to the cool shade and water of the night paddock. Then Harrison stretched out in the shade and ate his meal, brought to him in a woven basket covered with a snowy crochet work cloth by his wife, walking barefoot and graceful through the bush, the basket on her head. Beyond the kikuyu were the tobacco lands, the main crop of the farm. Block after block of strong green plants on their long, straight ridges, pampered by great sprays of water throughout their short life. And all day long the hot sun looked down from a clear sky, the occasional high, white and wispy cloud accentuating the depth of the blue. It was a lovely time of day, and worlds away from the wind and rain swept Devon smallholding we had left. Harrison Alepha, my assistant shepherd, was a tall, lanky, good humoured young man who permanently wore a huge smile and a red T-shirt. His assistant was Shanghazi, a 'madala' (old man) who viewed me with a certain quiet suspicion until he heard from Harrison that I was attempting to speak Shona. From my first hesitant 'Mangwanani' (Good Morning) his manner changed and I even got the faintest glimmer of a smile.

The grass we had planted in the irrigated pastures was struggling gamely, but a wealth of donkey weed and khaki weed had appeared in appreciation of the irrigation. So Harrison and Shanghazi were each given a 'bemba' to swing at the offending weeds as they followed the flock and we hoped that the sheep would eat the rest when the first flush of grass had been taken.

Orbit, the night guard, was a cheerful, laid back kind of a guy who had been with the army for several years and therefore had some training should he have the occasion to use it, and he came each evening armed with an axe. Although there were leopards on the adjoining farm we knew his most likely raiders would be human, for the temptation of fresh meat was strong, and we knew that the flock could never be left unattended.

"O.K., Harrison?"

"O.K. Missus," he returned my smile and headed after the sheep, Shanghazi trying gamely to outflank them as they headed for the distant strip of bright green amidst the brown.

It was a twenty minute walk home, and at 6.30 the morning sun was already hot, casting dark shadows beside us as Orbit fell into step alongside, casually swinging his axe.

"You have more clothes coming?" he enquired conversationally.

From someone dressed in a buttonless shirt, patched shorts with torn patches and a hat with no crown it seemed rather a strange question. Admittedly I had packed for four weeks and was now into my fourth month, but I still felt I looked tidy.

"Clothes?"

"From England," said Orbit, "all your clothes."

Belongings, I thought,

"You mean 'pasha'?"

He grinned. "Ah," he feigned amazement at my brilliant control of the language, "You know Shona too much!"

I nodded; we did have some things to come. We had sold the farm eventually with very little left over after paying our debts. It had been a very depressed market when we had sold our surviving sheep, and land prices were also beginning to drop, so we had actually done well to cover our costs. We bought our air tickets and the rest had gone on a container so that we could bring our Suzuki jeep and all our tools with us. Had we know the state of the market in Zimbabwe we would have also crammed in the few pieces of agricultural machinery that we had, for they were just about impossible to get unless one had foreign currency to purchase outside the country. So we had more or less given away our old outdated mower and hay turner, to find that here they were like gold dust.

At the gates of our bungalow Orbit and I parted company and I went in to get breakfast ready. It wasn't a fancy bungalow. It was oblong, with walls made of home-made bricks and a corrugated iron roof, and set on the edge of a section of unclaimed bush land between the compound, where the farm workers had their own thatched, mud walled huts, and the burial ground. It had a big veranda which still had grenade guards on the windows left over from the war, an L-shaped lounge/diner, a kitchen without cupboards, shelves or working surfaces, an office, two bedrooms, and a bathroom with a limitless supply of hot water. After our old mobile home it was a real luxury to just have more than one room, and the bathroom was sheer bliss. In Devon we had used the old dairy as a bathroom. A wash-boiler and a hosepipe had proved the hot and cold water, and the 'bath' was a stainless steel free-standing sink in which, I had discovered, I could actually sit. The ambient temperature in winter had often dropped below zero, but there is no substitute for actually sitting in hot water and I had folded myself up into the sink with great determination and to much amusement from my husband. The dairy had been more than a hundred yards from the mobile home, and I had been a little worried that I might, one evening, become stuck and be found frozen into a cube, but it had never happened.

The bungalow stood in a garden of about two acres, within a high security fence. Lack of water had reduced the garden to a sandy desert. The lawns were brown, wiry roots devoid of leaf, around which a few Cannas and flowering weeds had survived. The weeds closed and wilted sadly throughout the day, but opened with a blaze of red and yellow blossoms in the evenings. We had a wealth of lovely old trees, though, and had started a vegetable garden. Neither John nor I had ever professed to be gardeners, but I looked forward to planning this one for, as promised, Fred had provided us with both a house girl and a gardener.

Tendai, a young Malawian girl took care of the washing, ironing and household chores while I still did the cooking. Misheck was our groom/gardener, as yet without a horse to groom but not for long. Horses were at the top of our shopping list.

We had arrived on the farm on the first day of planting tobacco. It had taken John a while to find his feet again learning Fred's methods, but it had taken him no time at all to lapse back into the strange mixture of Shona and other local dialects that he had spoken since birth. But although he conversed easily with all the locals I was told that I should learn pure Shona, and Tendai and Misheck were having an uphill battle teaching me. This may have had something to do with the fact that they were both Malawian! We had quickly got into a routine. John would go off to his mombies (cattle) or the tobacco barns while I checked the sheep and then we would come back to breakfast and plan the rest of our day.

John's motor bike could be heard in the distance as I finished setting the table with what had become our usual breakfast of chilled pawpaw, mealie-meal porridge with peanut butter and coffee. He arrived a few minutes later, covered with a film of fine sand from the top of his grey-gold hair to his sandaled feet. His T-shirt bore the slogan "Choose Life," which was a bit of a paradox when he was aboard the motorbike - but he was beginning to get the hang of it again now. The scars on his legs from the hot exhaust pipe had healed nicely, and the deep sand made for soft landings. It also grabbed the wheels now and again when he was least expecting it and had been the cause of the odd minor spill or two.

"Sheep on Thursday," announced my husband, heading for the bathroom.

I followed him.

"What sheep?"

"Fred is going to buy some more sheep. He's found some at Norton and so we'll go and look them over on Thursday morning and the lorry can go and pick them up the same day. "He dried his hands,

"Coffee?"

I fetched the coffee and the chilled paw-paw from the 'fridge

"So, how many sheep and what sort?"

"Dorpers, about 150 I think, so that will bring you up to near the 300 Fred wants."

"Wonderful."

In fact it was quite overwhelming. We had saved for our own flock practically sheep by sheep, and carried them home in Renault 4 load batches. To go and choose 150 and have them delivered was beyond my experience so far. John guided a heaped spoonful of sugar towards his coffee cup and then, remembering his new resolution, tipped in half and put the rest back in the bowl. He stirred vigorously so as not to waste any.

"And the Vet is coming tomorrow to vasectomize the teasers, so you had better sort out a surplus ram."

"I've sorted one. He's really ugly and a bully - he'll make a good teaser."

"It's a good job Fred kept that Simmental X bull," said John," he's ideal."

The Simmental had been the first calf born on the farm, a stocky fine-looking baby that had grown into a mediocre two year old.

"No way do we want him for a bull," declared John," but since Fred's so fond of him I'm glad we can provide him with a career."

It was all starting to take shape. John in charge of his beloved mombies and me looking after the sheep. A whole new beginning together. Could this perhaps be the top of the cliff in my dream?

Early next morning, with the help of Sadina who looked after the house cows, Kenyemba, Fred's gardener, and Misheck, we cornered the flock of rams and caught the proposed teaser. For those who have no reason to know of such things, a teaser is put out with the breeding flock, or herd as the case may be, and since it is vasectomized (not neutered) it will behave as an entire. He will convince the ladies in his life that he is the only one in the world for them, and they will obligingly come into season. Two weeks later he is taken away and replaced by a fertile male. The teaser has already done the ground work, as it were, and the new male finds a queue of females trying to attract his attention. So at the other end of the season when the lambs, or calves, are born the births are close together over a matter of a few weeks, making management much easier and more efficient.

The rumour that we were going to vasectomize a bull and a ram rippled through the workforce. That such a thing had even been considered met with surprise tinged with a fair amount of curiosity. The vet arrived at the appointed time, a tired looking, middle aged white man, with a quiet voice and a kind of detached air about him. His helper, an equally quiet and careful African, busied himself setting out instruments, prepared a disinfectant wash and filled syringes. We had penned the ram in some old dog kennels in Fred's garden, and there in the shade of a huge avocado tree he was flipped onto his side and rendered immobile by Kenyemba sitting on his head. A local anaesthetic was given, and whilst it was taking effect the African produced a single razor blade and holding it deftly between his fingers he shaved wool from the target area. The operation was soon over. Amidst incredulous exclamations from our little team the cords were found and severed and the wound neatly stitched. The ram scrambled to his feet, no longer a bully with an attitude problem.

Meanwhile the Simmental had been lured into a pen next to the cattle dip and was standing there patiently with the dairy bull. Sadina and Kenyemba went ahead and by the time we got there they had got him into the cattle crush. The Vet decided that it would be best to put him right out, so his assistant smacked a syringe full of dope smartly into his rump and we opened the gate and let him out. Within a few minutes he was lurpsing around drunkenly in circles, and then wisely decided to lie down before he fell down, breathing heavily and hazily watching us watching him. A few seconds more and he was out. I pushed a sack under his head to protect the eye that was on the ground and the vet's assistant looped a rawhide rope around one back leg and pulled it forward. He gave the end to two willing helpers with instructions in Shona to pull it tight and hold on. Then, putting himself in a very vulnerable position behind the roped leg he produced the razor blade again and started shaving. By this time two more had joined the team, and there were four men on the rope as well as Mishek on the head and Kenyemba sitting on the front legs. As the scalpel came into play all heads craned forwards once more. One of the men from the tobacco seed beds nearby wandered over and another came past from the barns, and these two both joined on the end of the rope and watched in silence. This time the cord proved to be fairly elusive and much probing ensued, whilst tension mounted on the faces of the onlookers. There were now ten people around the slumbering bull, five of them holding limply onto a completely slack rope. The cord was finally located and given the same treatment as before.

Soon it was all finished and the African assistant untied the rope and started to pack things away in the boot of the car. The bull came round, struggled into a standing position and stood with a leg in each corner and a "Where am I?" expression in his eyes.

"You can use him in about three weeks, " said the vet, "Take the stitches out in a week's time."

He gave us a brief, humourless smile, started his car and drove away. John and I looked at each other.

"Friendly sort," muttered my husband.

"Not a lot of charisma," I agreed.

CHAPTER TWO

Mornings started well before five. Down in the little village of thatched round mud huts where the workers lived with their families, Chiringwe the foreman started to bang the 'simbi', a metal gong that called everyone from sleep. Soon after, if response was slow, we would hear his "Enda, enda, enda, enda........." echoing across the fields from the banks of the river, "Go, go, go, go....". A little later the voices of the men were heard coming up the track which passed our bungalow on their way to the yards. Here they congregated until orders for the day were given and then irrigation teams, reaping teams, weeding teams, a steady stream of people dispersed on foot, tractors and trailers and in the backs of pickups to various parts of the farm.

John had already crashed around the kitchen making morning tea, but somehow I rarely woke until I was actually sitting up with a mug in my hand. Then he was gone, the sound of his motor bike following after the voices of the Africans, calling and laughing and shouting to each other.

I still had time for a cool bath before my walk out to the sheep pens, for it was already warm under the iron roof of our bungalow and little air moved through the wide open windows. I was pleased I had chosen a cotton caftan as a gown, and the waxed concrete floors were cool and welcoming to my bare feet. I had a leisurely bath and wandered back to the bedroom to find something cool to wear. As I did so something sort of crunched under my right foot. It felt like a soft twig or maybe a piece of the mosquito coil which we burnt each evening and tended to shatter easily. I lifted my sweeping gown and looked around, but there was nothing there. I had found cotton slacks and shirt and had half closed the drawer when I spotted a crumpled heap at the side of the bed. There on its back, eight legs thrown out in one final gesture, lay a huge spider. Then the terrible, shocking, repulsive truth hit me. I had swept it along under my flowing gown and trodden on it with my bare feet. I leapt onto the bed and crouched there, staring at it, tears of horror in my eyes, my fists clenched knuckle white as I fought down the panic that made me want to scream. A senseless loathing made my flesh creep. If a cobra had found its way through the waste pipe and into the shower I could have handled the situation calmly. The lizards that flashed up the walls as I passed, I enjoyed. The vicious looking hornets that buzzed me around the kitchen, I ignored. But spiders! A spider was the one creature in this world that could send all reason straight out of the window. My phobia only extended to spiders inside, outside with the earth beneath my feet and the sky above, a spider was just another of God's creatures about its daily business. Inside, a spider could paralyze me. It could zip open a jagged path through my realms of reason to the very centre of my being, leaving a tangled trail of nerve endings jangling uncontrollably against each other. I could still feel the scrunching sensation under the ball of my right foot and my toes curled convulsively. Wrapping my skirts tightly around me well clear of the floor, I edged cautiously around the body, for fear it could be feigning death. I guess a spider that survived sixty kilos on its head would merit caution. In the bathroom I ran a few inches of warm water into the bath and sitting on the edge put both feet in and scrubbed them hard with the nail brush, trying to rid my foot of that awful imaginary tingle. Marshalling my thoughts into some sort of calm, sensible order I dressed, got the long handled broom and swept the body, even more grotesque and vile in its mangled state, along the shining concrete corridor, through the kitchen and out of the door.

"Mmm," said John disinterestedly, when I took him to view the body at breakfast time, "that's a rain spider, we get lots of them about this time of the year, they're quite harmless, you'll get used to them."

He was quite wrong. As the build up towards the rains went on the rain-spiders became more and more of a problem. I steeled myself to ignore them when they appeared each evening, skittering across the slippery uncarpeted floors. I buried myself in a book, put my feet carefully up on the edge of the coffee table, and tried to switch off. I developed a sixth sense and, interesting as my book might be, the slightest movement across the floor would register in my sub-conscious, and a glance would tell me whether it was friend or foe. Geckos climbed the walls on their suction padded little feet, beetles the size of a matchbox, mosquitoes, praying mantis, moths and huge ants found their way effortlessly through the old, worn out fly screens and joined us for our evening meal. All were welcome, but going out to the kitchen for another cup of coffee I would scan every inch of the way. The evening I met one in the kitchen doorway and wordlessly stepped over it, I thought I had won. Then coming back from the tobacco lands late one night, having been out with John to switch off the irrigation pumps on the river, I opened the door to find a spider about five inches long sitting on the door post. I jumped past it, and it jumped with me. We landed side by side half way across the lounge, and I beat it easily to the kitchen. I watched round the corner of the passage to see which way it went.

John had put the truck away and came in whistling. He nodded briefly,

"I saw the leap."

"It's huge," I defended myself quickly; "It's gone towards the fireplace."

"Shut the passage door," suggested my husband, "Keep him down this end of the house."

There was a two inch gap under the passage door.

"That won't keep him out," I was in no mood for argument. If it was loose in the house it could come into the bedroom, and if I found that in bed with me I really would go off my head.

"I'm sorry, but it's got to go, they're not an endangered species."

"They are in this house," muttered John, and a few moments later I heard a series of loud swats coming from various parts of the lounge. I felt momentarily ashamed. I knew it was wrong to kill something harmless. It was just unfortunate that it had the power to make my heart stop, but reason didn't come into the matter.

So my sixth sense developed into an automatic scanning device. I was always aware of the likelihood of their presence, and would take in at a glance the emptiness or otherwise of any room that I entered. There was no doubt about it, I had a problem. Perhaps the Lord would take the phobia away from me. How could I live in Africa if I was going to be so pathetic?

It was just two weeks after meeting the five inch monster that I made my way sleepily out to the kitchen with the tea tray around five thirty a.m. The teapot dregs went into Mishek's new compost system and with pot in hand I pushed open the back door. In the corner of the small porch, less than three feet away, a dark sinuous shape quickly coiled itself and struck in my direction. It was incredibly fast, but I was trained. I slammed the door, carefully put down the teapot and thoughtfully scratched my head. I went out of the front door and looked around. There were a few people way down the track out of earshot so I went to look for Mishek who, I knew, would be busy sorting out the shed that was going to be stables for our horses. Mishek always reminded me of a gerkha, and was coming across the paddock at his usual double time pace.

"Good morning, Mishek."

"Good morning, Medem."

"Mishek, there is a snake in the back porch."

He looked blank.

"A snake, Mishek."

"Ah, yes Medem," recognition of the word dawned, "Where is snek?"

"On the back porch, can you.....?" I made a hitting motion with my hand.

"Yes, Medem," Mishek nodded quickly, and picked up a heavy stick. Fred had the same policy about snakes in the gardens as I had about spiders in the house. Most of them were deadly, and there was no snake bite serum in Zimbabwe.

"Big snek?" enquired Mishek, casually, as he marched away in front of me.

"No, not very big. About five feet long."

Two madalas met us on the track, the news was passed to them in rapid Shona, and they fell in behind Mishek and his big stick. At the side of the house Mishek slowed and looked back at me.

"Where is snek?"

"It was just inside the porch."

He advanced, stick in hand, and peered cautiously round the corner.

"Aiee!" hissed Mishek, jumping swiftly back and handing the stick to the old man behind him. This brave man, suddenly promoted from onlooker to centre stage, reached around the door post and delivered a heavy blow, following it up with a series of quick stabs with the end of the stick. Then he bent, grabbed the twitching tail and marched off with a triumphant grin, trailing the corpse behind him.

"What kind of snake, Mishek?"

"Mamba," he replied, "Black Mamba."

Well, the Lord works in mysterious ways. How often recently had I questioned His wisdom in building into me the overpowering spider phobia? In a few short weeks He had installed into my system a kind of automatic radar that could only be to my advantage. Outside, snakes would usually move away when they heard you, outside I didn't mind spiders. Inside, snakes were on the defensive, and so was I!

"I don't expect they knew what it was," said John when I told him my story at breakfast time. "They tend to call them all Mambas. Let's face it, it doesn't really matter to them, because if they get bitten they are dead pretty soon afterwards."

It was probably a fact. Medical aid was very basic in the rural areas, and transport even more so. You don't get far on a bicycle or in a wheelbarrow after you've been bitten by a Cobra, and you could die from old age just waiting for the ambulance station to answer the 'phone.

Our new sheep had arrived. We had been to inspect them at Norton the previous week, leaving 'at sparrow' as Fred called it, soon after the 'simbi' had sounded. As we had left the rest of the farm had been up and moving too, a stream of people chattering loudly made their way up from the village, past our gates and out to the fields beyond. Children, the boys in grey cotton shorts and shirts, the girls in dark green pinafore dresses, ran barefoot on their way to the mission school, hoping for a lift on a tractor trailer or in the back of a pickup for at least part of their five mile journey. Women in sleeveless tops, brightly coloured cloth skirts wrapped around and tucked in place, babies on their backs in casually tied blankets, moved gracefully past balancing impossible loads and shapes on their heads, on their way to who knew where.

We drove past Harrison and Shanghazi, moving out from the night paddock with the sheep running eagerly ahead of them and the egrets flocking after them, and returned their waves. Out of the farm and onto the narrow strip of tarred road that led into Chegutu. Just before we reached the outskirts the road gave way abruptly to sand and gravel again, and we bumped across the ruts and potholes raising a cloud of dust in our wake. Women were already working in the poor soils edging the road, swinging badzas at the weeds invading their parched plots of maize. Still more children, running to school barefoot with their shoes tied together by the laces and balanced upon their heads. As we lurched back onto the tar road on the edge of town we passed more women, large enamel bowls on their heads carrying fruit, vegetables and eggs to sell from the pavements. A tractor and trailer under a roadside tree held chickens, sold live for the table, bought and carried casually away by the wings. We drove over a level crossing, looking very carefully both ways, and finally out onto the wide, straight road to Harare. There was little traffic, for cars were owned by a very small percentage of the population. The buses, packed past capacity, swept along these open highways at frightening speeds, belching out clouds of thick, black smoke on all the hills and at every gear change. When they weren't bearing down on us menacingly they were motionless by the side of the road, the familiar red triangle propped up fore and aft. All the passengers would be sitting around on their luggage, or relieving themselves amongst the sparse bushes or offering advice to the harassed driver or feeding babies. We frequently met overturned lorries and jack-knifed trailers, their loads spilled over the road. The temptation to travel too fast on these good open roads, coupled with the inability to maintain vehicles in good condition through lack of spares, made disasters commonplace.

We had found the farm easily, turning off the main road past brilliantly coloured bougainvillaea and onto a sand track beneath a cool, shady avenue of jacaranda trees. The Estate's head shepherd, his rank clearly defined by a white coat, Wellingtons and a clipboard, had already herded the ewes into a paddock and quickly issued a barrage of orders to his four helpers who were dressed in smart green overalls. The sheep allowed themselves to be shunted slowly towards the mouth of the race, but here they stopped, immovable, immune to waving arms, shouts, threats and the odd shifty kick. The head shepherd marched quickly through his minions, grabbed an empty yellow grain bag and shaking it confidently led the now eager sheep down the narrow passageway where they were trapped for closer inspection. My inspection was fairly broad minded, concerned mainly with missing teeth and missing teats, but several had undershot jaws and there was the odd suspicious looking tumour. The ones we chose seemed good, sound and healthy.

Unlike the cattle lorries used in England, our transport was a heavy lorry fitted with an open topped cage-like back. There was no ramp, and each sheep had to be lifted bodily on board. The driver backed up to the front end of the race, and loading began Zimbabwean style. Head shepherd grabbed the sheep and passed it to two assistants who flipped it on its back. One took the front legs and the other took the back legs and together, usually, they swung it up above the tail board. Here it was grabbed by it's nearest convenient part by another helper who deposited it in the straw, helped it to its feet and chased it to the front of the lorry. Back at Fred's farm the unloading procedure was marginally quicker in reverse, gravity aiding the catcher in the lorry and the main danger seemed to be that those on the ground could be knocked out by a flying sheep.

Our new teaser had been introduced to his ladies, and had instantly reverted to the insufferable bully that he had been before his ordeal with the vet. They had settled in well and Harrison was delighted with his new responsibilities

CHAPTER THREE

It was about this time that a thought kept coming into my mind. 'You must be baptized.'

It was just a quiet little thought, but it persisted and I knew it was one I should listen to. The idea was totally new to me. I had no friends who had been baptized, we didn't go to church and we didn't own a Bible. I didn't understand why I should be baptized, I had been duly christened in the Church of England as a baby and, as far as I knew, I was therefore enrolled into Heaven. But the thought persisted.

A few miles down a hot, dusty track from the farm was in interdenominational bible school for the Africans, so I thought that was probably a very good place to start. I didn't know the people who ran it, but one day on my way back from shopping in Chegutu, with butter and ice-cream melting in the boot, I followed an impulse and turned into their driveway. The track led down between white painted classroom blocks and shady goat pens to an old style farmhouse where the principle, John Valentine, lived with his wife Celia.

Celia answered my knock, and looked a little taken aback by this strange white woman who announced, without preamble,

"Hi, can you help me? I want to be baptized, please."

I was quickly introduced to her husband, and I repeated my request.

"Well," he grinned, "There's a bit more to it than that, you know!"

They held two church meetings on Sundays, he told me, one in English in the Scout hut in Chegutu, and one in Shona at the Bible school. He suggested I go along and join them for a week or two and see how I got on. And so I began to attend their Chegutu services. People came from all directions, on foot, by car, by tractor, on bicycles. There were very few white faces, and the service was literally worlds away from the occasional Anglican 'prayer book service' I had sat through in my childhood in England! Here the wonderful African singing in completely unrehearsed harmony threatened to take the roof off, and the Lord was praised in Shona, English and Tongues. I had never been part of such wonderful, happy and abandoned worship! Sundays couldn't come around soon enough, and I came away feeling deeply moved every time.

Meanwhile, back on the farm, Mishek and I were busy preparing the paddock for our new horses. Sally and Patrick were friends from the old days, when John had played the occasional game of polo. Hearing that John was back they had immediately guessed that he would want horses and had offered us two from their string of polo ponies at a ridiculously low price. They were half-brothers, by a thoroughbred stallion and both had taken after their father. One mare had been called Imp, and all her offspring had been named after the 'little people'. The one coming to us was called Leprechaun. The other one had been named Jack by a friend, and was going to be re-named as soon as I could think of something nice and before John got too used to calling him the Jackass! Leprechaun was seven and well schooled, Jack was just three with everything to learn. The paddock near our bungalow had originally been fenced off for the dairy mombies using the usual barbed wire and metal stakes, all well rusted and thoroughly dangerous. In England we would never have considered putting horses behind such a barrier, but here we had no option and could only do our best to make it as safe as possible. So armed with a sharp knife and a heap of yellow plastic fertiliser bags we cut out piles of yellow ribbons and tied them onto the top strand of the fence at intervals of three feet as a visual barrier. The tune, "Tie a yellow ribbon round the old oak tree," was firmly embedded in my mind and wouldn't go away, but Mishek politely ignored my tuneless singing.

The plan was that Sally's groom would ride Leprechaun and lead Jack over to us across country, leaving at about five in the morning and arriving around lunch-time. The three arrived, exhausted, at eleven thirty when the late October sun was at its hottest. Jack had not led well and Never, Sally's African groom, was relieved to finally turn them out into their yellow fringed field. The dairy cattle all came charging up to inspect these strange animals and then they quickly settled down to graze the dry, unappetising brown grass.

Never settled himself in the shade to enjoy a well earned cup of tea and a sandwich while we had a quick lunch before giving him a lift back home.

"Sally sent you a note and some biscuits," said John, handing me an envelope and a plastic bag of little bite sized homemade crunchy cookies. I popped one in my mouth and opened the envelope. My husband was looking at me in astonishment.

"You're not eating it, are you?"

"Of course I'm eating it." I knew lunch was on the table, but it was only a little biscuit. No criticism on Sally's cooking, but I wouldn't have actually sent them to anyone, although they were very healthy, extremely high on the roughage. I crunched steadily while John shook his head. A thought struck me.

"They're not for the horses, are they?"

"Of course they're for the horses!"

I read Sally's note. It gave full instructions on worming and dipping the horses and enclosed 'a few of the biscuits they enjoy in the evenings.'

Well, I suppose I was lucky she hadn't incorporated the wormer in the biscuits. We took Never back to his home and I spent the return journey trying to think up a good name for Jack. It had to be short and preferably rhyme with Jack and have the right feel about it. I came up with 'Anzac'.

"Isn't that a sort of nutty cookie?" grinned John, "Yes, good name. Suits him."

Next morning I informed Mishek of my decision. He looked relieved. Anzac he could manage, but Leprechaun took some remembering. We went out to look at them before breakfast, and Mishek was already there picking up their feet and patting them, he seemed as delighted as we were to have them.

"Leetle one good," his smile was enthusiastic, " leetle one be no problem. Big one not so good to catch," he prophesied gloomily.

They came up to us and sniffed us all over while we petted them and John examined them closely. Leprechaun had taken a small round lump out of his fetlock, probably over-reaching in his tired state the day before. Anzac was gentle, nuzzly and quietly pushy to get the most of the attention. Leprechaun was a little aloof, probably expecting to be caught for another six hour ride in the hot sun. Then they followed us companionably to the gate and leaned over for more fussing, Anzac licking my hands carefully. There was little in it for size really, Anzac was a little smaller but at three he had a lot of growing to do and he was already much bigger that the 14.2hh I was generally used to.

"You choose," said John, "You have whichever one is right for you."

In my heart I had already chosen Anzac. He had a gentle, affectionate nature and would stand with his nose pushed into the angle of my neck and shoulder with his eyes closed, lapping up the affection. They both had to be dipped against ticks weekly, and we did this by sponging their coats, manes and tails liberally with cattle dip solution. For this we insisted Mishek must wear big yellow, rubber gloves, as some guard against the lethal qualities of the stuff. I held Anzac and he stood quietly while Mishek soaked his coat.

"Did you do his ears, Mishek?"

"No, Medem."

"Best do his ears, that is where the ticks go."

"Yes, Medem," agreed Mishek dutifully.

Two seconds later Anzac's head shot up in the air and he snorted protestingly, one ear up and the other hanging down. As usual Mishek's enthusiasm had run away with him.

"Not pour it in, Mishek," I tried to explain, "Just use a wet cloth."

"Ah," agreed Mishek, "wet cloth."

And he scrubbed firmly away at the other ear. Being groomed by Mishek must have been like being mugged by an industrial vacuum cleaner.

We tied Anzac onto a clump of bamboo and Mishek held Leprechaun for me to take my turn at the dipping. He handed me the gloves which had as much dip inside as outside. This I pointed out, whereupon he apologised profusely and wiped them dry on his shirt. So much for protective clothing. Anzac was still shaking his ears and pawing clouds of dust up.

"He wants to roll," I commented, slapping dip onto Leprechaun and spreading it around.

"Yes, Medem. He is rolling," murmured Mishek fondly.

And he was. On his side, first one way then over onto the other, then up on his feet, a mighty shake and a snort, then standing quietly on a slack halter. He really was a very laid back three year old.

Dipping over, we took them for their first walk around the farm to dry them off. I went in front with Anzac, passing tractors, sheep, hysterical chickens, cows that went hightailing away with their calves at their side, and dogs that rushed at the fences barking fiercely. He took them all in his stride; his sensitive ears and calm unworried eyes took in all the new sounds and sights and left him quite unruffled. He faltered once at a group of Africans with umbrellas for sun-shades, but after a good look decided that they were harmless. I was delighted with him. Here was a horse I could have fun with and, more than that, Anzac and I were going to be friends.

The next day was Saturday, and John was away by five thirty to attend to the vital irrigation. I had given up trying to beat Mishek to the horses for their first feed, so it was just after six when I carried the tea tray back to the kitchen. The horses were tied to the bamboos in the corner of the garden, their heads in their feed buckets and Mishek was standing quietly by the back door.

"Anzac has a big sore," he greeted me," A very big sore, on his chest and on his neck."

My first thought was that the dip must have affected his skin, and I went over to have a look. He raised his head from the bucket as I approached and turned a little towards me. His chest had a hole in it I could have put my fist into. The swollen lips of the wound gaped open four inches and it was just as deep. Skin, fat and muscle had been torn apart. On his neck was a shallow slit about three inches long, and his knee was scraped and so was his stifle joint. He heaved a deep sigh and turned back to his bucket. I didn't know how it had happened, but I knew that treating it was beyond anything I could do. I was well used to treating prolapses in the sheep and dealing with minor injuries, and I wasn't squeamish, but this needed a professional. It was still very early and I decided that if I was quick I would be able to get the vet on the telephone before he left home. Leaving Mishek in charge I sprinted through the paddock to Fred's house, let myself in quietly and dialled the vet's home number. For once the telephone worked and I got straight through. The vet's mother answered, and then went to get him. The quiet, tired sounding voice came on the 'phone and I explained the situation.

"How bad is it?" he asked casually.

"Well, he's laid his chest wide open and it's going to need the muscle stitching at well as the skin."

"Oh," he was quiet for a moment, "You see, actually I don't work on Saturdays."

I couldn't believe I had heard correctly.

"Did you say that you don't work on Saturdays?"

"Yes," he confirmed, "that's right."

"Well, who can I get to stitch this up on a Saturday?"

"I'm afraid I really don't know."

The conversation seemed to be over, but I desperately wanted to get some help from him, he was the only vet in a hundred miles.

"Well, what do you suggest I do?"

"Mmm.....well, I really don't know."

I was furious.

"Well, don't you worry about it," I told him sarcastically, "I'll find somebody."

"Good," drawled the quiet voice, and I dropped the 'phone back on its stand. I stood there fists clenched, breathing heavily. I wished, oh, how I wished those uncaring grey eyes could have been there in front of me, I would have changed their colour so quickly. But, they weren't and suddenly Fred was there instead, looking down questioningly from his six foot four. I explained.

"No," he confirmed, "He's a Seventh Day Adventist, or something, won't do anything on a Saturday, or a Sunday either come to that."

"Well, I hope his Christian soul benefits from leaving a helpless creature to suffer," I fumed.

I went back to Mishek and asked him to just stay with the horses in the garden while I found John.

I drove out to the tobacco lands and found John riding his motorbike along the tracts of green, waist-high plants in his own little cloud of brown dust. His attention had been attracted by the big cloud of brown dust approaching at around 80 k.p.h. along the dirt road, and when he recognised me in the centre of it he came to meet me. I told him the story. His face darkened,

"The miserable little ......," he muttered, "Let's go and see the horse."

They were still standing contentedly with Mishek, and John could see at a glance how bad it was.

"You talk to him," I suggested," He may come out if he knows it really is serious and not just some woman being hysterical. After all, it's only a journey of about 40 kilometres for him."

So back we went to Fred's house and miraculously the 'phone worked again and soon the vet's mother was answering. No, she told us, her son was not there and could not be contacted. The telephone rocked back on its cradle.

"Ring Sally," suggested John, "She may know someone."

Sally's voice answered almost immediately. She sounded tired and I had the impression that I had wakened her and felt surprised.

"No, he won't come," confirmed Sally. "We all get left in the cactus by that ..... How deep is it?"

"About four inches wide and three deep."

"O.K. Give him a shot of penicillin, 25 c.c. and then 20 c.c. a day for five days. Use a syringe to wash out the wound with salt water, and use hydrogen peroxide if it's dirty, 'cause that will bubble the dirt out. Then slap plenty of acriflavin lotion into the wound and spray it well with wound spray to keep the flies off. That should keep it fairly clean 'til that, that...... 'til he comes to stitch it up on Monday," she finished vehemently.

We both knew it wouldn't heal well if left that long.

"Or, would you like to have a go at stitching it, Judy? I've got all the stuff here."

"No, it's so deep Sally. Way beyond me, I'm afraid, it needs layers of stitches."

"Ja," she agreed, "Well, you could ring Mike in Harare, John will remember him, but I think he will tell you the same. Welcome to Africa," she gave a tired laugh, "We were sabotaged last night."

"How?"

"Two thousand bales of straw set alight right next door to the stables."

They had lost all their straw but the horses were alright.

"We're pretty sure we know who did it," said Sally. "But proving it is a different matter. Anyway, keep me posted about Jack."

"If you go back and start cleaning the wound," said John, as I rang off, "I'll be along in a minute, I'm going to ring Mike."

Mike had been a good friend and a super vet from many years back, but now he was 150 kilometres away.

Back at the bungalow Mishek was beginning to look bored, but Anzac was bright and unconcerned. I gave both horses a couple of Sally's biscuits, fetched a syringe and a bowl of salted water and started to wash out the chest wound. Through the split skin the muscle was sliced apart and an even deeper hole disappeared down into the depths. Luckily it seemed pretty clean and wasn't bleeding at all. Anzac stood quietly with his nose on my shoulder and his eyes closed. The cut on his neck was fairly shallow and all the cuts seemed to be on one side.

"He may not like this, Mishek," I warned as I shook the wound dressing aerosol.

Most horses hated the hissing sound of the propellant. I talked to him and gave the neck cut a short burst. He ignored it. He also took no notice of the long burst into and around the chest wound. That was as much as I could do until I could get to town for the acriflavine.

"Here is boss," said Mishek.

My husband's expression was one of relief mixed with amazement,

"Mike will have a vet here by mid-day. He would have come himself, but he's booked up."

Well, thank You, Lord, for a vet that not only worked on Saturdays, but would travel 150 kilometres to someone else's area.

We made a thick bed of straw in one of the cattle barns and put both horses in together with a heap of green cut grass, into which Anzac dived without so much as a thank you.

"Breakfast!" demanded my husband.

The vet arrived at 11.30. The sun was hot and his car like an oven, but he refused even a cold drink before seeing his patient. He examined Anzac closely then began laying out his stitching gear on an old oil drum.

"Shall we need a twitch?" he asked John.

"I think just try him without," suggested my husband, "I don't think he'll hassle."

And he didn't. For all his young years he stood immobile as the vet gave six injections of anaesthetic deep into the wound itself. Two more went around the neck cut and he began to shave the hair from around each stitching area.

"Have you been with Mike long?" asked John.

"Oh, only a year or two," he patted Anzac and stood back, waiting for the area to become numb. "Mike tells me he knew you about a hundred years ago." He smiled, a warm genuine smile, full of warm genuine feelings.

"My name's Dave, by the way, we didn't have time for introductions. Mike is very well and hopes to call and see you very soon."

He threaded a short, curved needle and began to stitch the muscle together, leaving a small hole at the bottom for the wound to drain. Then he drew the skin together making a neat long line of blue stitches.

"This stuff is like wire to use," he commented," but the stitches are easy to take out."

Several more went into the neck and suddenly it all looked a whole lot better.

"I won't bother with pain killers," said Dave, "because I don't really think he's in pain."

John nodded in agreement.

"No brain, no pain," he suggested, glancing sideways at me.

Dave wisely refrained from answering.

"He'll be pretty stiff tomorrow, let him move around outside as he wants to."

"Tea and a sandwich?" I suggested.

"Oh, no thanks. I've got someone to see yet in Shamva, best get going."

He started to pack his kit into his truck. Shamva was 200 kilometres away. John fetched a bucket of water for him to wash his hands.

"I need a uniform," stated Mishek, out of the blue.

He had been standing quietly watching the proceedings and I had forgotten he was there.

"A uniform?"

"Yes, Medem," he nodded briefly, "and Wellingtons."

He had certainly chosen his moment.

"You mean overalls?"

He considered this for a moment, then nodded again.

"Yes, overalls Medem, and Wellingtons," he added quickly, lest I should have missed that bit.

Now one thing that had really surprised me was the general addiction to Wellingtons. In cold and muddy Devon I had lived in the things, but here with the temperature at 32C and not a cloud in the sky, I had been more than happy to swap them for sandals. Here, I discovered, they were a status symbol and every African just loves a uniform. I had no doubt that in a uniform and Wellingtons Mishek's stature would metaphorically zoom well above his actual five foot nothing.

"O.K." I agreed, "But when we get paid, eh? At the moment, no money."

The vet's bill was going to be horrendous with all the travelling involved.

"Yes, Medem," agreed Mishek. He waved a hand towards the horses, "Now I have stables to clean," he explained.

I had to admit I wouldn't be too keen to muck out stables barefoot either, but having seen him sifting chicken manure with his hands I couldn't help but feel he was cashing in on the situation. The average African can negotiate the rocks, thorns and baking sands quite happily barefoot from the toddling age, and one often saw women walking back from town in their best clothes with their shoes on their heads. Being barefoot presented no problems, but if it was Wellingtons he wanted then Mishek should have Wellingtons. It was a small price to pay for his unfailing enthusiasm around the place.

Dave started up his truck and waved as he bounced away down the track.

"And Compound-D," went on Mishek.

He'd obviously got out his mental shopping list.

"Compound-D? What's Compound-D?"

"For the garden, Medem. The garden needs Compound-D. And mealie seeds."

"Mealie seeds."

"Yes, Medem. I have prepared four plots for mealies."

I looked at him.

"For you," I suggested.

Mishek smiled and waved a hand expansively, "For me, for you, for everybody," he explained, "we can *sell* mealies."

It was only then I realised Mishek had a business mind.

CHAPTER FOUR

My attempts to learn Shona were not meeting with any great success. Tendai, being from Malawi, had learned Shona at school and as it wasn't her native tongue I found she had to consult the few books I had in order to keep one step ahead of me.

"Ah," said old Sinoya, the builder, nodding his head wisely, "Bechana, bechana, bechana."

Little, by little, by little. And it certainly would be if I listened to him, because for my benefit he was speaking Chilapalapa.

Mishek had a go too.

"Door knife," he demanded one morning at the kitchen window.

I looked around. I could see door, door frame, door key, door latch, door step. Door knife?

"No such thing," I informed him firmly.

"No," he laughed patiently, "TORA knife. When I say 'tora knife' I mean you give me knife."

"Oh, O.K. " I offered him the set of kitchen knives from which he selected one and went away.

I went and found my English/Shona dictionary. 'Give' was not tora. I followed him out to the vegetable garden, where he was busy carving up a wet sack to make stable rubbers. I showed him the book.

"Where's 'tora'?"

He examined the page closely.

"Not there," he confirmed, " Not a very good book."

I gave up and went indoors.

Five minutes later he tapped on the window again.

"Means 'I TAKE knife'," he corrected himself.

I looked up 'take' - tora. O.K., now I had a bit more to play with. That afternoon he was back again.

"I need broom."

"You mean, 'tora broom'."

"Yes, Medem," he chuckled happily, "Tora broom."

"What's 'broom'?"

"Mutsvairo."

It took several attempts to get my tongue around that one. Anyway, now when I wanted him to groom the horses I could say ' Tora mutsvairo'. I suggested this to him. He shook his head sadly.

"I do not groom a horse with a broom," he stated emphatically.

When he had gone I looked up 'brush' in my not very good book.

Bhuracho.

I decided to try it out on Tendai before making a fool of myself again.

"Tendai, what is 'brush' in Shona?"

She gave me a long, hard stare and then shrugged.

"A bhuracho is a bhuracho," she declared flatly, in her heavy accent.

Well, of course it was. They had fooled me again. Theirs was an ancient language, unwritten for hundreds of years. New words were simply adopted from the English and given a splash of African colour. A brush was a brush was a bhuracho. A bucket was a bucket was a bhagidhi. A motor car was a motokari, a motorbike was a motobhaki. Maybe I would get the hang of it after all!

With the help of my dictionary and an old school book someone had given me I had picked up a few phrases. But invariably when the opportunity to use them arose and they were on the tip of my tongue, I would be greeted in English, for the few words that I had learned were equally well known by the locals in my language. In Shona, however, you don't just return good morning with good morning. There is a ritual. Translated it means:-

Good morning.

Good morning.

Did you sleep - or - How did you sleep?

I slept, only if you have slept.

I slept.

This comes out as:-

Mangwanani.

Mangwanani.

Marara sei?

Ndarara kana marara-ow.

Ndarara.

I was word perfect until someone said it to me then my mind would go completely blank. One of the older women, however, was determined I should learn and I frequently met her on the track going past our bungalow.

"Marara sei?" she would demand, brimming drum of water balanced on her head, hands on well padded hips.

If I faltered she would immediately follow it up rapidly with

" Ndarara kana marara-ow!"

repeating it several times to drum it into my thick scull.

The problem was that I didn't always meet her in the mornings. Often it was in the afternoon and then we were into a whole new ball game.

Good day.

Good day.

Have you spent the day?

I have spent the day if you have spent the day too.

I have spent the day.

And this comes out as:-

Masikati.

Masikati.

Maswera here?

Ndaswera kana maswera-ow.

Ndaswera.

The best time to go out was in the evening, when all you said was 'Manheru'.

However, I really wanted to get over my stupid tongue-tied inclination to stick to the language I knew, so when early one morning I met my self-appointed tutor coming through the trees I answered her 'Mangwanani' with one just as good.

"Marara sei?" she demanded, slowly and distinctly, looking closely into my face for any sign of hesitation.

It was there, but as her mouth opened for the next part I put up my hand in the universal sign for stop, shook my head, and closed my eyes tightly. Out it came, like a cork from a bottle,

"Ndarara kana marar-ow!"

I opened my eyes and looked at her. The shining round face broke into a huge grin and the women with her got a fit of the giggles.

"Hey-HEY!" yelled my teacher, triumphantly kicking one leg out sideways and giving me a double thumbs up sign without slopping a drop of water from her drum. Then correcting me slightly,

"Ndalala malalow".

She waited until I had repeated it and then walked gravely on. That, I learned, was the local friendlier greeting than the formal one.

I took a phrase book with me whenever I went to the sheep pens. Harrison's English was as non-existent as my Shona but then, of course, he was Mozambican. I frequently had to look up words. I remember with pride the alacrity with which he responded to my first "Bata ino," catch that one, as I pointed to the sheep I wanted to examine. Within seconds it was pinned to the ground awaiting my inspection. It was then that I realised that I hadn't a clue what 'let go' was, and no amount of prising his fingers off would make him release the poor animal as he shifted his grip grimly. Finally I remembered ' Nda pedza', I have finished, and he let go.

The other problem was that sometimes there just didn't seem to be a word available. I asked in vain what a ram was. 'Murhuma', Harrison assured me, and certainly 'bata murhuma' always got the right result.

"Murhuma is 'man'," said John, "You've been saying 'catch the man'."

"So what is a ram?"

"Bull," said my husband.

Another thing which fascinated me was the fact that in Shona all names, unless they are taken from the English like Harrison's, mean something. When the horses arrived and I was asked their names they also wanted to know the meaning. Leprechaun was fairly easy, but Anzac's 'nutty cookie' seemed totally unfair. The origin of some names defied imagination. Sadina, for example, meant 'brick'. How could any mother call her new born baby Brick, unless it had been an exceptionally difficult labour? So whenever I saw that quiet, friendly, smiling old man in the mornings and politely said,

"Mangwanani, Sadina,"

I was really saying

"Morning, Brick."

I was talking to Orbit about it one morning.

"Yes," he agreed," They always have a meaning. Like my son," he added, "He is called Tegawirra."

"What does that mean?"

"It means," he grinned wickedly," that they make me marry my wife for the sake of my son, but I didn't want to!"

Back home I looked it up. 'Tegawirra - we fell.' Well, I suppose it is all in the interpretation.

Meanwhile the horses were settling in well, and Anzac's wound was healing slowly. The stitched gash still looked a mess. It was draining, as it was intended, and the surrounding hair had matted and hardened. The swelling had gone down now; his knee was suppurating a little but had also reduced to normal size. The flies were being a nuisance, although no more than usual.

"I'd give it a wash off," said John, straightening up after a close look at the stitching which, luckily, Anzac hadn't tried to remove. It was late afternoon and Mishek had brought them in for their evening feed.

"We've got Dettol soap, I should use that, and it could do with something like Vaseline to keep it soft."

After their feed I got Mishek to take them into the barn whilst I collected soap, a bucket of warm water and a cloth. Anzac stood patiently while I sponged away the gunge and scraped off with my finger nail the loosened hair which came away in small chunks. The act of putting his head down to graze was still painful for him and he had learned to splay his legs like a giraffe to ease the pressure. With normal, every day movement the stitches had opened a little and the drainage hole was larger than intended, but it all looked very healthy. The minor cuts had healed now, leaving long hairless lines into which I rubbed castor oil, and I had been slipping a few cloves of garlic into a handful of cubes each morning, hand feeding them while I fussed him. I sponged off his knee and his neck, and mopped it all dry with the cloth wrung out in warm water. It looked much, much better.

The next day I rang the shippers. Our container had still not arrived and it was slightly worrying that no-one seemed to know exactly which country it was in. I re-introduced myself to the young lady in the shipper's office, but I got the impression that she already knew who I was.

"I have today telephoned the National Railway," she said hurriedly, before I had time to ask, "And it is not yet on their computer."

"And is it on the South African computer?"

"I do not know."

"Have you telephoned them?"

"I have not."

"Why not?"

"Because first I do not know their number and also I do not know who to speak to."

"Is this container your responsibility now, or still the responsibility of the English shippers?"

"It is ours when it gets to Zimbabwe, but" she went on quickly,"I have today telephoned the National Railways........."

"... and it's not on their computer," I finished for her.

"I will telephone you when I hear that it is at the border," she added helpfully.

I gave up. "Thank you, please do that."

I put down the 'phone. TIE-TIA. Take it easy, this is Africa.

Until our gear arrived we could do very little with the horses. Amongst our few possessions was a hamper holding all our horsey gear and a few saddles. In the meantime we were using a length of washing line fashioned into halters and improvising with locally bought brushes. However, it would give Anzac's wounds time to heal, and they had also had their horse-sickness vaccinations which came in two stages a fortnight apart, and were followed by a three week period during which they were supposed to take things easy and not sweat up. So although we were unable to ride them we were able to walk them around the farm in the evenings. It was cooler then, an hour or so before the sun sank down amidst its fiery gold and crimson pillows. The flying ants were beginning to emerge in their millions and the swifts and swallows were always there, diving and twisting and swooping through them, catching them on the wing with a snap of their beaks. It was a brilliant flying display, and I marvelled at their ability to keep their eye on the target and still effortlessly avoid the rest of the darting, banking, and wheeling flock. We stopped to let the horses graze whilst we watched them. They took no notice of us at all, skimming past Anzac's nose as he cropped the grass nearer and nearer the hole from which the ants were emerging. A flight on new wings which was to be pitifully short. I tugged on his halter and moved him around away from them as collision looked inevitable. John looked at me enquiringly.

"He'll get a swallow up his nose if he stays there," I explained.

"And you think it's kinder to turn him around?" asked my husband.

Plum coloured starlings were there too, shyly coming down to scoop up a mouthful and then returning to the safety of their tree to enjoy them. Further down the track the huge grey shape of a gymnogene hunched below the excited airborne throng, daintily picking up the tasty morsels with its huge curved beak. They all ignored us, so busy were they harvesting their bountiful crop. We walked on through keeping mouths firmly shut and eyes half closed as the fat little winged creatures, like manna from Heaven, drifted around us. The gymnogene took off and flapped a few metres down the track, but wasn't really worried by us, and the horses on their washing line halters lowered their heads and walked through snorting.

The walk had two purposes. One was to get to know the horses and their reactions to the various things they were likely to meet every day. The other was to check that all was well with the irrigation.

Anzac and I led the way as it was better for the younger, less experienced horse to meet and face any monsters by himself, rather than just follow Leprechaun blindly and be influenced by any hang-ups that he may have developed. We weren't sure if they had been close to irrigation pipes and it was something they would have to get used to. A network of pipes stretched throughout the crops, from which standpipes threw great jets of water skywards. Pulled down by gravity to a graceful arc of spray, it was forced through the ingenuity of man to rotate fairly briskly, watering all plants within its circle. The water falling on the huge, broad leaves of the tobacco plants made a fairly loud noise and moving in a circle the noise and water came quickly towards you and over you if you didn't judge it right. It was icy cold and took your breath away.

One of the methods we had used in the past to load difficult horses into a horsebox had been to suddenly splash a few drops of cold water on their rumps. Although quite painless the effect was often electrifying, causing the horse to leap forward and into the box before he had time to think about it. Now, with an untried three year old at the end of a ridiculously inadequate halter I was about to walk through Fred's immaculate tobacco lands with bucketsful of icy water streaking towards us from all sides. Furthermore, the four inch pipes feeding the water from the river criss-crossed the track at intervals, looking and sounding like fat brown snakes in the grass as the water hissed through them.

"O.K.?" called John.

I took a deep breath.

"O.K."

If he did spook and I did lose him there could be a mangled trail of tobacco plants from here to the horizon a few seconds from now.

Despite his injury Anzac paced along with long, ground-covering strides which were difficult to keep up with over rough ground. We were going into the setting sun and it wasn't easy to see the direction of the sprays. Anzac looked unconcernedly at the first one we passed. It was on the right of the track and distributing its water away from us. The second one sneaked up on me, catching us at the very end of its range. It was on my side, so I got most of it. Anzac turned his head towards me, snuffled my arm and kept walking. The next one drenched us and except for his mobile ears, he showed little concern. We came to the first pipe across the track which he noted, then stepped carefully over.

"You're catching them all," yelled my wet husband.

"It's good for him," I yelled back doggedly, and as I turned to look back at John we reaped full benefit of a freezing deluge what left me gasping.

"Of course it is," grinned John.

I was happy sloshing along in the wet sand with my hair plastered to my neck, my new found friend swinging along beside me on a loose rope. And if I was happy so was he.

CHAPTER FIVE

Mishek's house took ten days to build. He and his wife Maagi and his two children Meridia, who was six, and Besta, who was about three had been living quite happily in a shack in the garden until such time as a house became vacant in the village. Quite often, in the mornings, while it was still dark and Chiringwe still had to sound the simbi, I would wake to Maagi's quiet singing as she swept clean the little area around the shack. Meridia was a shy girl who seemed to spend most of her days playing with the children of Fred's cook, Mwanza, whose little cluster of thatched huts, housing his two wives and seven children, nestled beneath the trees just outside our gate. Besta was a strong, solid little boy with an excellent pair of lungs and a self-willed nature. His mother seemed to naturally adopt the 'Dr. Spock' attitude and his temper tantrums and furious screams which he bombarded us all with several times a day were met with a gentle laugh and then ignored until they subsided. There was little peace to be found in the garden, and as it seemed unlikely that any house was going to become empty we decided to build them one. We chose a site just outside our boundary fence and adjoining Mwanza's yard.

The bricks had been made on the farm from clay dug from the anthills, which rose like grey turreted ruins all over the farm. A small paddock had been set aside as a brickyard, and there a waist deep pit had been filled with clay and water and puddled by foot until the right texture had been obtained. Then it was slapped into wooden moulds and the resulting bricks turned out in long lines to dry in the sun. When dry they were built into a stack with tunnels at the bottom which were filled with wood and coal. The whole stack was then plastered with more clay, the ovens fired and the stack left to cure slowly.

The round house was four metres in diameter and the walls two metres high. A doorway was the only opening, a little light and ventilation being let in by a couple of brick triangles worked into the wall. A few yards away, with doorways directly opposite, another three metre diameter hut was built. This was the kitchen. Simon the builder took the house to eaves level then Sampson the thatcher took over. Long, dry, brown grass was cut on the farm and brought in bundles to the site where two madalas did the combing. Two uprights were driven into the ground and a crosspiece with a couple of dozen six-inch nails driven up through it as teeth. Taking it in turns the madalas would swing a bundle of grass down on the teeth, drawing it through and leaving behind all the loose, dried leaf and rubbish, to finish with a bundle of smooth, strong, shiny brown stems. Four inch diameter blue gum poles formed the rafters, like the skeleton of an umbrella wired together at the top and sitting on pegs at the eaves. Then Samson and his assistant made long mats of the grass, stringing small bundles together at one end with twine. The mats fitted snugly over the rafters and were stitched into place. Another was fitted on top with its untied fringe covering the stitching of the first one, and so on until the roof was complete. A little upside down cone of thatch covered the hole at the top.

The plastering was woman's work and Simon volunteered the services of his wife for sixty dollars. Again, the medium was clay and this was brought up from the river banks on her head, heavy bucket after heavy bucket, until John realised what was happening and organised a tractor and trailer. She used her hands to mix it and put it on, smoothing it expertly over the bricks. From our garden she fetched the orange coloured soil which lay beneath the sand in some places, and mixed it with her clay to make a warm, golden colour. With this she made a wide band around the bottom of the house, inside and out, contrasting prettily with the sun dried white of the walls. She did the floors, mixing in cow dung in her traditional way to create a finish as hard as concrete. Then she plastered and coloured the kitchen to match.

Mishek's contribution was the 'stoop', a metre wide brick step encircling the hut which would be his sitting out place. This he covered with a clay rendering, made black and shiny by rubbing in old engine oil. Within an hour of moving in he was out digging his new garden. We gave him a pack of mealie seeds to start him off and his world was complete.

Our own garden had really not come up to expectations. The rains had not arrived and were later than anyone could remember. Consequently our newly dug beds, even with the addition of our carefully gathered chicken, cattle and sheep manure, had produced little.

Jenny, who held down a job as a rep. for the Farmer's Co-operative, and advised on stock feeding, was a person I took an instant liking to and looked forward to her rare visits when I could natter woman to woman in English for an hour or two. She called unexpectedly, soon after Mishek and his family had moved into their own place, and I decided that morning coffee in the garden would be a new luxury now that peace and privacy were ours. She sat with me on the low stone bench beneath the M'soro tree and looked around.

"Gosh," said Jenny, "It reminds me of that book."

She thought for a moment.

"I can't remember the name of it, but it was about a woman whose husband brought her to live in a place like this. They had no water, so she couldn't do the garden," she gazed around at the brown, sandy lawn space and the wilting weeds, and then went on, "The house had a tin roof and was hot at hell, she had no-one to talk to and absolutely nothing to do....." She stopped, obviously thinking she may have got a bit too close to the truth. "She went mad in the end," she finished lamely.

"I can see how it could happen," I agreed, pouring a couple of stiff coffees.

"Have you got snakes here?" asked Jenny, changing the subject, "You often find if a house has been empty a while they tend to move in."

"Yes," I agreed, "We've found quite a few, I had one in the porch a while back which they said was a mamba. John thinks it was more likely to be an Egyptian Cobra. It didn't actually worry me too much; it's the spiders that terrify me."

She laughed,

"What is it about you English? You are all afraid of spiders. Do you get told fairy stories about them as children, or something? Mind you," she went on, "I remember as a child I was having a bath with my sister. I put my shower cap on and then thought my hair had slipped down so I pushed it up under my cap. But it was actually a huge rain spider, not my hair. It fell into the bath and my sister rose vertically, she didn't touch the sides, and I was left with the spider swimming around me."

Mishek came past at that moment, and stopped with a shy smile and a "Good morning, Medem," for Jenny, then marched away Gurkha like towards the vegetable garden. Jenny watched him, open mouthed.

"Oh," she whispered, "Isn't he cute!"

We finished our coffee and had a brief wander round the sub-desert and Mishek passed us again at his usual pace, balancing a 45 gallon drum on his head. Jenny's startled gaze followed him.

"I cannot believe that man," she confided, "where did you find him?"

"Actually, he found us," I said, "It is such a shame about the lack of water, because his energy and enthusiasm seems to be limitless. I mapped out a plan for the garden the other day and showed it to John. He agreed with the plan but made me promise I wouldn't show it to Mishek, only a little bit at a time, or he reckons the whole place would erupt."

She laughed,

"Hold on to him," she advised me seriously, "that sort of enthusiasm is hard to find."

The news that afternoon that our container had arrived in Harare seemed so unlikely that neither John nor I could work up much enthusiasm. It wasn't until we got into town early the following morning and actually saw it standing in the shipper's yard that we allowed ourselves to believe. We still didn't expect things to be simple and we were not disappointed. Before the container could be unsealed, we were told, we would have to bring a customs officer to the yard. Customs officers had to be booked, and our intention to be back with one by midday was met by superior smiles and shaking heads. We went away determined to prove them wrong. At the customs office we sought the aid of a very pleasant and efficient woman official who had dealt with us when we had first entered the country and whose name we had carefully written down. She recognised us and kindly found the diary of the person who we needed to open the container. Nothing was booked for that afternoon so she would, she told us, pencil us in but we would have to come back at 2.00 p.m. to verify it. At five minutes to two we were back, first in the queue as they unlocked the doors. We went straight to the appropriate desk and found the gentleman we wanted sitting on top of it, swinging his legs and looking pensive. Yes, he would have liked to have helped us, but unfortunately he had forgotten his glasses and couldn't read without them.

"Try mine," suggested John, fishing his reading glasses from a pocket.

The official was impressed.

"They are very good glasses," he agreed, "But unfortunately I have no transport."

"No problem," smiled John, "we will take you there and bring you back."

He sighed.

"All right," he agreed with some reluctance, "I will come."

By half past two we had whisked him through the traffic and accompanied him triumphantly through the swing doors of the shipping agent's office. He greeted them as the old friends they undoubtedly were, and we all marched through into the yard beyond. As appropriate in moments of such great drama a roll of thunder echoed around the tall buildings, and the patch of city sky changed from blue to black. Mr. Madzura, our customs man, broke the seals on the container and the doors were swung open.

There in the centre of Africa were all the familiar, every day things from our Devon smallholding. We had no furniture to speak of, having lived for so long in the old mobile home, but there were the tools and the feed troughs, the buckets and rolls of wire that we had crammed around our only valuable possession, our Suzuki jeep.

"I need the forms, and some carbon paper," stated Mr. Madzura.

The inventory appeared from a slender file, and Mr. Madzura marched back inside, beckoning us to follow. He gave me a piece of scrap paper and a pen.

"I tell you what I want to see and you write down the numbers," he instructed.

He went through the inventory, calling out the item numbers of all the electrical goods. The transport manager came in looking apologetic.

"It is raining," he explained, "It is impossible for us to unload in the rain."

Outside the window a few spots were trickling down the glass.

"I wouldn't call that rain," said John.

"No, but it will rain," insisted the manager," and we cannot take the responsibility of unloading all your beautiful chairs and furniture in the rain."

We assured him that the responsibility would be ours.

"If we have some tea," suggested Mr. Madzura, with some authority, "The rain may stop."

The tea arrived and the skies opened. The manager allowed himself a satisfied smile.

"You come back tomorrow," he stated.

"Why do we have to unload in the rain? Why can't you back it into an empty garage?" I asked.

"We do not have an empty garage."

"Yes, you do. There's one just behind the container."

"It is only a small space."

"It is only a small container."

We could see that he wasn't happy.

"Alright, I will get a driver to back it up to the garage," he agreed at last.

At that moment a loud siren began to wail.

"After the tea break," said the manager, "The driver is now having his tea."

We watched the water pouring off the corrugated iron roof and went back to find Mr. Madzura chatting up two pretty secretaries.

We drank our tea and filled out the forms that were going to be necessary eventually. A driver was parted from his tea and the trailer backed up. By this time it was after four, and the manager was looking reluctant again. Mr. Madzura looked at his watch.

"I am going to inspect this container today," he stated, "no matter how long it takes."

Within minutes a team of workers had been assembled, all dressed in blue overalls and looking exactly like the Smurfs. Quickly they unloaded the boxes into the garage and found the boxes with the numbers that had been noted on my list. Mr. Madzura wanted the registered model numbers on the cooker, 'fridge, freezer, television and anything electrical. By the time all the boxes were found it was nearly five o'clock and everyone became wildly enthusiastic. The requested boxes appeared as it by magic, wrapping was torn off, numbers found and called out to me, because by now I had the clip-board and was working with Mr. Madzura. One number called was B.S. something. I pointed out that this was a British Standards number but, as Mr. Madzura said, it was a number wasn't it? Then the blow fell. They couldn't clear the Suzuki jeep because they didn't have a ramp, and all the documents had to be stamped by customs at their offices.

"You must come back tomorrow," said Mr. Madzura.

Tired, wet and frustrated we decided that there was no way we were going to travel all the way back to the farm and then into town again the next day. So we begged a bed for the night with one of Fred's friends in town and were back at Customs House by seven fifty next morning.

It took one and a half hours to get the documents cleared and then we went back to the shipping agents who had, by then, unloaded the car and hitched on our little trailer. The transport manager was all smiles, having managed to get us back next day, and pronounced the papers as being all in order. Our container was cleared.

"There is one small problem," he added.

We just knew there would be.

"We must have photocopies of all the documents before we can let the goods go. Unfortunately our photocopier is being repaired. I wonder if you would mind getting copies done - there is a place two blocks away?"

It seemed a small price to pay.

"Oh, we will pay," exclaimed the manager generously, and gave me 75c out of his petty cash tin.

"I wonder," he added thoughtfully," we have a few other things we need copied......., since you are going anyway.......?"

We went off with a file of papers, three of them ours.

When, at last, all the paperwork was copied, all the files in order, all the rubber stamps in the right place, we were finally allowed to load up our trailer with a few essentials like saddles and chainsaws, leaving the rest to be delivered to the farm the following week. Then with John driving the Suzie and me following in the truck we drove thankfully home, glad to leave the city and the crowds and the officialdom behind us, happy to be heading for the open country and home. It was well after dark when we drove through the gates of our bungalow, and only minutes before the kettle was on for a life saving cup of tea.

John was searching feverishly through his pockets as I carried the tea tray into the lounge. He looked up sheepishly.

"I seem to have mislaid my reading glasses," he muttered as I handed him his cup, "We may have to go back tomorrow."

CHAPTER SIX

We were glad that our bungalow was surrounded on three sides by open bush land. Lack of water on this part of the farm made it difficult to grow crops or pasture cattle, so it had been left to nature. As the garden seemed a natural extension of the bushland many birds - and snakes - treated it as part of their patch and took very little notice of us.

On the telephone wire above the kitchen window a red-headed weaver bird had started to build. The intricate nest of woven grasses took shape steadily over several days. A funnel entrance on the lower side and a thatching of dead leaves on the top against the coming rains completed the little home, and it was proudly shown to his wife. Mrs. Redhead was actually yellow-headed and did nothing except sit in a tree nearby and twitter. Occasionally she came to inspect the nest closely, but apparently it wasn't to her satisfaction, for the day following completion her husband started building again on the next door plot, half a metre along the telephone wire. I marvelled at the way the little bird was programmed to create such an intricate and practical structure. However, his wife was unimpressed and before the last leaf was laid he started on number three. He was fairly expert by now, and the familiar structure positively mushroomed. This he decided to decorate with green M'sasa leaves picked fresh from the bough. I was drawn to the window soon after watching these final touches being made, by a furious exchange of unrepeatable weaver bird language, and in time to see Mr. Weaverbird beating up Mrs. Weaverbird with all the frustrated anger that only three dud nests could bring. Every time she tried to land he flew straight at her, knocking her off branch, wire and post alike. It was a while before I realised that there were two lady weaver birds. I guess an unattached one had come along and given the thumbs up sign to his housing estate. We shall never know which one inherited his wealth in the end. One imagines that he remained faithful to his fussy, shrew like, nagging wife and chased away the newcomer. But how many men would take that option? Perhaps the newcomer did win, knowing the best way to a weaver bird's heart is through his love nest. Or did Mrs. Weaverbird capitulate when she saw that she could lose everything to a less demanding mistress? The eternal triangle appears at all levels of creation. But, as in many cases, the honeymoon period was a short one. About ten days later I saw our beautiful red-headed neighbour sneaking a beak full of grass from nest number two and starting wearily on number four, as his little yellow headed partner chirruped impatient instructions from the M'sasa tree.

I loved the fireflies. They followed John home at night when he walked back from the tobacco barns, obviously mistaking his torch for some mega-firefly. Then they followed him through the house and into the bedroom where I was usually already asleep. I would wake and see them drifting around the room, like fairies with torches caught out after dark. Their light threw shadows around the room like candlelight.

It was as well to be first in bed. John had this firm belief that if we switched all the lights off, including the bedroom, and left the passage light on until last, then all the mosquitoes, beetles, moths and gnats would migrate towards the light and leave the bedroom free. This was fine in theory. Unfortunately for me it always took me longer to prepare for bed, and the light switch was at the far end of the passage. So with spiders inevitably on my mind I would switch off the passage light, grope my way along the walls of the passage in complete darkness, being buzzed by beetles and not wanting to actually touch the walls because of wall spiders, and canon through the bedroom doorway. I would reach blindly for the curtains and pull them open to let in any breeze there might be, fish around for the radio lead, follow it to the wall plug and switch it off. Then I would find the end of the bed, leave my slippers at the end and clamber gratefully towards my pillow. On one night in particular it was a tie and I jumped into bed before John could kick his slippers off and beat me to it.

"Oh," he said suddenly," now be careful, there's a big old scorpion."

It was the first I had seen, and I left the sanctuary of my bed to go and have a closer look. Out from under the chair it marched, almost black, about four inches long with a three inch stinging tail curved menacingly over it's back and pincer claws out in front. It was dispatched quickly with a sandal and John looked at me enquiringly.

"He didn't really worry you, did he?"

I shook my head.

"Women," he sighed, kicking off the other sandal and hopping into bed, "Switch the lights off, would you?"

Mishek had killed another snake in the garden; he brought it proudly to the kitchen door one morning, dragging it by the tail. I looked at it closely.

"Now, that is the same as the one that was in the porch," I told him," So what kind is it Mishek?"

Mishek shook his head,

"Ah, I do not know, Medem."

"Let's put it up on the wall and show the boss when he comes in to breakfast," I suggested, "then he can tell us."

I picked it up by the tail and flipped it over onto its back. It was around five feet long, grey on top and whitish underneath, the description I had read of a Mamba. Mishek gathered it up and put it on the wall by the kitchen door, and I went in to get breakfast ready.

"Mishek's killed a snake," I told my husband when he came in, ""I'm sure it's the same as the one that was in the porch."

We went outside to look.

"Mmmm." said John, standing back a few paces, "It's an Egyptian Cobra, and it's still breathing."

It was now very obviously still breathing, its body swelling and contracting deeply and evenly.

Mishek was standing next to his compost heap, trying to make the hose stay on the tap by twisting strips of old bicycle inner tube around the join.

"Mishek," I called, "It's still breathing."

"Eh?"

I pointed towards the snake,

"Still breathing. I think you had better kill it again and then bury it."

"Yes, Medem," said Mishek without his usual enthusiasm.

"A lesson well learned," said John as we went in to breakfast,"Cobras can, and often do, sham death."

A few minutes later Mishek passed the window with the snake looped over a garden fork held at arm's length.

It had occurred to me then that Mishek wasn't quite himself, although it was difficult at the time to say exactly why. Later that day he confessed to feeling very sick and not being able to keep food down. I went into the kitchen and made a brew of basil tea, and when it was cool I put it in a Martini bottle and presented it to Mishek.

"One cup about an hour before meals," I told him.

"Yes, Medem," he gave an obedient nod and marched away to put it in his house.

Next morning he positively bounced across the garden, a broad grin on his face.

"That medicine ver' good, Medem. Aiee! It is too strong. I am well now."

"Good," I told him, "We will go and cut some bana grass."

The rains had still not arrived and it was almost Christmas. The horses needed the bulk of the grass as well as their horse cubes, or 'orsey coobes' as the man in the Farmer's Co-op called them. They could eat about four sacks a day of the tall bana grass which was still growing lush and green at the end of the irrigated section of the farm. It took no time to fill two sacks and as we started on the third I asked Mishek conversationally where his parents were.

"Not far," said Mishek, "Near Harare, at a mission."

He grinned,

"My father he make medicine like you give me, that strong medicine. He is N'anga; you would call him witch-doctor."

Still new to Africa and to Christianity I knew nothing of the spiritual side of a N'anga's role in African culture. I was fascinated. In England we had a very good friend who had become a master herbalist, and he had quickly infected me with his belief and enthusiasm in herbs. I had just started learning a few of the healing properties of the wild plants around our Devon farm, and had used them successfully on our sheep, when we had moved to Africa and all the plants were strange to me once more. I had tried unsuccessfully to find a book on the subject, but a real live witch doctor must surely be better than a book.

"Would he teach me?"

"Teach you?"

I explained my interest.

"Yes, yes, Medem, he teach you."

"Does he speak English?"

Mishek laughed.

"No, Medem, he speak Chinyanja. My mother speak Shona. You speak to her in Shona and she speak to my father in Chinyanja."

I couldn't see that this would be much help with my current command of Shona.

"Do you see him often?"

Mishek shook his head.

"Ah, no, Medem, I do not have much money to go. I have not finished paying yet for my wife," he added sadly.

I tried to look suitably sympathetic.

"Does a wife cost very much?"

"Ah, yes Medem, wife cost too much," he slashed at a clump of grass with feeling. "About seven hundred dollars. I pay one goat, this big," he held a hand at waist height, "and four hundred dollars and still I have three hundred to pay. If I don't pay," he explained," they can take my wife back, but the children, they are mine."

I could see his problem. At least if one's car was reclaimed you didn't have a heap of little ones to find petrol for.

It was several days later when Mishek again complained of not feeling well. Although he didn't exactly look pale, there was a certain lack of tone to his dark features, his eyes were downcast, his manner subdued. He had already fed the horses and was holding Anzac for me to rub Vaseline over his wound which was almost completely healed.

"How do you not feel well?" I asked sympathetically.

"It is my stomach, Medem. Yesterday, last night and today it is not well," he pointed vaguely at his lower abdomen, "And I have a lump."

A hernia, I thought. He was always lifting things that would normally make three Africans grunt, and took a pride in doing so.

I plastered a liberal amount of Vaseline down the line of the chest wound. Mishek, in his debilitated state, held the halter lethargically and Anzac, mistaking my ministrations for a biting fly, took a swipe at his chest giving me a crashing blow on top of my head with his jaw bone. I stood up, stars and rainbows playing in front of my eyes.

"Aieee!" commented Mishek, stroking Anzac soothingly, "I think that place is sore too much!"

I gently fingered my head where the lump was already rising and felt marginally less sympathetic towards Mishek's stomach. Bravely I carried on.

"If you don't feel well," I said, still blinking spots away from before my eyes, "I think you should go and see the doctor."

Mishek looked quietly disappointed in me, but agreed. There was no way I was going to attempt advice on a hernia. Word had spread quickly that I was interested in herbs, but instead of people coming forward to share their knowledge, they began to come with symptoms. A sore toe there, a swollen ankle here. They didn't come to me, but casually mentioned their problems to John. Without any training, a very little knowledge gleaned from my herb books and very few herbs to play with I was very unwilling to advise. One morning, however, John described symptoms and I ventured that this particular man's problem was probably his liver.

"What should he do?" asked John.

"Give up tea, coffee and beer to start with,"

"He won't like that," my husband shook his head.

That evening, after dinner, he said,

" By the way, Tobias was most impressed. His doctor had told him the same thing."

He had obviously been hoping for a kinder remedy. Duplicating a diagnosis with the doctor gave me, I suppose, a degree of credibility, for within days people began coming to the kitchen door. Tobias himself came, his ankles and wrists swollen. All my books pointed to parsley, which would help clear the fluid from his body. The next best thing seemed to be chicory, and as pure chicory was available as a coffee substitute we bought him a large jar. His doctor and the hospital had given up on him, and I was sure that the few herbs I had couldn't hurt. I arranged with Fred's gardener that he should have a large bunch of parsley each day and asked to see his hospital card, which diagnosed 'swollen ankles'. A few days later I sent Mishek down to the village to find out how he was.

"I find him, Medem," reported Mishek, half an hour later, "He had gone into bush to make the pee."

Well, maybe it was working.

Mwanza brought his little girl with a nasty sore on her chin that had defied doctor's treatment stubbornly for months. We tried witch hazel, bathing it twice a day. To my surprise and delight it healed.

Burns were commonplace, the tobacco curing barns were places of hot pipes and steam and back home in the huts children quite often rolled into the embers of the central fire during the night. Both children and adults came, receiving a dressing of comfrey, vitamin E oil and honey mixed to a paste which healed them quickly. One man came with a burn about four inches square to his upper arm, the whole area contrasting white to his black skin. We used the same comfrey mixture and left it untouched for three days. During this time the wound began to heal cleanly and the dressing peeled off easily without pain or damage. The procedure was repeated and after a further three days the brown pigment was beginning to creep back over the wound and three days later it was completely healed.

Jameson, one of the cattlemen, came. He had hit a metal spike hidden in the undergrowth whilst walking in the bush and driven it into his shin to the bone. His face, when I applied a liberal amount of cayenne pepper, was a picture. But the bleeding stopped at once leaving a solid crusty scab to protect the hole. I was worried about this particular deep puncture wound. After I had cleaned and dressed it I went up to find John who was talking to Fred and Paul, the tobacco foreman, outside the curing barns. I explained Jameson's problem.

"He should have a tetanus injection," I told John.

Fred smiled,

"Tetanus injection? What's that?"

"Judy," he went on patiently, "You'll see all sorts of horrendous things here. I've seen'em walking around with axes in the tops of their heads, ears sliced off...."

"...fingers bitten off," put in Paul, grinning, "Old Kaferenje's missus bit his finger off at the joint because he pointed it at her, took him a while to live that down. She did," he assured me, "Right off at the joint. Must have spat out quite a lump." He chuckled, his deep rumbling laugh kept in check, "Imagine coming home in the evening to your mud hut, and there's your wife, crouched on the floor snarling and spitting....".

"Reminds me of a notice I saw once," put in John, "Dogs are O.K. but watch out for the wife."

It was clear I was getting nowhere.

"If it doesn't fall off he'll be alright," stated Fred, firmly, "Rule of thumb."

It was true that most of the Africans seemed to have a good supply of antibodies. John had a cow go missing. With a history of calving problems she had carefully given the herdsmen the slip and vanished. They found her two days later, when anyone for a mile around could have found her, and I had gone out with John in the truck to see. She had calved and her heifer calf, fine and healthy, was well hidden under a thorn bush. The body of the mother was upside down and distended, and it was possible that the calf had been able to suckle what was left in the udder after the cow had died. We lifted the baby into the pickup and she laid there quietly, her black coat glossy and her blue-black eyes bright under the long, curling lashes. I sat in the back with her as we bumped and lurched our way across country to the cattle pens, where the herdsmen had rounded up a newly calved Tuli cow. I had been with John that morning when he had dosed them all, and had been amazed at the anger and indignation displayed by most of these African bred animals. The simple act of sticking a dosing gun in their mouths and pulling the trigger had been met with roars and bellows and snorts of fury. Milking one was likely to be worth watching. In fact John did remarkable well, getting a good one and a half pints before he got kicked. We poured the warm, colostrum rich milk into a gin bottle with a teat on top and I offered it to the calf. She got the idea immediately, sprang to her feet and drank so enthusiastically that we were both in danger of falling out of the pick-up. Having got at least a pint or so of colostrum into her the herdsmen, Shadrak and Robert, took the Tuli back to her own calf and came back with another cow whose calf had died. We left her penned closely with the orphaned calf, hoping that they would take kindly to one another and that the calf, now that it had a taste of milk, would be fairly determined about finding some more.

      Chiringwe arrived with a tractor and trailer and the dead body of the cow, followed by a cloud of flies and the smell of decay. Fred followed in his truck a few moments later.

      "What do you think we should charge?" he asked John.

      "I don't know," said John, "a dollar a kilo?"

      "Charge for what?" I asked.

      Fred inclined his head towards the dead cow,

      "The meat."

      I was horrified, "No-one would actually eat that?"

      Fred laughed, "Of course they do, they'll eat it when it's green."

I looked at John, who confirmed with a nod.

      "Well, what would you do with it, Judy?" asked Fred.

      "Bury it!" I suggested.

"Well, we could," agreed Fred," But it would need a very big hole, it would take a lot of time and energy, and it would only be dug up again when we had gone"

"Well, couldn't you just let anyone who wanted it have it? It just seems a bit mean to actually charge them for that."

We always charge something," explained my husband, quietly," Because if it was free then others would 'die'."

"Worse anyone will get is a two day stomach-ache," Fred assured me.

"And it's Friday, anyway," I pointed out.

Fred gave me an approving smile,

"So everyone will be fit for work on Monday. You're learning."

The cow's carcase vanished and no-one was ill, and the drums, singing and merriment coming from the village that night suggested that it was an ill wind that blew nobody any good.

Mishek took my advice about seeing a doctor, and together with his wife and two children they set out to catch the tractor and trailer that went into Chegutu early every morning to deliver eggs and collect supplies. For the whole weekend his house was deserted and it seemed strange not to hear little Besta's temper tantrums at regular intervals throughout the day.

As I left the house on my way to feed the sheep just before six on Monday morning, the horses were in, their noses deep in their manger and it was obvious that Mishek was back. His new house was quiet still and empty looking, the door closed and the man himself not in sight. Feeding the sheep and counting them had evolved into an efficient routine as both shepherds and sheep now knew what to expect and what was expected of them. By the time I reached the night pen each morning Harrison had made an inspection with Orbit and any sick or sorry ones were pointed out to me. The troughs, brought from our Devon farm, were already placed in three well spaced rows outside the fence and Harrison was waiting to take the bags of maize from the back of the Suzuki. He filled the troughs carefully, dribbling the corn from the corner of the sack, being scrupulously fair in his distribution. When he had finished the sacks he checked it all again, and carried odd handfuls from one trough to another until he was quite satisfied. The last stage was really quite unnecessary but the secret of successful shepherding, as with all stockmanship, is attention to the smallest detail, and having found that rare quality to be a natural part of Harrison's makeup I was careful not to upset it in any way. Shanghazi then opened the gates, having learned the hard way to stand to one side and not in the middle, and a tide of sheep broke through to engulf the troughs. Within a few minutes it was all gone, and as they finished and began to drift away towards the pastures Orbit and I counted them.

Orbit waited for his lift back, which had also become part of the routine, settling himself in the passenger seat with his overnight lunch bag and his axe. We lurched across the paddock and back onto the sandy track, under the archway of tall jacaranda trees covered in brilliant blue blossoms, and back towards breakfast.

"You have seen where I live?" asked Orbit, casually.

"You mean, have I seen the village?"

"No, have you seen my house?"

I had to admit that I hadn't.

"I think," suggested Orbit," that it would be nice for you to see my house."

"You mean you want a lift all the way home."

"Yes," he laughed.

"No," I said firmly, "You can walk from the bungalow."

Orbit chuckled; it had been worth a try.

Mishek came through the gate as I parked the car and was looking solemn. I caught up with him by the back door.

"Are you well, Mishek?"

"No, Medem," his eyes were downcast," I am not quite well."

He paused a moment, then,

"I have to go back to doctor on Friday for more injection."

I really didn't know what the treatment for a hernia was, but an injection didn't seem quite right.

"This lump," explained Mishek, pointing to himself, "It is a disease given me by that Maagi."

I was really surprised, Maagi had seemed a model wife.

"Yes," said Mishek, "She have boy friends and give this disease to me. I do not have girl friends and give disease to her, so she must go. She cannot stay in house with me."

He was strong in resolution and voice, but his eyes when he looked up were very sad.

"So, yesterday," he continued," I take her back to her mother. I have paid four hundred dollar and I have no wife, so the children they stay with her until they are eighteen and then they go to my mother."

Poor Mishek, he loved his children. Little Besta was always at his father's heels, 'helping' with the garden, swinging a badza manfully. 'Baba' was the constant cry whenever Mishek was around. And Meridia too. Only a few days ago he had been telling me proudly that she was going to start school. Now the lovely new house with its pretty thatched roof and softly patterned walls stood quiet and empty, whilst all around Mwunza's children laughed and played while his two wives chatted. Poor Mishek. I hoped it was a simple form of the disease. In England, the newspapers and television had driven home the message that in Africa AIDS was rife. Here, on the spot, amongst these poor but happy people, in this beautiful country, it was difficult to believe. The statistics we had heard were frightening.

CHAPTER SEVEN

Before leaving England we had gathered together four saddles and bridles and various oddments of tack. Both Leprechaun and Anzac were a lot leaner than our horses in Devon, and it was a matter of trial and error to kit them out from the selection we had. John had a lovely Western saddle, which was like an armchair to sit in and of which I was slightly covetous. We had agreed that Anzac should be mine, now came the distribution of tack. It was the fourth bridle that John tried which fitted Leprechaun to perfection and as he threw on the Western saddle it looked as if that was good too. Leprechaun had a very high wither which could easily rub on a low pommelled saddle.

"Looks good," commented John, his expression a mixture of relief tinged marginally with sympathy on my behalf, "Where's the cinch?"

I handed it to him. John quickly attached it and pulled it up. A perfect fit. Next he picked up the Australian stock saddle. We had got it very cheaply at a sale in Devon, because no-one else seemed to know what it was. It had broad padded flaps of leather which fitted above and below the thigh of the rider, designed to give protection from thorn and scrub when riding through the bush. It was ideal for our purposes and looked very comfortable, although neither of us had tried it. Some woman at the sale had said authoritatively and in a loud voice that it was for disabled riders, and so no-one else had put in a bid for it. It fitted Anzac perfectly and, as John pointed out, the 'horizontal hold' might come in quite handy when we backed him.

Now his education could really begin. We found a curb chain to use as a mouthing bit, giving him something to play with and jangle, but attached long reins to the noseband of his stout head collar to get him used to his various commands and signals before graduating to a proper bit. Daily long reining now became part of the morning routine after feeding the sheep. At first we took Leprechaun too, Mishek leading him and bringing up the rear as they hated being separated and we felt it was important that Anzac should be relaxed during these first lessons. He soon got the idea, and I loved these early mornings with Anzac swinging along in front of me, ears pricked, tail swishing lazily, the long ribbons of reins held loosely in my hands, guiding him easily from the noseband. The long grass, heavy with dew, soaked my legs and flashed rainbows at us as the strengthening sun began to take control of the new day, dispersing the dampness of the night and darkening our shadows. Behind me came Mishek's gurkha like tread, two to my one, as he followed with Leprechaun marching barefoot along the sandy tracks. Bauhinia trees, decked with their delicate white honeysuckle shaped flowers, filled the air with a lovely, elusive perfume which mingled sweetly with the spicy smell of the warming grasses. High in the clear, deepening blue sky the rock pigeons clapped, beating their wings beneath their bodies in a staccato tribute to life and the wonder of flight, and through the dense leaves of the fig trees and m'futis flashed the jewel bright blues, yellows and reds of the weavers, starlings, kingfishers and bishops. Hidden from sight the turtle doves scolded their cousins in the sky with their 'go tell fa-a-ather, go tell fa-a-ather." Sometimes we would see the dark shapes and light underbellies of the monkeys which roosted in the high blue gums, slipping soundlessly away as we approached, and sometimes a tortoise, lumbering along with old wrinkled face on scrawny neck viewing the world suspiciously from dark, wet eyes. Always there were the scurrying lizards, running with their peculiar swimming motion from the warm, sunny path into the dark jungle of grass edging the track.

Africans with bicycles would suddenly appear out of the scrub, women glided past following parallel tracks, disembodied, laden heads above a sea of grass. They all played their part in Anzac's education, and he learned with confidence. Soon I would be riding him, and I looked forward to the day.

It didn't seem like Christmas. A couple of weeks ago I had dashed into the Chegutu butchery, very aware that my other shopping was warming up quickly in the back of the Suzi, and had been quite startled to see 'Merry Christmas and Happy New Year' complete with holly and snow, stencilled on the glass swing door. The butchery itself was still a place of wonder to me. Heaps of unidentifiable offal, chickens feet, and great slabs of fatty brisket lay at one end of the counter where the Africans lingered. At the other end at practically throw away prices lay the rump steak, fillet pork and lean cuts of meat. Occasionally one of the butcher's assistants would walk past bearing a whole cow's head or a pair of front legs complete with hooves. The manager was a very efficient Indian and the whole place was scrupulously clean.

The Christmas message had prompted some very hasty shopping and I still had to post presents to our family in England.

"Medem," said Orbit, as we left the sheep pens the morning after pay day, "Your two dollars."

He handed me a note, repayment of a loan given a week previously. I was agreeably surprised. Loans were not always repaid, but I had felt that a two dollar bet on Orbit's honesty wouldn't be too serious a loss. I glanced at the note in my hand.

"This is ten dollars. Ah!" I feigned understanding, "Interest."

I quickly put the note in my pocket.

"T'tenda,' I thanked him, gravely.

"Ah, Medem," laughed Orbit, "You give me eight dollar, eh?"

I spread my arms,

"No money," I stated truthfully.

"Eh?" There was a slight sob in his voice and he was looking worried.

"This morning I go to town," I promised, " This afternoon I give you eight dollar."

I had a morning of queuing ahead of me. The Bank to deposit our pay cheque and get some cash, that would be a good hour. Then the post office to post the Christmas presents to England, that would be at least an hour and a half. Then there was the household shopping, butcher, baker and garage for petrol.

Orbit looked doubtful,

"I have a lift back, eh?"

"Of course".

"Perhaps," suggested Orbit, as we headed for home, "I get change and give you two dollar," he sighed, "You see, I have no more money."

"You were paid yesterday evening."

"Eh? Oh, yes, but ....oh, I owe so much to the store. They take all I have."

The store in the village, run by a fellow African, allowed unlimited credit and then charged an unbelievably high percentage in interest for the favour.

"Well," I reasoned, "If I keep these ten dollars, then I have saved eight dollars for you."

He gave a resigned grin,

"So, this afternoon I come and get it?"

"Right!"

"Sure?"

"Sure!"

I dropped him at the gate of the bungalow and went inside to start packing parcels for the post. Ten minutes later there was a knock on the kitchen door. Mishek stood there resplendent in a bright red shirt I hadn't seen before.

"This man want to see you," he announced, jerking a thumb over his right shoulder.

Behind him stood Orbit, in clean, white shirt and neatly pressed trousers.

"I come to town with you, it's O.K.?"

He obviously intended riding shotgun on his eight dollars.

"You can," I agreed, but I shall be another hour before I am ready to go."

"O.K." he chuckled, happily," I go to get some beer," he confided

"You've got no money," I reminded him.

His grin broadened,

"I get some from my wife."

I went back to my packing.

A few moments later there was a knock at the front door. Mishek stood there again.

"Sadina want medicine for headache," he explained, inclining his head towards the patient who stood meekly at the end of the path. I fetched the 1000 tablet pack of Aspirin provided by Fred and gave four to Sadina.

"Two now, two this afternoon, and if it's not better come and tell me."

Mishek gave a quick translation, and Sadina nodded and went away.

I had just stuck down the last parcel when I heard another knock. Mishek stood at the back door again, and handed me twenty dollars.

"Harrison give me for Boss," he explained, "Boss lend him ten dollar, now he need ten dollar change."

"O.K. I'll give it to him when I pass on my way to town."

Boss had told me not to lend Orbit two dollars and had given Harrison ten. Boss as big a pushover as me. The sound of Boss's motorbike reminded me of breakfast and I quickly cleared the decks to reveal the breakfast table that Tendai had made ready.

"Ye gods," exclaimed John, kicking his way through brown paper and boxes, "Are you winning?"

"I've won," I assured him, passing him Harrison's twenty dollar note.

"Return of loan," I explained, "He needs ten dollars change."

"Oh, right," said my husband. He paused, "Would you give the ten dollars to the new guy with the mombies? He's a bit short, and it's a month to pay day."

Breakfast was a hurried affair as reapers were piling tobacco into the barns. I finished my cereal and drained my coffee cup.

"I'm off then; I want to be somewhere near the head of the queue at the Bank."

Collecting my parcels, list, cool box (a real luxury for shopping) and handbag, I gave my still munching husband a hasty kiss and headed for the Suzi.

Orbit was sitting outside the gate in the shade with a ten gallon plastic drum. He jumped to his feet as I drove up, opened the back door and loaded the drum.

"Isaac, he goes to town too - to the hospital," he pointed to Isaac who was further down the track, loitering hopefully. Isaac wore a Hawaiian shirt, shorts and a wide brimmed straw hat, and didn't look particularly sick. I waited as Orbit crammed him into the back with the barrel and the cool box and then hopped into the passenger seat himself. We bumped our way along the track away from the farm, and out past the sheep being herded across the pastures by Harrison and Shanghazi. I stopped and waved to Harrison who came running, and taking ten dollars from my bag I handed his change through the window.

"T'tenda, Missus," Harrison smiled broadly, and softly clapped his hands in thanks. I smiled back and drove on. Orbit was staring at me.

"You have no money," he stated, slightly accusingly.

"No, that's right."

"But you give him ten dollar?"

"That was yours," I explained, gently.

"Eh?" There was that sob again. Orbit turned swiftly, looking over his shoulder at the quickly diminishing site of his cash.

"Don't worry, I promised you eight, didn't I?"

"Eh?"

"You will get eight," I stated firmly.

We reached the tar strip road into town, and I put on my seat belt and waited for Orbit to do the same. The local police were quite hot on seat belts.

"You like Paul Simon?" I asked, putting a tape in the cassette player.

"Aieee!" agreed Isaac and Orbit.

Gracelands needs to be played loudly, and where better to enjoy that wonderful rhythm than bowling down a hot, dusty African road, with cicadas singing along from the bush lined track.

It was strange how my taste in music was changing, however. I still enjoyed our old tapes, but when I was by myself I had this deep longing to sing. None of the songs I knew seemed to satisfy, the words were mundane and the music worn out. At the little Chegutu church service that I attended each Sunday the music lifted my spirit and the words were full of meaning. I had come to know a few of the wives of the missionaries at the Bible College, and one in particular was always singing choruses and hymns to herself. My early unworthy thoughts had been that it must be very difficult to keep up such a show of holiness. Now I would often find myself humming these same choruses to myself. I wanted to sing, but I didn't know any of the words off by heart, so I learned a few and the Holy Spirit helped me. I would wake up with a tune on my mind and maybe a couple of words which I would hum and sing over and over until, suddenly, the whole chorus would come to me. Now I sang for the sheer pleasure of singing. It was my first indication that the Holy Spirit truly wanted to be my teacher, for soon after the experience came the confirmation, discovered (I thought) quite by chance in the Bible. "Speaking to one another in psalms and hymns and spiritual songs, singing and making melody in your heart to the Lord." (Eph.5 v 19).

We covered the distance to town in no time, and I asked Orbit where he wanted to be dropped.

"Here is good," he pointed, "By that tree, where that guy is with bicycle."

He got out and retrieved his ten gallon drum, while Isaac took his place in the front seat for the short trip to the hospital.

"What time you come back?"

"Back? I'm not coming back."

"Eh?"

The prospect of walking home with a ten gallon drum of beer on his head didn't seem to appeal. Isaac giggled.

"Well, I shall be a long time," I told him. "First I have to queue in the Bank for eight dollars........."

Orbit nodded, he could see the sense in that.

".... and then I have to queue at the post office, and do shopping. If you are here when I come back I'll pick you up."

Orbit nodded, and then his face brightened.

"I can wait in the bar, it's no problem."

"Well, wave at me if I don't see you."

"I will," promised Orbit.

I took Isaac to the gates of the hospital and then headed for town.

The queuing took three hours. The Bank wasn't too bad, but having queued at the post office for nearly an hour I then had to fill out two forms for each of my six parcels and also tie them with string, as they didn't think my sticky tape would hold. For this the counter clerk kindly gave me one long length of string, which he separated from a large roll by sawing it frantically across the edge of his desk, and left me to decide how I would tie up six parcels with it. I sorted through my bag and found a penknife, and eventually everything was tied, stamped, labelled, documented, rubber stamped and hopefully on it's way to England. As I left the garage on my last stop a heavy shower of rain started, and I couldn't help but think that if nothing else it might sober Orbit up a bit before I got there.

He had placed his barrel half way across the road and was sitting on it, flapping both arms like a large, waterlogged bird. I steered round him, pulled off the road and stopped. He came running up with another guy, carrying the heavy barrel between them.

"He can come, too?" asked Orbit.

"He can, but you spill beer in the car you clean car, right?"

"Right," grinned Orbit, "Sure!"

I drove on gently. African beer has a sour, pungent smell, the barrel had a loosely fitting lid which was jammed on with a plastic bag, and the road was far from smooth.

"Can we have music?" whispered Orbit.

We drove home to the second part of Gracelands, and Orbit's face was a picture of contentment. We reached the bungalow and I took out four two dollar bills and counted them out before him.

"Six dollars for the lift and two dollars for the music," I told him.

"Eh? Ah, Medem," laughed Orbit, taking his eight dollars.

I left them at the gate, kneeling on the ground, peering into their barrel. As I packed away the groceries a knock came at the back door.

"I need a one litre jug," explained Mishek, "That guy at the gate, he is selling beer."

As the day wore on it seemed more and more likely that the rains were going to break. It was oppressively hot. The clouds built up into great piled masses of deep grey and straight sided curtains of grey showed the path of the rainstorms across the open countryside to the north. Lightening forked wildly, its brilliance heralding the great, majestic boom of the thunder which rolled across the parched, brown sandveld. The air was charged with a force that could be felt, and the smell and taste of rain was on the wind. The storm touched all the senses, moving towards us with a steady inevitability which emphasised the power it held over us mere mortals. An ocean held in the sky. The rain we needed so desperately was minutes away. For most it was new life, for others it would be death and for others devastation. The clouds could bring hail that would reduce the crops to stunted stalks in a sea of mud. Or, it could bring steady rain that would feed and nourish growth and fruitfulness. A few heavy droplets scattered noisily across the corrugated iron roof of our bungalow, a few seconds pause and then the deluge. Deafening in its intensity, the solid wall of rain enveloped us, drowning even the sound of the thunder, which was felt rather than heard. The lightning switched the lights off and on as if showing its contempt and superiority over man's puny attempts to harness the power that was its life.

I thought of the horses out in the paddock with just trees for shelter. I thought of Tobias, off on swollen feet that morning to see a faith healer. I thought of Harrison out across the open pastures with the sheep.

The storm hit Chegutu, ten kilometres away, with merciless ferocity. Hailstones the size of a man's fist caved in roofs and wrought havoc amongst the red blossomed Flamboyant trees that lined the streets. The lightning claimed two lives; four more were killed when unsafe houses collapsed. Telephone and electricity lines toppled as the storm rolled on towards the south, and was gone. On the farm we knew little of its fury. The rain was torrential, but when it had passed the sun came out to warm the backs of the dairy cattle in the paddock and to steam them dry. It had been a heavy shower in African terms, a welcome break for the crops from the hot sun, but it would have done little towards filling the river or restoring the dams.

CHAPTER EIGHT

Christmas came and went amidst brilliant sunshine and sweltering heat. I was happy to be away from the commercialised Christmas of England. There were no carols on the radio until Christmas Day, no great advertising campaigns, no hard sell. We bought charity Christmas cards and should have bought more, but two days before the holiday they had been taken from the shelves and were unavailable. We had piles of cards from England, a taped message from our daughter and her family, and as if to christen our new telephone which had been installed mid-December, we had 'phone calls from the family which were wonderful. Suddenly Africa and England didn't seem so far apart and the line was so clear we could have been sitting together in the same room. The home-sickness I had expected didn't come. I was completely happy in my new home, and although I looked forward to seeing our children soon, I wanted to show them Africa much more than I wanted to go back to England.

When our container had arrived John and I realised that we now had a number of 'thievable' items and came to the conclusion that we would need a guard dog. I had always had a dog, and in England we had two, a Doberman and a spaniel. Both had been rescue cases. Mutt the Doberman came to us as a skeleton, Sam the spaniel had been dumped at a picnic site. The spaniel was John's the Doberman mine, and he had left a big hole in my heart. I had treated him for years for a skin condition which became gradually worse until we came to the inevitable decision and took him to the vet for the last time. Sam had followed a friend's car late one night from our Devon smallholding and had been killed by a car on his way home. So when we left England we were dogless, and now we decided that a puppy would be an ideal Christmas present for me, and I began to search the newspapers and farm magazines that Fred sent down to us, via Mwunza, each week.

I didn't want a Doberman, although tears still came into my eyes when I saw one, but I did want a big dog and there were plenty to choose from. It was a sad fact that they were necessary. Gangs ranged out from the towns, raiding isolated farms and everything and anything is saleable in a country with severe monetary controls and widespread poverty. In England our belongings were few and poor pickings, but here they were enviable. So every farm had its pack of dogs and the crosses were frightening. Rotweillers, Alsatians, Great Danes, Ridgebacks, Staffies, Irish Wolfhounds and Dobermans. They had all been jumbled up to produce big, strong, potentially ferocious animals that patrolled inside security fences and you passed the gate by invitation only.

I saw an advertisement for Bouvier x Great Dane puppies and liked the idea. Jenny, from Farmer's Co-op, had a Bouvier x Irish Wolfhound which was waist high and looked like 'Animal' in the Muppets. I tried, unsuccessfully, for a week to get through to the telephone number given, but eventually I was answered by the maid.

"Do you have any puppies left?" I asked her.

"We haf nineteen," came the answer.

They hadn't gone like hot cakes.

"Can I make an appointment to come and see them?"

"You want puppy, you come get puppy," was the quick reply.

I got the impression that cleaning up after nineteen puppies was becoming a chore. I made an appointment to go the following day.

We found the house in an expensive suburb of Harare, and were met at the gate by two Bouvier bitches, both with wagging tails and both in milk. The maid came and opened the gates for us to drive in and John parked in the shade. I looked around hopefully for a Great Dane.

"Puppies here,"

the maid waved an arm in the direction of her little annexe, adjoining a large, white, villa type house, and led the way across closely cropped lawns, fringed with flowering shrubs and palms. The Bouviers followed, tongues lolling, happy expressions on their faces. They were quite small, but I had never seen a pure bred Bouvier so didn't know what to expect.

"These are small," agreed John, "they're very young."

"Fourteen months," said the maid.

The puppies came tumbling out of the wash-room at the back of the house, some black, some spotted, one or two brindled and the rest brown. They were healthy, cuddly and wriggling with friendship, as all puppies are, but small with small feet, which made us feel that they wouldn't gain much altitude.

"Where is the father?" I asked.

"He is next door."

"I'd like to see him."

She nodded and I followed her across the back lawn to the neighbouring house. A high wall separated the two properties, and finished at a tall dense hedge and a clump of big, spreading trees. A piece of wire netting bridged a small gap between the wall and the hedge and the maid headed for this gap. There she quickly shinned up a tree, and balancing herself against the trunk, put two fingers to her mouth and whistled loudly. Immediately several large sounding dogs began to bark, and I could hear them coming closer. She called something in Shona and two young African men, dressed in the white uniforms of house staff, came to the fence and indicated that the dog I wanted to see was somewhere behind the wall.

"You come up tree," suggested the maid, "You see him."

I managed the first couple of branches, which was enough to let me see the dogs. Three Alsatian crosses were standing there, sniffing the air suspiciously and when they caught sight of me they all bounded towards the now insecure looking wire, barking and snarling. I found I could manage another couple of branches for a better view.

"Which is the father?" I asked my fellow tree dweller.

"This one," she pointed to the one leaping at the wire, jaws dripping saliva.

"Right. Well, I think they can take them away now, "I suggested, "I've seen him."

She spoke to the laughing Africans, and the dogs followed them obediently into the house, growling, hackles raised.

I slithered to the ground. What had happened was obvious. The most aggressive dog had jumped the wire and sired two litters of puppies. The bitches were far too young and still had some growing to do themselves. Where the Great Dane idea had come from was a mystery.

"Tell the Boss the puppies are very nice, but we don't think they will grow big enough," John told the maid, "We really want a big dog."

She nodded, her disappointment showing.

I was disappointed too, but we had never had a puppy, always other people's mistakes and tragedies, so our first puppy had to be the right one. I don't know why we ever considered the advertisement for Jack Russell pups. They were certainly unlikely to grow any bigger than the ones we had seen, but they were just down the road (30 k) from the farm, and looking at pups seemed a nice thing to do on a Saturday afternoon. We came back with two. They were absolutely irresistible, and having not resisted very hard about the dog puppy I chose, John didn't argue at all when I suggested he should have the little bitch he liked and they would be our Christmas presents to each other.

"What shall we call them?" I asked John, as we drove home with them curled up on my lap in a fat, warm heap.

"Yin and Yang," said my husband promptly.

I didn't want to be a wet blanket, admittedly it was an apt and original idea, but somehow it didn't feel quite right. I couldn't see me striding through the bush yelling 'Yin, come here. Where are you Yang?' I kept quiet about names for a day or two and then suddenly, when I wasn't even thinking of names, I looked at them playing together and it came. Porgie and Bess. If John was disappointed about Yin and Yang he put on a brave face and Porgie and Bess they became. He immediately dubbed them Porkie and Bess, and no amount of kicking his shins would stop him, but it was true that Porgie was very much of a podge to start with. There had been two litters, sired by the same dog and it soon became apparent that not only did we have one from each litter, but neither of them was really a Jack Russell. A wide variety of dogs come under that heading, but Porgie soon developed Fox Terrier legs and towered above Bess who had an alert, foxy little face and also grew legs, but not to the same extent. They fought from their first waking moment until their last exhausted growl. They were quite independent, with a huge garden to play in and explore, but they also adopted each of us as if they knew how they had been chosen, Porgie coming to me and Bess going to John. Porgie would suddenly leave Bess in the garden, come rushing in to find me and ask for a cuddle. Cuddle given, he would rush off again to continue battle.

I fed them according to the natural feeding diet suggested in my Herbal Veterinary book. At 8:00 a.m. they got milk and honey, and at 12 noon cereal and milk with a little oil or butter. At 4:00 p.m. they had raw shredded meat and at 8:00 p.m. more shredded meat with chopped parsley and a sprinkle of bran. Their internal clocks never failed them, and they grew rapidly, their coats sleek and silky and their energy boundless. From the very beginning, I took them with me when I worked with the sheep. The ewes soon put them in their place and for a couple of weeks they knew that the safest place was under the parked Suzi, as the sheep couldn't crawl under there, although they did tend to get surrounded. As they got bigger and braver they ventured out for brief sorties, diving back if a ewe charged them. Within a month they were all great friends. A group of ewes would stand heads down, eyes half closed, as the pups bounced around them, tail stumps wagging, delightedly licking their faces and pulling at their ears. Two or three of the ewes we had bought in had lambed unexpectedly, and the lambs were fascinated to find other animals their own size and came running up to them to play. This often caused the pups to be bowled over by their mothers, whose natural instincts didn't allow for such un-natural friendships.

They greeted Harrison with unqualified enthusiasm each morning, and every day his grin became broader as he made a fuss of them. Even Orbit came under their spell, barking and growling at them and then running away across the paddock with the pups in hot pursuit. Although in the villages there were many leggy and ribby dogs to be seen, I found that most Africans on the farm, especially the women, were frightened of dogs and horses. This was easy to understand as most dogs were kept by the whites to protect them from Africans, and I was just as uneasy walking through their villages. A contributing factor was that the risk of rabies was a very real one, and very few villagers bothered to have their animals vaccinated. One morning, before I had the dogs, I had walked out to the sheep pens and chanced to stop at the top of a small kopje and look back. There I saw a jackal sniffing along my trail. I hadn't been worried, but when Orbit reported seeing six jackals near the sheep pens a few days later, and everyone began to arm themselves with axes then I began to wonder.

"Carry a stick," John had told me, "They often have rabies and they're not frightened of you."

He went on to say, that two women had been attacked on the adjoining farm the previous year, and had subsequently died.

It was well to have everything vaccinated. It was law to have the pups done, but cattle and horses could also be affected. There were a heap of things to vaccinate the sheep against, but as ours were all bought late in the season they had already been done - or we thought they had.

The rains had still not come, but the few heavy showers were heavier than anything I had ever seen. One of these squalls gave us two inches of rain in one evening, and Porgie and Bess sat side by side looking out of their flap-less cat-flap in the veranda door, staring in disbelief at the solid wall of water outside. They didn't stare for long. One gave the other a push and they were gone, haring round and round the house, rocketing through all the puddles until they were soaked and breathless.

Next morning Harrison and Orbit were both in the night watchman's hut when we drove up. They seemed deeply engrossed, so I left them to whatever they were discussing and heaved the sack of grain from the back of the Suzi. I had got it as far as the troughs when Orbit came up behind me.

"This lamb, it is dying," he announced, "you come see."

Inside the hut the end of a log more than a foot in diameter was smouldering over the ashes of his fire. As it burned it was shoved up a bit further. How he had got it going in the first place was a mystery to me. The hut at floor level was filled with smoke, and the lamb lay flat out on a sack, its back to the fire. Its mouth opened and closed soundlessly in the final stages of exposure, and death was not far away.

"This hut is no good," stated Orbit, with feeling," The rain come, and straight through here," he indicated the gap between the wall and the roof," and I am wet to here!" He held his hand just below his chin.

"Just like England," I told him cheerfully," only there it's cold as well."

Having spent weeks at a time soaked to the skin and up to my knees in mud, battling against sleet, snow and hail to lamb our sheep in Devon, I had little sympathy for Orbit, gently steaming in the hot morning sun.

"I'll take it home," I told him, gathering up the lamb. Harrison nodded, his face full of concern. Anyone who says that the African has no feeling for animals has never met a person like Harrison.

I put it gently in the back of the Suzi, propped it up on its chest, covered it with a sack and jumped quickly into the driver's seat. Orbit, seeing he was about to miss his lift, grabbed his bag and axe and dived for the passenger door as I moved off.

At the bungalow I carried the limp little body to the bathroom, filled the washbasin with warm water and popped the lamb in. I massaged the water gently into its cold, closely curled wool, topping up with hot water. Once she felt warm I towelled her dry, found a deep cardboard box, lined it with an old wool sweater and put her in, covering her over and tucking her in until only her nose was showing. I put the box in a sunny corner of the veranda and left her to sleep - she would live or die, I could do no more. Back at the sheep pens Harrison caught the lamb's mother and taking the jug I had brought with me I knelt in the damp sand to milk out the udder so that I could tube feed the sick lamb. One side of the udder was quite empty, the other swollen with milk. I drew thumb and forefinger down the teat and got a bead of milk. I tried again. Nothing. Feeling gently along the milk canal I found a small swelling. The milk came as far as the swelling and no further. Rummaging through the glove compartment of the Suzi I found a hairpin.

How it had managed to stay hidden there I would never know, it was ages since I had used hairpins, but now I was delighted to see it with its long straight sides and tiny smooth bobbles on the tips, it was ideal. Harrison watched open mouthed as I straightened out the pin, pushed it carefully up through the teat opening and worked it up to the blockage. The ewe didn't move. With my left thumb and forefinger I held the blockage and wriggled the pin around inside in a circular movement. Then I pulled out the pin and squeezed the teat. Milk spurted out and Harrison gave a triumphant squeak of delight. It was thick, creamy and lots of it. Driving carefully with one hand I bore my life-giving milk home. Having collected stomach tube and syringe from the kitchen I trotted through to the veranda and dropped to my knees by the box. The little black head peeped out from the warm wool covering, her eyes still closed, and she was quite dead.

I called Mishek and handed him the box with its sad little bundle to bury. What was I going to say to Harrison?

"Mishek, how do you say 'dead'?"

"Fa," said Mishek, "Kufa is to die."

He glanced at the box he was holding,

"Just say 'y'fa'," he suggested.

That evening I went up to check the sheep into the night pen.

"Picanin?" queried Harrison, smiling expectantly.

"Y'fa," I said quietly, and opened the gates.

It was soon after the lamb died that we lost the mother of the twins. Three of the bought in ewes had lambed and we fed them separately to make sure they had their fair amount of grain to keep the milk flow coming. They all became very tame and on the day she died I had been making a fuss of her when she had finished feeding. She was bright, fat and healthy. Two hours later she was fat, in superb condition, and dead. I just couldn't understand it. Two days later the same happened to another one. This one was black, and the sheen on its coat was a mark of absolute health. Again, death was swift. I began to panic slightly.

We loaded the carcase onto the truck and I took it into the vet, hoping that Monday wouldn't be another day that he didn't work. It was. The gardener told us that he wasn't expected in that day and once again we had been left in the cactus. I took it back to the farm, where it was eagerly skinned, cut up and distributed to eager buyers. Then a thought struck me. I checked my vet book as I felt it was almost certainly pulpy kidney against which they were supposed to have been vaccinated. I rang Fred who was spending a few days in Harare and asked if he would bring back vaccine to bring them in line with the rest of the flock and he came back with the same 8 in 1 vaccine that we had used in England. I had asked our local vet if such a thing was available in Zimbabwe and had got the cold smile and the answer, 'wouldn't it be lovely'. And now, here it was in my hand.

Within a few days we had enough to do the whole flock and they had their initial dose, the second injection would be done two weeks before lambing and then their lambs would also receive immunity from their mothers. The timing actually couldn't have been better and I was more than relieved that they were all protected. And then the other one died. This one didn't die suddenly. She was obviously not well, hanging back behind the rest of the flock and not eating much. I gave her a broad spectrum anti-biotic but there were no real symptoms to work with. She was a little laboured in her breathing, and I suspected pneumonia. Pneumonia was not in Harrison's vocabulary.

"Bad cold," I explained, "'flu."

At 'flu' his face lit up in recognition.

"Ah," he nodded readily, "'flu. Or maybe," he ventured, "malaria?"

"She has eaten," said Orbit, with a degree of authority," a very small, white frog."

"She could have too," agreed John later, when I was pouring over my faithful vet book, "they're extremely poisonous, and sometimes cattle graze them up with the grass."

At last I decided to bring her into the garden where I could keep an eye on her, and when I went to fetch her she was much worse, her breathing difficult. Something struck me about the colouring around her mouth and when I opened it I found that her tongue was quite blue. I had heard that there was a viral disease called Blue Tongue, about which I knew nothing. The local sheep manual gave nothing about symptoms and just stressed the need for vaccination. I rang the farm that had sold us the sheep and spoke to the manager.

"Yes, they've all been vaccinated," he assured me, "it's done as a matter of course. Leave it with me and I'll find out the dates from the head shepherd."

I rang back that afternoon.

"The manager had to go out," said the secretary," but he left a note for you to say that he is very sorry, but it seems that none of them were vaccinated for Blue Tongue, it was overlooked."

Suddenly, I could see history repeating itself, sheep dying everywhere and nothing I could do about it.

In desperation I rang the vet in Harare who had stitched up Anzac. I needed to talk to someone whose opinion I trusted. I was lucky he was there.

"Well," he said, "In Blue Tongue you actually have blood clotting at the base of the tongue, and it swells, turns blue and goes hard."

"It's not hard, just blue and her breathing is very, very laboured."

"Temperature?"

"Normal".

"I should say she's more likely to have pneumonia, have you got antibiotics?"

"Yes, I've given her teramycin."

"Well, that's right. That's what she needs."

"But her tongue is blue."

"Well, " he explained patiently," If her lungs are damaged and she can't breath, she's not getting the oxygen and she will go blue."

"Oh, well, that's a relief. I thought they were all going to get it."

"They could if it's viral pneumonia," he told me, cheerfully.

Viral pneumonia had been one of the eight diseases that we had just vaccinated against.

"Can you tell me more about this Blue Tongue," I asked, "I've just found out that none of them have been vaccinated and they should all be in lamb now."

"No," he said, without hesitation, "You can't vaccinate pregnant ewes. It's a live vaccine and you would cause abortion storms and have malformed lambs. You'll just have to sit it out this year. It's actually most prevalent in the wet seasons," he added comfortingly, "and no-one can call this season wet!"

I put the 'phone down feeling much better. In his opinion it was pneumonia and the treatment I had given was right, there was nothing more I could do. She died the next day and vanished the way of the previous two. I couldn't help but think that the local Africans must have blessed the day that I came as shepherd.

CHAPTER NINE

Tobias died at the end of January. The village mourned his passing from the evening of his death to two evenings after the funeral. A drummer such as we had never heard before beat an intricate rhythm on a strange drum, deep, dark, rolling black notes that led the shrill singing of the women. The storm clouds gathered and the thunder added its own dimension.

I drifted off to sleep each evening and woke at four thirty the following morning to the same sounds. In the morning they worked as usual, but at mid-day the drum began again and the women joined in. Soon after noon on the day of the funeral Mishek led the tall, slim figure of Gomo through the gates.

"This man is sick," he explained, "Boss John say you have medicine."

Gomo looked very sick. His eyes were half closed and his pallor unhealthy.

"How is he sick?"

Mishek hesitated, and then explained hopefully in Shona.

I shook my head, "Sorry, Mishek, I don't understand."

Mishek sighed and resorted to graphic sign language, which was instantly understood.

"Diarrhoea?"

"Yes, Medem," Mishek beamed in relief, "Diarrhoea."

I had no medicine for diarrhoea, although the Farmer's co-op sold it by the litre.

"I can make him a drink to stop him being sick," I suggested, "You know, like the one I gave you."

"Yes, Medem, "agreed Mishek, faithfully," That good medicine."

"And if he has nothing to eat for a day, it may help to stop the diarrhoea."

"Yes, Medem," Mishek nodded to the prescribed treatment.

The beating drum reminded me of Tobias and the parsley. Tobias and his hospital card that said 'swollen ankles'. Tobias off to see a faith healer. None of us had helped Tobias in his search for a cure. No-one could, for

Tobias had died of AIDS. What was wrong with Gomo? I felt desperately inadequate. The only experience I had was from raising two children and reading herbal books. A little knowledge was so dangerous, but what alternative did he have. The alternative, I knew, was the witch doctor, and he had chosen to come and see me.

Gomo said something quietly to Mishek.

"Medem," said Mishek, quickly, "Gomo say he need malaria pills."

Malaria pills. So that was the medicine Boss John said I had. I fetched the large plastic pack and counted ten pills out into an envelope and wrote on the packet. Four now, two at six o'clock, two tomorrow and two the next day. I went back to find Gomo sitting on a boulder in the rockery beneath the trees, his head in his hands. I sat beside him and read out the instructions on the envelope. He nodded quietly, thanked me and walked slowly away towards the village, the drums and the singing. I got into the Suzi and drove up to the tobacco barns. John was talking to Paul by the tractor sheds, I waved and he came over.

"Gomo came for some pills. He looks really very sick."

John looked puzzled, "Gomo or Godfrey?"

"Gomo".

"I sent Godfrey."

"I sent Gomo," put in Paul, "His guts are playing up."

"He said he wanted malaria pills."

Paul shook his head, "Wouldn't have thought so."

"Well, I gave him some."

"Don't worry," said John, "They won't hurt him."

A couple of hours later he came into the bungalow and handed me back the envelope of tablets.

"Gomo collapsed in the compound. He's unconscious and we took him to hospital."

My nagging doubts leaped into guilt.

"He shouldn't have had the tablets."

John shook his head,

"They were fine," he assured me, "The hospital says its malaria."

Late that afternoon the drums and the singing and the whole village, it seemed, moved nearer to the small graveyard outside our northern boundary fence. For a short while afterwards there was silence, then later, after darkness had fallen, the deep drum began a lonely tribute as if to say, 'You have left us Tobias, and we have laid you to rest, but you are remembered by all who hear the drum.'

And the thunder echoed the drumbeats, sending the message still further.

"There are many," said John, standing quietly by the veranda window, gazing unseeingly out into the night, "Who say that AIDS is Nature's way of saving Africa. Too many people, having too many children, all wanting to farm, taking more from the soil that is given back. Nature balancing herself. But they are all like Tobias. Do we weep for Tobias, or do we weep for Africa?"

All like Tobias, I thought, all like Gomo. And I think we both quietly wept for them all.

The bucket I picked up in the garden shed had a bar of green soap in it which looked like the herbal soap that I had brought with me from England. It was precious to me as I wasn't going to get any more easily, so I picked the small cake up and sniffed it. The strong carbolic smell hit hard, and I put it down quickly just as Mishek appeared in the doorway.

"Yours?" I enquired.

"Yes, Medem, it is mine."

He looked serious.

"I wash my hands every time," he explained," and then if I get this disease I don't give it to anyone else."

I was touched by his thoughtfulness, although I felt that his understanding of the problem was probably a bit hazy. He had refused to go back to the clinic for the rest of his treatment, but had consulted someone in the village who knew African medicine, and had pronounced himself cured. Maagi had reappeared a couple of times, each visit coinciding with pay-day, but her visits had been short. Mishek was looking very well. He was still without Wellingtons, but I had given him a white coat to wear whilst dipping the horses, and he had fallen upon it with great enthusiasm, and it was now his 'uniform'. He wore it everywhere, and it was always brilliantly white and neatly ironed. It was one that I had worn the summer before in England, when a friend had persuaded me that it would be fun to show our goats at the local show, and it fitted Mishek to perfection. He usually wore it with the deep red shirt, the collar folded neatly over the top of the coat, which set off his dark features very well. He had also grown a moustache, which suited him. The finishing touch was a wide brimmed straw hat, with a red ribbon to match his shirt stitched around the crown. He reminded me of a very sunburned ice-cream salesman, but to the ladies of the village he cut a very dashing figure.

The garden, however, failed to flourish and it wasn't now due to the lack of water.

"The Boss is cross," I told him," There are no lettuces in the garden, How can we have salads. You must plant the seeds when I give them to you."

"Yes, Medem," said Mishek with great humility.

The next morning I went out to the garden and found a whole bed of freshly watered lettuce plants.

"You make magic, Mishek?" I asked.

He looked down at his feet, and grinned.

"No, Medem," he admitted," I go see Kenyemba, he give me out of Boss Fred's garden."

They were destined to be short lived lettuces. I had impressed upon Mishek the value of picking the vegetables we did manage to grow when they were young and in prime condition, so that I could store them in the freezer. So when the first ones began to heart up nicely he picked the whole bed.

Weekends were always fairly wild down in the village, and the drums played from sunset on Friday until early Monday morning. I wasn't too surprised to see Mishek's head glide fairly slowly past the window on Monday morning, as he tried to walk without moving up and down too much.

"Good morning, Mishek," I greeted him," Are you well?"

He looked at me, painfully.

"No, Medem, I am not well. Last night I get drunk," he confessed, "And that woman she say, 'Why you sleep there? You must get up, and I have fall asleep on the ground by the store. This morning I am not well. I cannot work today."

He had chosen his moment, as usual. John had a rare day off, and wanted to work with the horses.

"Well, you had better tell that to the Boss," I told him, swiftly passing the buck, "He'll be here in a minute. Tell him."

I walked away. John used to have red hair. He also had the temperament to match. Some years later, after his baptism, he began to mellow as the fruits of the Spirit ripened in the life of my born again husband. Love, joy, peace, long-suffering, kindness, goodness, faithfulness, gentleness and self-control (Gal.6 v 22,23) had all been there and were the qualities that I loved, but some took longer to ripen than others!

A few minutes later John came in looking grim.

"Mishek's reeling around out there. He's a bloody nuisance. The one day I get off for months and he does this. I'd made up my mind to go for a good long ride," he gave a fly a hefty swat that would have stunned an elephant, "Poncing around in a white coat and a hat with ribbons on it. He can get his act together or he can go!"

He dropped into a chair for all of ten seconds, then bounced to his feet again and went to glare out of the window. I must say, I felt the same. The horses were difficult to separate with the flimsy barbed wire fences we had. If we took Leprechaun away then Anzac panicked and vice versa, but without a safe place to put them we couldn't let them panic for a while and get used to being alone, it was very frustrating. The fencing team had been kept busy doing repairs and alterations in the tobacco barns so all we could do was leave one with Mishek whilst we worked with the other. Tendai looked around the door.

"Mishek, he want to see you. He is at the door."

"Is he," growled John, "Well, he may wish he wasn't".

He was back in less than a minute.

"He says he needs to go to the hospital clinic, he's expecting a lift!"

Even if Mishek hadn't been in the dog-house, trips to town were rationed for all of us, petrol prices being what they were.

"I told him to catch a tractor, there's one going into Chegutu."

With the rest of a free day ahead, we tried unsuccessfully to think of a way to utilise the horses. We gave up, took the motorbike and went for a tour of the farm to check the cattle fences - something John had hoped to be doing on Leprechaun. Coming back we met Tendai, looking for Chiringwe.

"I didn't get paid," she explained, "I think he has my money."

After a cup of coffee we re-examined the horse question.

"If I rode and you long-reined Anzac we could swap half way," suggested my husband.

This decided we tacked up and set off.

Anzac soon took the lead and John purposely kept Leprechaun back so that the distance increased by over a hundred metres. Safe in the knowledge that his pal was back there somewhere, Anzac went well and we had gone through the farm and out along a bush lined track when he suddenly veered to the left and started pulling to get his head. Simultaneously I heard Leprechaun call. The effect was instant. Anzac put down his head, gave two hearty bucks, turned and dodged the other side of a tree. I tried to pull him round towards me but the tree hampered the action of the rein and he pulled them easily through my hands. In a last desperate attempt I tried to use the tree as a snubbing post but he had too much rein and I had to let go. I yelled to John that he was coming and caught sight of my husband's blue shirt through the trees. He was leading Leprechaun. Anzac ran to his friend like the big baby he was and John caught him easily. He was holding a stirrup in his hand. Leprechaun had given a fair imitation of a bucking bronco when we had gone out of sight and his stirrup leather had broken. Luckily John had stayed on.

"What now?" I asked.

"Press on," said my husband, wearily.

"Are you getting up?"

"No, I won't bother. There's no pleasure riding him in this mood."

Anzac went ahead again and John kept Leprechaun way back as before. We did a circle and came back onto the path to the bungalow without further mishap. Leprechaun looked as if he had been in a foam bath. He was running with sweat and had walked no more than a couple of miles. Anzac was completely dry.

"Well, I think that is pretty conclusive," said John, "They're too highly strung for the sort of job we want them for."

He looked at me, closely,

"Are you all right?"

I was a lighter shade of puce,

"I'm hot."

We put the horses out, put the pups in the Suzi and went for a short drive and a long walk along the river. It hadn't been the best of free days. The next evening John came back at four-thirty.

"I'm going to take Leprechaun out," he announced, determination in his voice. "Mishek can stay on 'til I get back and keep an eye on Anzac, it won't hurt him."

I put the kettle on for a quick cup of tea whilst he rummaged around the spare room, finding a saddle and all the bits he needed to replace his broken Western. He also picked up a crash-hat which showed he meant business. He went through the kitchen carrying head collars and lead reins and a few seconds later I saw Mishek heading towards the paddock at the double. He had been on his best behaviour all day. John drank a quick cup of tea and followed him and as he went through the door a rattle of thunder shook the air ominously. I finished washing the spinach that I had just picked, with a tight feeling in my stomach as if I was about to be put on an untamed horse and let go.

'It's silly,' I told myself, 'you don't even have to be there. He's never been thrown off in all the years you've known him and Mishek's responsible for Anzac. What are you in a state about?'

I hurried to be there. A few heavy spots of rain were falling and I took John's mac with me. He came to meet me at the gate leading Leprechaun, all tacked up and ready to go. Anzac was grazing peacefully inside the paddock gate, held on a long lunge rein by Mishek, in his white coat and hat with the ribbon on. John handed me the reins while he put on the mac, and I looked up at Leprechaun. His head was high, his eyes worried and his breathing quick and nervous. He knew they were going to be separated. John was up in the saddle before I knew it, and then realised that the new stirrups were too short. He was sitting slightly sideways, one foot in the stirrup and the other leg hanging free as he lengthened the leather, when Leprechaun exploded. He shot backwards, dragging the reins from my hands, and as John shortened the reins to take control he reared. He went high, and to stop himself from going over backwards he somehow moved his back legs off the path and into Mwanza's mealie patch, which was deeply hoed. He lost his balance in the soft sand and went down on his chest, but sprang up again almost immediately. He reared high again and then started to plunge. John had stayed with him until then, but on the last rear he had been hit hard on the bridge of his nose. Mid-plunge Leprechaun twisted sideways and John half fell, half slid to the ground. He still held the reins and having got him off the horse stood snorting and shaking. Blood was pouring down John's face as he took off the saddle and then as he handed me the reins the heavens opened.

"Chuck him out, would you?" he said quietly, his temper tightly held in check, "That was his last chance."

I turned him out in the paddock with Anzac and followed my husband inside to find him sitting in a cold bath with a cube of ice on his nose.

I suppose I have always had a misplaced sense of humour, and my husband had long since come to expect weakly suppressed giggles more than sympathy. The bleeding had actually stopped and as he looked cross eyed at me past the ice cube I could see a small but deep cut. A year previously I had been standing casually in front of a four year old thoroughbred mare when something had frightened her. She had, without any hesitation, knocked me flat and gone over the top of me. I well remembered lying in a heap on the straw with warm, sticky blood dripping very rapidly past my eyes. That had earned me bruised ribs, seven stitches across my nose and eyebrow, two Technicolor eyes and several days of uncontrollable laughter from my husband every time our eyes met. I gave as good as I got. It did seem, though, that thoroughbreds were definitely not for us.

Later that evening Mel rang. Johnny and Mel lived in Nyanga, Johnny and John having been friends for many years prior to John coming to England, and their home was set amongst beautiful mountains and streams in the wild, unspoilt countryside of the Eastern Highlands.

"Hey," shouted Mel above the crackles of the phone," Why don't you folks come up this weekend, we want to see you."

"Oh, Mel, that would be great. We would really like to come, can I just check with John?"

"Sure."

"Are you well?" I waited for John to cover the last few yards to the phone.

"I am," she laughed, briefly," But Johnny's had an accident."

"Oh, no. What's he done?"

"Well, we've got this Santa Getruda cow with a two day old calf. Johnny went to let her out of the pen. He knew he had to be careful, and he opened the gate and gave her a wide berth. She went through alright, then turned round and came back for him. She knocked him down and danced on him, I've actually just come back from the hospital with him.

"So, what has he done?"

"She got him in the head too, so he's got black eyes, swollen face and neck and he's broken three ribs."

I relayed things quickly to John, who took over the phone whilst I went to rescue supper as they went over it again.

"Well, Melly, do you really want us there at the moment?" asked John.

The answer was obviously in the affirmative as he laughed and said,

"O.K., what can we bring?"

"Food and drink," answered Mel, promptly.

"Right" agreed John, "See you Saturday."

"You're going to make a lovely pair, "I told him, "I'm glad I've got a colour slide film in the camera."

We were just going to bed that evening, when there was a quiet knock on the back door. Phineus, the witch doctor, and someone else stood there in the shadows. He said something to me in Shona, but the only words I understood were the English ones, 'telephone' and 'ambulance'. I called John to come and find out what the problem was while I dialled the number. It was engaged, and I gave it a few minutes and tried again. Still engaged. John came in,

"It's a woman with breathing problems."

I found another home number and tried that. No answer. I went back to the original number and it rang.

"The ambulance is out," said the woman, who eventually answered, "when it comes back there is someone else waiting and it will come after that."

John relayed the message to Phineous and they went away.

I lay in bed later, looking out at the brilliant moonlight and the stark outlines of the big old trees near the window, listening to the sounds of the night. Frogs, crickets, nightjars. A child began to cry in Mwanza's house and down in the village I heard a woman shouting. Much later Fred's dogs began barking and the pups joined in. I heard the ambulance, changing up and down through the gears as it negotiated the bends, rocks and potholes on its way to the village. A brief silence and then it bumped its way back again and sped away down the long drive towards the hospital. The next thing I heard was John's watch peeping insistently. I buried my head under the pillow and waited for him to turn it off and reset it. Obviously it was still set for his mid-day 2.00 siesta. To my surprise he slowly sat up, swung his legs out of bed, located his slippers and crashed his way towards the kitchen. Down in the village Chiringwe began to beat the simbi and I realised it was, indeed, morning.

"I organised a raid on Orbit's house, last night," said John, handing me a mug of tea.

I was still mostly asleep and thought I had misheard.

"Orbit's house?"

"Mmm..." he gave me a sideways look from two eyes that sported every colour except black. "I've been told that at nine in the evening he goes home and sleeps, and then gets back to the sheep around four next morning."

In a way it didn't come as a surprise. Orbit always looked pretty fresh in the mornings for someone who had been awake all night. I had often been tempted to go and check on him, but the chance of him being there and putting an axe through my skull had always deterred me.

"Who told you?"

"Classified information. Actually, it is best that you don't know. I asked Chiringwe to go to his house with a witness after nine last night, and if Orbit was there then that's it - he's on his bike."

I hoped they were wrong; he was such a likeable rogue. It was with relief, therefore, that I found him with Harrison as usual when I reached the sheep pens later. He was either innocent or too quick for them! I suppose I felt relieved because I had a difficult subject to broach with Mishek that morning. He was grooming the horses when I got back.

"Mishek, did you collect Tendai's money for her on pay day?"

"Tendai? Yes, Medem, I collect it."

"Where is it? She's still looking for it."

Mishek's eyes were still furry looking and he stammered slightly.

"I get it and put it in my house. Then when I get drunk and go to sleep by the store, someone come and take it."

"You mean it's been stolen?"

"Yes, Medem, it is stolen."

No wonder he had managed to get so drunk.

"You must tell Tendai as soon as she comes today," I told him.

"Yes, Medem, I tell her."

How could he be so stupid? He was good with the horses; he had a good mind and was meticulous in his work. He was neat and tidy and enthusiastic, and he was falling to pieces. Mishek the thief, swindler and drunkard. It could well be Mishek the jobless if he didn't pull his socks up. Later that morning he marched across the garden to meet me, looking down at his toes in an ashamed manner.

"I tell her, Medem," he said, "And I say that next pay day she can collect my wages and take all of it, for what I have lost."

And he was true to his word.

Our weekend in Nyanga was wonderful. Warm and welcoming as ever, Johnny and Mel came to meet us as we drove up to their lovely, deeply thatched stone cottage, standing on the edge of their eight thousand acre ranch, surrounded by the high wooded hills and distant peaks of the Nyanga Mountains.

Johnny was leaning against the front of his truck, nursing his cracked ribs and trying hard not to laugh.

"Hell, it's like looking in a mirror," he chuckled, peering from his blue, black and purple eyes into John's.

We had a quick lunch, and then relaxed on the terrace with a bottomless tea pot and endless news to catch up on. Then I went with Mel to inspect her new chickens and geese, whilst the men wandered out to see the new building works and the mad cow that had surprisingly still survived her attack on Johnny. They had invited Lou, a neighbour from the next door farm, for supper. He arrived just as dusk was falling and when Mel went out to meet him we heard her shriek with laughter. Lou walked in with a black eye.

"I was castrating this calf," explained Lou, "My chap was supposed to be holding the rope tight on it's leg, but he leaned forward for a better view and you can guess the rest!"

I took a photograph of the three of them.

"How are the sheep, Judy?" asked Lou, as we settled into deep lounge chairs after a wonderful supper.

"They seem fine. There was a sick one just as we left this morning, isn't it always the way? But we gave it a jab of long acting antibiotic and hope that it will be better by Monday."

"Ah, sheep!" said Lou, with feeling, "Sometimes they die just because a friend did."

"I used to have sheep," he went on," in fact I had 780."

"You did?" I was impressed.

"Yeah, but I lost 252."

"How?"

"Predators. I shot over seventy jackals. Then we've got leopards, and hyenas, and then we've got whatever everyone else's sheep die of."

The conversation drifted on.....

"I think we use too many weed killers," Johnny was saying.

"I was reading the other day," I remembered," that if you plough at night you don't get the weed regrowth."

"Really?" said Lou, "Why's that then?"

"Apparently the weed seeds need just a split second burst of light to make germination begin. So when you turn the soil and the weed seed is exposed to the sun, even for a short time, it's enough to start it off. If you plough at night they don't see the sun. Simple, eh?"

"Well, I'm blowed," said Lou. "It's the same as asthma and Chihuahuas. Did you hear about that?"

"No," said Mel, "What's that?"

"Well," said Lou, "They've proven that if you suffer from asthma and you have a Chihuahua then the asthma goes away."

"Go on!" said Johnny, "How many do you have to take a day, Lou?"

Chris arrived just as Lou was leaving. Chris was a friend who lived on the ranch and helped Johnny with the cattle and horses. He was an avid bird watcher and his great love was for the eagles and hawks of Africa. Most weekends, it seemed, were spent on some precipice or other, watching them. It was then that I had my brilliant idea. Chris was also very, very good with horses.

"Chris, how would you like to come for a week's holiday and back Anzac for me?"

Chris blushed, shyly.

"I would love too," he said, sincerely, "I would really love to."

"Great," said Mel," Why not go back with them on Monday? We've been trying to make him take a holiday for months," she explained, "We can't make him go!"

Next morning John and I rose early. We walked out across the ranch, cool and clear in the high mountain air. We came across Johnny's horses, ten or so of them standing grazing and dozing, belly deep in the high brown grass. 'Number Four', one of Johnny's tame Brahman heifers came up for a chat and a big cuddle. We found ourselves on the wrong side of a stream and waded across, the water sharply cold and the rocks smooth and slippery. An African lad appeared from nowhere, driving a Brahman x Jersey cow in front of him, on the way to the house to be milked.

We arrived back to find Mel and her cook Kefus, frying eggs and bacon on her outdoor kitchen stove. Beyond the kitchen door they had set up a wood burning range under a canopy. Next to it a big tank over a wood fire heated gallons of hot water for the house and on the table next to the stove Kefus chopped tomatoes and aubergines. Their white bull terrier, Jaws, stood by hopefully.

That afternoon Johnny drove us further up into the hills to an hotel, where we browsed around a huge selection of African handicrafts on display and then sipped wonderful fruit laden drinks by the swimming pool, looking out towards the mountains. Johnny grinned at me,

"Tough in Africa, eh?"

Next morning we were up early again to pack. We jammed Chris into the back of the Suzi with our cases and set off on our five hour journey home. Before he left Africa, Nyanga had been John's home, and he was always sad to leave it for the hot lowveld where we now lived.

"I'm really looking forward to the next week," said Chris, "Just lazing around, riding new horses, and maybe spotting some different kinds of raptors. It's going to be great!"

Little did any of us know!

CHAPTER TEN

For Chris and the pups it was love at first sight. They leapt around him wriggling uncontrollably with delight, licking his face and tugging at his beard. We had left them in the combined care of Tendai and Mishek, and Orbit had come as night guard and fed them kapenta and sadza. Paul had come each evening to feed them their main meal. They were overjoyed to see us back. Porgie had somehow managed to pull one of his nails quite badly and was limping, but it didn't interfere with his bouncing. Chris sat on the floor with them, talking to them quietly in his 'animal language'.

"Mopped shmopped," he told Porgie, seriously," and mupped shmopped, and shmibbled wopped and mupped shmopped."

He looked up and grinned, "They understand,"

He looked back to Bess, "Wobbeklsk?"

Supper was a makeshift affair of sausages and spinach, which was none the less welcome.

"I know where you're going to sleep tonight," Chris told the pups, as we cleared away the plates and set the kettle to boil for coffee, "In my bed."

"Oh, no they're not," I told him firmly, "They sleep out on the veranda, and they're quite happy there."

Chris just smiled. He had brought his sleeping bag, as our funds hadn't yet accumulated enough for spare bedroom suites. We did have plenty of blankets, pillows and a mattress or two though, and that's where we found them neatly made into a comfortable bed - on the veranda. The pups were in the sleeping bag as if they had done it every night of their young lives, and Chris moved them over and crawled in too. Who were we to spoil the happiness of three?

The next morning we introduced Chris to the horses. They both got a big kiss on the nose and a quiet chat, understood by them alone. It was difficult to believe that the man standing cheek to cheek with Leprechaun had fought the terrible bush war which ended Rhodesia and gave birth to Zimbabwe. He had served in a mounted unit, was deaf in one ear from grenades and had been blown up by a double landmine explosion. It was almost impossible to believe that he could raise his hand in anger against any living thing. After the war he had worked with horses, training youngsters and retraining those spoilt by ignorance and heavy handed riding. It was easy to see that he would have been in his element there.

Mishek tacked up Leprechaun, and after another quiet chat and another kiss on the nose, Chris sprang lightly into the saddle and walked him away. The horses called to each other until Leprechaun was well out of sight, but he kept going. We tacked up Anzac, putting his head collar over his bridle and attached the long reins once more to the nose band. I had been driving him for some time with both saddle and bridle and he was quite settled in them after the first few bucks. Mishek and I had backed him both in his box and outside in the paddock, but he was understandably wary of such liberties, and we had found it difficult to get any further than walking round in a circle as long as we had Leprechaun with us. We did try walking them both out one morning and Mishek had hopped up on the way back while I led him, but it was a dismal failure and I still have the scars. So we had decided to wait until we could do it properly, rather than create a negative attitude on Anzac's part. We took him out in the opposite direction to Chris and he went really well. We got back just minutes before Chris, who came ambling into sight singing at the top of his voice, reins dropped on Leprechaun's neck, completely at ease. They had a lovely ride.

That afternoon Chris mapped out a twenty metre circle in the dairy paddock and Mishek, armed with a badza, hoed a narrow, sandy path. Leprechaun was tied to the lower branches of a big, shady tree and Anzac had his first lunging lesson. Mishek led him to give him the idea and Chris held the lunge rein and gave encouragement. At times it was difficult to tell whether he was lunging Anzac or Mishek, but he eventually got him to understand and Mishek was able to stand back and regain his breath. It wasn't bad for a first attempt, Chris decided.

Next day Chris rode Leprechaun off again without any problem, and Anzac behaved perfectly on his long reins, weaving in and out of trees and answering to the bit which we used instead of the noseband for the first time. That afternoon, after ten minutes lunging, Chris put the saddle on him and hopped up. Mishek led him round the circle, and Chris started singing his usual 'mopped schmopped' song. Anzac progressed uncertainly, every few steps he would give a flip with his back legs which couldn't be called a buck, but you could see he was thinking about it. Chris took him around a couple of times in each direction and then decided that he had done enough for his first lesson.

So each morning we worked the horses and at last I felt we were really getting somewhere. In the afternoons Chris went fishing. We had borrowed a rod and line from Paul, begged worms from Kenyemba who knew just where to dig for them, and off he went in search of the monster bass that could be found in the river or the dam. He came back with one six inches long, gave it an understanding kiss on the nose and popped it in the freezer.

"Poor l'il animal," he said sadly.

That evening we lunged Anzac again and Chris put his foot in the stirrup to get up. Immediately he laid back his ears and flipped his back legs in a threatened buck. Chris ignored the protest, got up after a few minutes between flips, and he soon settled down. John came back just as we were putting away the tack, and suggested that maybe it would be a good time to go back to the river and catch a proper fish. We left Mishek to settle the horses and went to get the fishing rod and bait. Chris had discovered a wealth of huge, fat, white grubs, the larvae of rhinoceros beetles, buried in the dung heap and had collected them for bait. It was then that we discovered that they had made a break for freedom and were no longer in the earth filled jar. Porgie found one half way across the veranda, I found another on its way into the sleeping bag.

"We can catch some grasshoppers, or something," suggested John, undeterred.

So off we went to the dam, where in the coolness of evening the golden clouds of sunset were reflected in its smooth surface and the fish rose to feed spreading ripple after tell-tale ripple.

"Just look at them," breathed Chris, "Look at that!"

Not far off shore a heavy silver fish threw itself skywards and landed with a great splash. Chris baited his hook with a single worm while John and I went looking for grasshoppers.

Catching a grasshopper in your fingers is easy if you say it quickly. In practise it is much more difficult and they seemed to head instinctively for the tall reeds, where we knew a python had been seen and were a bit hesitant about diving in after them. An excited yell from Chris coincided with one from John as by sheer luck a grasshopper dodged the wrong way and he held it triumphantly in cupped hands. Chris had caught a bass. Like the previous one it was about six inches long, and he had scooped up some water in the plastic bag carrying his one remaining worm and popped it in. It was treading water furiously.

"Poor l'il animal," I told him, "His Mummy will be looking for him. She'll be swimming round and round the dam calling 'Robert, Robert....'"

I pushed my lips out in a big 'O' as I said the name, giving the impression of a gaping fish.

"Dear God," said John, "You're as bad as him."

He carefully passed the grasshopper over to Chris, who gave it a big kiss on the nose for luck and baited his hook. We sat quietly on the bank watching the colours fade from the sky as night came quickly down over us. The frogs started calling and a million crickets began to sing. Across the reed beds from the river a flight of ducks came in and landed, black shapes with silver wakes. Cattle egrets flew gracefully past, dipping low across the water heading for the dark woodland beyond. Chris sighed and reeled in his line, once more the big ones had evaded him. He took the grasshopper off the hook and threw it to the fishes.

"Let's put Robert in the reservoir," suggested John.

We stopped by the high round brick tank which held the water pumped up from the river for the cattle . From there it was gravity fed to the water troughs and the top of the open tank was rich in water beetles, water scorpions and drowned insects. Robert could grow big and strong there. We went back to a meal that, many years ago, our children had christened 'chilli gone barmy', cold beer, ice-cream and bed.

Next morning, out of beer, lemonade and dog meat I had to go to town. Orbit asked for a lift 'next door' to a farm five or six kilometres down the road, where his mother lived.

"I'm going at nine o'clock," I told him as, sheep counted and all well, he rode back with me as far as the bungalow.

"Ah, it is too early," he shook his head.

"So, you must walk."

"O.K."

He got out of the Suzi and mooched off in the direction of the village. Eventually, however, by the time we had loaded empty crates, the cool box and Tendai - who could smile her way to the front of any queue and made shopping much quicker - it was nearly ten, and Orbit was waiting by the gate with two women and a small child. He opened the gates for me and closed them behind me, then came to the window.

"I am going to the farm, "he told me," and she - ," he pointed to a young, heavily pregnant woman, "- is going to the hospital."

"I only have room for one," I said, reasonably, putting his chivalry to the test.

He called the woman, opened the back door and settled her in. She was pouting and frowning and looked near to tears. Orbit gave a rapid order to the other woman, who began to walk back towards the village dragging the unwilling child, then quickly squeezed himself in beside the pregnant girl and slammed the door.

"I am in," he announced unnecessarily. Ah, well. It was only a few kilometres.

I stopped by a cluster of thatched mud huts beyond the next farm and Tendai let Orbit out of the back. He crossed the road quickly, then called back,

"Please, Madam, you give my wife two dollar, I have no money," and was gone through the bush.

The nerve of the man! So, this was his wife, eight months or so pregnant, to be dropped in town with a two hour walk back if she didn't get a lift. And she wouldn't get a lift without a two dollar fare, which I now felt obliged to give her, as few Africans would transport her for free, as I was doing. Orbit, I decided, was going to pay me back those two dollars if I had to go with him to collect his pay.

The week passed quickly, and Chris was doing wonders with the horses.

"We'll have you riding Anzac by the week-end," he had told me cheerfully.

So when Saturday dawned I was greeted by Mishek holding two horses tacked up and ready to go. Anzac gave me a snuffle and lick or two, as he always did and stood quietly as I made a less dignified ascent than Chris. Gone were the days, I told myself sadly, when I could easily mount a seventeen hand horse from the ground. Now even fifteen two was a challenge.

"Mishek, I think it would be a good idea if you build me a granny-ramp," I told him, "Just a wide step at the end of the tethering rail, so I can stand on it."

Mishek grinned, "Ah, Madala, Madala," he muttered.

Anzac moved off quickly as Chris turned Leprechaun away from home, anxious not to be left behind, and he fell in step beside him. His ears were turned back towards me and he moved cautiously, the unfamiliar weight changing his centre of gravity and stiffening his back. A couple of times he gave the little flip that I had seen him do with Chris, but it was very minor and not at all worrying. I patted the long, shining, brown neck and talked to him, still unable to believe that I was actually riding him at last. As we moved away from the farm and onto the sandy tracks that crisscrossed through the scrubby bushland, his long, swinging stride suddenly clicked into gear, taking him on past Leprechaun and into the lead. Once out in front his ears flicked forwards and he strode on confidently. We rode for just over an hour and I came back, my spirit singing. He hadn't put a foot wrong, had led the way for almost the entire ride and passed everything from man-eating dead tree trunks to tractors and rattling bicycles. I couldn't wait to go out again.

So on Sunday morning we were out by six, so that I could get a ride in before Church. Wonderful, wonderful.

"You must ring Sally," said John, when I got back, "She would love to know that he's going so well and perhaps we could go over one afternoon and show Chris their other horses."

I rang her.

"Great," she laughed, obviously amused by my enthusiasm, "And yes, why don't you come over this afternoon. Come and have a cup of tea about 4.00."

I had just put the 'phone down when Chris rushed in. He dashed past me, through to the spare room where he had stowed his bag, then back to the lounge. He grabbed a small phial from the dresser and ran to the kitchen gasping for breath. I followed him quickly. He had just managed to pour a little water into a cup when he slowly began to collapse at the knees, making choking noises in his throat. I took the phial from his fingers and shook out a tiny blue tablet, pushed it hastily into his mouth and sloshed some of the water after it as he gradually slid down the wall and sat in a heap on the floor, still gasping. I shouted to John, who was in the bath and he came sliding wetly down the shiny waxed corridor.

"Chris has passed out."

He hadn't - quite. In fact his breathing was slowly coming back to normal.

"What happened?" asked John.

"Bee," said Chris, briefly, "Stung me on the bum."

Within minutes he was back to his old self.

"That's one hell of a reaction," I told him.

He nodded.

"I died once, but they jumped on my chest and pulled me round. Some stupid medic in the army gave me the injection in a vein instead of the muscle - when I came round I hit him," he added, with satisfaction.

"Well, do you feel like going to Sally's?" asked John, concerned. "We can easily put it off and go next week."

"Oh, no, I want to come," declared Chris, "I'm fine, now."

"Bring those pills," I said firmly.

After lunch we changed, settled the pups and piled into the Suzi. We left the farm, turning onto the narrow strip road with its wide sandy verges. John was driving and just before we reached the place where the tar petered out and the bush track began he braked slightly and glanced in the rear view mirror. He stopped the car and stuck his head out of the window, peering down the road behind us. Chris was peering, too.

"Was that a snake?" he asked.

"Think so," said my husband, and began reversing.

There, on the sandy shoulder lay a young python, about two feet long.

"Oh," breathed Chris, excitedly, "Let me out. Oh, please! Let me out."

He bounced up and down like a child. I let him out and he sprang past me, across the road and scooped up the snake.

"Mopped schmopped and mupped schmopped," he sang delightedly, "You ALWAYS get a big kiss on the nose from me."

And so saying, he delivered a hearty kiss on the top of the python's head. The snake didn't seem to mind too much.

"You hold him," said Chris, generously, "He won't hurt you."

I took it gingerly, whereupon it turned its head towards me, opened its mouth impossibly wide and hissed a warning. It needn't have worried, I had no intention of kissing it and hurriedly gave it back to Chris. A car came past and it was Paul, grinning broadly and shaking his head, but not stopping.

"We will put you somewhere safe," promised Chris, and strode off through waist high grass and thick bush scrub at the roadside, in shorts and flimsy sandals, risking puff adders and cobras to set a python free away from passing cars.

The rest of the journey was uneventful, and Sally and Patrick were waiting for us surrounded by their five dogs and with tea and scones at the ready. We had tea and saw the horses, most of which got a kiss on the nose, and then Sally suggested that we might like to see the horses they kept at Patrick's mother's farm. It was on our way home, so we went in convoy. It began to rain heavily when we got there, and we dodged from stable to stable admiring their beautiful horses. A mare and foal, a three-year old colt, Leprechaun's full sister, who was really beautiful and had the same head as Leprechaun, and their oldest mare which John remembered riding about twenty years before in a race. Then we came to a lovely little black mare with gleaming coat, a wide strong chest and well muscled quarters.

"This," smiled Sally," Is Jack's - sorry, Anzac's - mother. We wondered if you would like her. She will make you a first class foundation mare and we want her to go to a really good home."

I didn't need to look at John. I knew as soon as I saw her that she was just his kind of horse.

When John had left Africa he had given his favourite horse to a friend to look after, knowing that there was a possibility that he might never return. Now, ten years later, she had offered him a young Arab stallion in its place. She still had the old horse, happy and well cared for. John loved Arabs and loved having a stallion around, it was a wonderfully generous offer. With the little black mare we would have the opportunity to breed some really lovely horses, and get away from the thoroughbred breeding that didn't really suit us.

"She's been ridden, years ago," Sally was saying, "but she went blind in one eye and couldn't be used for polo."

Chris had his arms round her neck and she was quietly dozing off.

"Think of the price you want," said John, "we'll find out when we can collect the stallion."

Sally smiled, "She's yours."

Next morning as Chris and I walked back from the horse paddock together after an early morning ride, a snake moved away quickly from almost under my feet. It was between three and four feet long and brownish.

"What sort was that?" I asked Chris.

I felt I really must get to know them in case I ever had to identify one that had bitten me. Chris immediately ran through the long grass after its disappearing ripple. The snake went to the right of a big tree and Chris went to the left. Suddenly he jumped back, turned and ran for the house. I ran after him.

"Did it get you?"

"Milk," yelled Chris, "Milk!"

He held one hand over his eyes and with the other he scrabbled along the shelf for the backdoor key. Not finding it he ran for the front. The door wasn't locked, so I went in and got the milk from the 'fridge, handing the jug to him as he rushed through the house. Leaning over the sink he poured the milk into his eyes as best he could, for eyes are not designed to be easily filled from a standing position.

"Water," gasped Chris, "Lots of water."

Our water was fairly high in solids.

"I've got a saline drip," I remembered," That's sterile."

I found a china egg cup and the drip and stood by, refilling it as he washed his eyes thoroughly.

"Mozambican spitting cobra," he stated emphatically, in answer to my recent question, "I mustn't rub my eyes."

"Are you O.K. now?"

"No," said Chris, "I had better go to the hospital."

Luckily there was petrol in the Suzi. I called to Mishek to tell John the story, barricaded the pups inside in case they found the snake, and we headed for town. There was a hospital there of sorts, a cluster of white huts on the outskirts of town. It wasn't wonderful by all accounts, but it was near and they must, I thought, have a good local knowledge of snake bites and spits.

We got there in record time, weaving our way around the ruts and potholes down the entrance drive. There were no signs so I parked by the nearest building and found the first inevitable security guard. He heard the problem, looked sympathetic and ushered us to a nearby building where half a dozen Africans sat on benches waiting to be seen. A boy with sores and spots all over his legs, a woman with a sleeping baby on her back, two men and an old, old woman. It was the end wing of a long, low block, teaming with people of all ages in clothes of all colours, not one white face amongst them. It was the first time since my arrival in Africa that I had sought one, but at that anxious moment I would have dearly loved to have seen a fellow European to share the problem with.

"I can't see," said Chris.

I took his hand, led him through the door and settled him on a bench. The security guard spoke to an orderly who found a large, amply proportioned African nurse who listened to Chris's account of what had happened with a slight smile on her face. She seemed more interested in his grasp of Shona than his injury. She went away and came back with an outpatient card and a pen which was reluctant to write. Slowly and laboriously she filled in name, address, age......., and Chris was getting more and more distressed, his eyes streaming. I knew that any remark that seemed like a criticism would bring down the portcullis and would get us nowhere, so I said

"What is the treatment, exactly?"

She hesitated.

"We give you some eye drops," she said eventually.

"Good," put in Chris, " Yes, please."

She smiled at him and went on writing.

I desperately wanted some action.

"Is there a doctor he can see? Someone who can tell if his eyes are damaged?"

"A doctor?" She savoured the thought, "Yes, there is a doctor."

"Can he see the doctor?"

"I will find out."

She handed me the pen and card to hold. On it she had written:-

'c/o (complaining of) spited with an Cobra since this afternoon. Has already irrigate the eyes. Not seeing well. Running nose.

o/e (?) 1. Redness of eyes

2. Running nose. '

"I can't stand this," Chris screwed up his eyes with pain, "Where is there water?"

One of the men in the queue led him outside to a tap, where he washed his eyes again. I stood up and paced around frustratedly. The nurse came back and gave me a superior smile,

"Sit down. The doctor is coming."

I sat down, and Chris came back led by the sympathetic fellow patient.

"I go to get the keys," said the nurse," for medicine cupboard."

She walked away, hips swaying, as if she were about to break into a dance. Five minutes later she came back, keyless. She had a brief search around an adjoining room, went away again and came back with another nurse with keys. They opened a huge wall cupboard which I could see was almost empty, just four or five large bottles on one shelf. The nurse peered at the labels on these, shut the cupboard and then had second thoughts and opened it again. She took out a two litre glass jar with a little liquid at the bottom, brought it to Chris and showed him the label, like a wine waitress.

"We don't have eye drops," she explained, apologetically, "we just have this."

"I can't see it," Chris muttered, "What does it say?"

She passed me the bottle.

"Chlorophenical..... something, take with syrup."

"That's O.K." confirmed Chris, "It's a bit like my bee tablets, I've had it before."

The nurse looked from one to the other of us for confirmation, and then went away again. Next time she came past she handed Chris a small plastic beaker of bright blue peppermint smelling liquid. He drank it thankfully. We had been there just over an hour. Suddenly the nurse appeared again, with a half-squeezed tube of eye ointment, also chlorophenical, a doubtful 'sterile' stamped across it. Chris quickly gave each eye a liberal dose. The nurse smiled at him benevolently and took the card from my hand.

"I have to show this to my senior," she explained.

"Oh, God," whispered Chris," She's going to see if she's done the right thing."

Here my misplaced sense of humour overtook my frustration. The thought of some even larger African lady inspecting the card and putting large ticks and crosses against the irreversible actions noted thereon caused a fit of the giggles. Chris, despite his predicament, joined in and soon we were sitting side by side, both giggling with streaming eyes and runny noses. The nurse had given Chris a loo roll to mop his eyes and nose and I helped myself to a piece.

"Please come!"

The nurse was back and held open the door next to where we had been sitting. Chris went in and I went out into the hot sunshine for a breath of air. Alongside the main path to the centre block stretched a wire upon which dozens of rubber gloves were hung in the sun to dry and presumably sterilize. Three truck/ambulances had arrived and were parked next to the Suzi, their drivers looking her over with great interest. Chris came out clutching his free loo roll.

"She gave me an injection, and I must say she was very good," he admitted, "African woman, but not a doctor."

"Feeling better?"

"Much better. I can see now."

"Well, thank Goodness for that. Now, promise me you won't kiss another one of those on the nose."

"I promise," grinned Chris.

Chris was fine next day, although he said he felt as though someone had beaten him up. But Porgie was sick. My lovely, cuddly, fat little pup had been off his food for a couple of days, but I had put it down to his pulled nail being so sore. Now he was sick, and not wanting to move from his bed. John looked at his gums and they were very pale.

"Biliary," he said, "Take him to the vet."

I had no faith in the vet but biliary, the tick borne disease that causes anaemia and death was common and I reasoned that he must have the remedy on hand. I carried Porgie to the car and made him comfortable on a blanket. Harrison wanted a lift in with his young son to the hospital, and I dropped him at the gates knowing now the scene awaiting him. The vet wasn't there, but his African assistant assured me that he was coming, so I sat in the back of the Suzi with the door open, my arm around Porgie, trying to look on the bright side. The vet eventually drove in, smiled his humourless smile and asked me to wait five minutes until he got organised. The assistant was asked to weigh Porgie and get his temperature. The vet looked at his gums and confirmed biliary. He gave him two injections. Looking around the room as I held the pup I noticed bunches of dried herbs hanging from the cupboard handles.

"Do you use herbs?" I asked, immediately interested and hopeful of finding at least something in common with this strange man.

The vet's expression changed.

"I love them," he declared fervently. He dropped the syringes into a kidney basin and went over to one of the bunches. Breaking off a piece he crumbled it in his fingers, sniffed it deeply and then came back and poured the dry powder into my hand.

"Rosemary," he whispered, "Just smell it."

I nodded, "its lovely, what do you use it for?"

"Oh, I don't use them medically, I just love to have them around." He turned back to Porgie,

"Keep him quiet for about a week. He has to make up his blood again, see if you can get him to eat liver."

"He's pulled a claw, too," I said, "Will it drop off or should we do something about it?"

He glanced at it, briefly.

"Yes, it must be sore. It may drop off, although it hasn't separated. If not you will just have to catch hold of it and rip it off."

My opinion of the man plumbed back to its old depths.

Porgie was sick on the way home and as I put him back in his bed Bess came bouncing up. Her sparkling vitality accentuated his illness. Chris put him in his sleeping bag and he stayed there, a model patient, all afternoon. That evening Chris and John went for a long ride and came back happy. Anzac had behaved beautifully and even Leprechan had settled down half way. They had taken them through all gears and thoroughly enjoyed themselves. That evening Porgie ate a little of the liver I had cooked for him and went back to Chris's bed. He was brighter next day, wagged his tail and crawled towards me when I took Chris his tea at 5.00 a.m.

Over the past week we had settled into a routine. First came the sheep, then back with Orbit to the bungalow where Mishek would have the horses fed, groomed and tacked up ready to go. By six thirty Chris and I were heading out in the early morning sunshine, through grass soaked with dew, passing the workers on foot and the women heading for the fields in their long, colourful skirts, with bundles, oil drums, bags and baskets on their heads. Children trotted past us on their way to school along bush tracks, running barefoot and tireless - future Olympic medallists in the making. Anzac dawdled when behind and went best out in front. He stretched out his long neck and got into his swinging stride so that I was just holding the buckle on slack reins. Alongside, Chris was holding no reins at all as Leprechaun paced calmly along, completely relaxed. And that was how we were when Leprechaun suddenly went bananas. I think he either saw a snake or thought he saw one. The effect was the same. He jumped violently over nothing and gave a hearty buck, then shied. Chris flew gracefully over his head and landed with a thump on the ground and luckily Leprechan got his reins wrapped around a spent tobacco stalk and stood tethered. Had he made for home there was little doubt that I would have gone too. As it was, Anzac stood quietly and waited until Chris had remounted.

"Funny," said Chris, conversationally, as we moved off again, "I haven't fallen off for ages."

"It's good to keep in practice," I told him, "But as you get older you tend to lose a bit of bounce."

"True," nodded Chris.

"Stein bock," he pointed out as we rode over little cloven prints in the sand and later ,"Jackal," and "Look, that's a Genet track."

A Chongololo, the fat black millipede, passed busily across in front of us.

"Cures warts," remarked Chris, "You cut them in half and they're full of a yellow liquid. Put that on the warts and it eats them away."

I was glad that, although an ugly step mother, as yet I had no warts to practise on.

We arrived home to find someone waiting to have a headache cured and Jameson the cattleman waiting with a red, elevated finger. He had managed to chop a lump right out and it was bleeding profusely. I gave the first patient magic aspirins and mopped up Jameson who was being very brave until I approached with my usual cayenne pepper. He turned his head away and whistled through his teeth as I packed it into the hole. John had just arrived back and came through the house as the whistling started. He chuckled as Jameson turned towards him, his eyes seeking signs of sympathy.

"It's good," confirmed my husband, laughing, "Nkosikas va shuper sterek, eh?"

Jameson agreed heartily that the Madam was indeed causing him grief. I put a bandage on top of the now staunched wound and showed him my hand, which had healed completely after Anzac's indignant bucking session, when Mishek had attempted to back him some weeks ago.

"Pepper," I told him with confidence.

"Judy's clinic," commented Chris, as he watched him go.

"I've told a chap to come and see you after lunch, "said John, "His picanin has some nasty spots, and the stuff she got from the hospital isn't helping."

At 2.00 p.m. they were sitting at the gate, a little girl of about eight with her father. She had whitish spots all over her arms and legs, and they had shaved her head to uncover those on her scalp. I thought it looked the same as the sore Mwunza's child had on her chin. Mwunza was sitting outside his hut, so I called him over to see.

He looked at the child closely.

"It is the same," he confirmed.

So they went away with a bottle of witch-hazel and cotton wool, and instructions to come back if it didn't improve soon.

That evening, as we finished supper, there was a soft knock at the back door. John answered it and called me. A woman had brought her young son, a boy of about twelve, who had stepped on a broken bottle. We brought them into the kitchen and Chris dragged a chair forward for him. He left a trail of blood across the floor, and had obviously cut a small artery.

"See if you can staunch the bleeding," said John, "I'll just get some shoes on and then take them into hospital."

The cut was deep and stretched across the ball of his foot below his big toe and the blood was pouring out. I pressed a thick gauze wound dressing over the cut, followed by a thick pad of cotton wool and bandaged it tightly. By the time I had tied the knot the blood was welling up through again. To keep it clean I wrapped an old hand towel on top and put his foot in a plastic bag, at which his mother nodded her approval. She was very worried about the mess all over the kitchen. John backed the farm truck up to the back door and we helped them in.

"Go and have a good scrub up," said John, his face suddenly full of concern, "How stupid of me, I just didn't think........"

I hadn't thought either. My hands were covered with blood. Working with animals, as I did, my hands were very rarely without a fresh cut or open graze. If the boy had the AIDS infection it was too late to think about it now. I would put plastic gloves on my next shopping list. It was very late when my husband got back.

"That place! It's like watching a play in slow motion. Everyone walking around and no-one actually doing anything or going anywhere."

They had waited over an hour before getting the boy's wound stitched. They had made a very good job of it, but no sense of urgency and he had lost quite a bit of blood.

His mother must have been happy with 'Judy's Clinic', however, as she came back with him each morning for the next week so that I could change the dressings. He had ten stitches. We gave him one of John's old socks to keep the dressings clean, and his mother's gratitude was overwhelming!

Chris's week long holiday had already stretched into three, and he had faced up to the fact that this coming week really had to be his last. I was riding Anzac happily and confidently, but before he left Chris had promised to take him out on his own. He was now quite calm on his own in the paddock when John took Leprechaun away, but he hadn't been ridden away from the other horse yet. Harrison had sent a message that he needed some more crushed maize for the lambs and whilst I was elsewhere Chris had decided to take it up on Anzac. He had ridden up to the sheep pens with the sack of meal slung across the saddle in front of him, and Anzac hadn't given a damn. When I arrived back at lunch time Chris greeted me with a very triumphant grin, and had made up his mind to go out for a proper ride on him that afternoon. I was really pleased. Anzac really did have a laid back sort of attitude; it was just his occasional impetuous pig headedness that made me wary. I put it down to his father's side, as both John and I loved the Arab more than the Thoroughbred.

"I'll take him out towards the big dam," said Chris, adjusting my hard hat to fit him, and buckling it under his beard. He wore it under protest, but after the bee stings and the snake spits we were taking no chances with him during his last week.

He gave Anzac the customary kiss on the nose and sprang into the saddle. They moved off down the sandy path, Chris ducking low under the branches of the bauhinias that spread over the track. Through the shade and out again into the sunshine, Chris turned and gave us a cheery wave as he turned right by the barns and out towards the dam. Mishek stayed with Leprechaun for a while until he stopped calling and settled down to graze, and John and I went back for a second cup of tea before the simbi sounded for the end of the lunchtime siesta.

A quarter of an hour or so later Fred's dogs began barking, joined by Paul's dogs and then came the excited screams and yells from Mwunza's children, followed by hoof beats. Anzac came flying down the track minus rider, his reins broken and his stirrups flapping. He scorched round the corner on two legs and screeched to a halt next to Leprechaun who came galloping to meet him, calling frantically. Mishek was already running to catch him and John was backing the Suzi out of the garage as I threw open the gates.

"Which way?"

"He was going towards the dam."

"Which dam?"

"The big one."

There were several ways he could have gone, and John stopped at the first crossroads and got out to look at the tracks.

"It looks as if he went that way," he indicated straight on, "but that's Anzac's prints coming back down this way," he pointed to deep, slurred tracks coming from the right.

We followed the outgoing trail and rounded a bend to meet Chris marching along purposefully, hard hat on, swinging a long, twiggy stick. We were very relieved to see him so mobile.

"Just suddenly put his head down and gave one almighty buck," explained Chris, without waiting to be asked. "I came off, and he gapped it."

"Are you O.K.?"

He rubbed a grazed arm and peered round at a scratched thigh.

"I'm alright," he grinned, "Cowboys don't cry."

He had no reason, according to Chris, just decided that was enough and he was going home.

Mishek had taken off his tack when we got back, and Anzac was grazing peacefully.

"Put it all back on, Mishek," commanded Chris, "He's not finished yet."

This time we followed at a distance, but he was clearly in a fractious mood, disputing at each change of direction and moving sulkily. When they eventually turned for home he became very bouncy and John slipped out of the car to walk near him whilst I followed. He did as he was bid, albeit with little grace, and the ride finished with Chris the master, but it was a small margin.

The next morning we rode again together. Again he argued at each corner and flipped his hind legs. I gave him a quick flick with the light stick I always carried, and he shook his head angrily and squealed, but he went on and eventually settled down and relaxed. Someone waved to us from the barns and I recognised with joy the tall, slim figure of Gomo. I couldn't have been more relieved to see him.

"Are you well?" I called.

He laughed," Yes, Madam, I am now well."

"I thought he was going to die," I told Chris, as we rode on, "He looked so ill."

Mishek was waiting for us to get back with great excitement.

"There is big snek in village," he burst out, before my feet had touched the ground. "Last night it come and take chicken, and now it has gone into the house of Phineus."

It couldn't have happened to a better chap. Let him witch-doctor his way out of that one.

"But now it is gone again," went on Mishek, "We go look for it?" he asked Chris, hopefully.

He really didn't have to ask, Chris already had that eager expression on his face and my brain immediately came up with the information that there was petrol in the Suzi and some of the blue syrup in the medical kit.

We walked down to the village to find John already there, with several women excitedly explaining the last seen whereabouts of the snake.

"Sounds like a big cobra," said John, as we arrived.

Chris and Mishek were already off through the tall, dry mealie patches to join a group of Africans beating their way through shoulder high grass between Phineus's hut and the bare, open ground surrounding the gardens.

"Oh, boy!" John watched him go, "Let's hope it's gone to ground, good and deep."

It seemed that it had, for no-one found sign of it and, deeply disappointed, Chris was persuaded to come home. Soon after John had gone back to his work Mishek came pounding on the back door.

"They have killed snek, come and see."

"I'll bring the camera," I suggested.

"Yes, O.K." agreed Chris.

By the time I had found it and my sandals Chris was back with the snake.

"It deserves a photo," he declared, "Have you got a tape measure?"

103

It was a black Egyptian cobra and measured six feet ten inches. Chris held it up by its head, his arm way in the air, then jumped up on a step so that its whole length could be seen. I took the photo.

"I'll skin it and portion it, and put it in the 'fridge," said Chris.

"You'll what?"

I thought he was joking. He wasn't.

"They're good eating!" he assured me. He held it in one hand, it's still twitching tail twining itself around his ankles.

"Chris, if you want to cut it up and barbecue it outside you are very welcome," I told him, "But I'll have quiche and salad."

He shook his head, sad that my unadventurous attitude was denying me the pleasure of a cobra steak.

"O.K." He draped it over the clothes line, "Which knife can I use?"

I went inside and found a bucket with three large bass in it on the draining board.

"You are being offered fish," explained Tendai, "Seven dollars."

They were lovely fish and I paid up happily. Tendai took the money out to the African woman who had caught them and who was waiting by the gate.

"I'll clean them for you," offered Chris, selecting a kitchen knife.

"Before the snake," I suggested.

"Yes, yes, before the snake."

He cleaned, scaled and washed the fish by the garden tap, wrapped them carefully and put them in the freezer. Then he started on his supper. Surrounded by an interested audience of women, picanins and passers-by, the cobra was skinned, gutted and thoroughly washed. I left him to it to rescue my 'Pommy fodder' of quiche and double crust rhubarb pie from the oven. Twenty minutes later he came proudly into the kitchen bearing a tray laden with a fleshy pink coil.

"Wonderful," I greeted him without enthusiasm. I felt guilty that he looked slightly hurt, but I really couldn't help it. I didn't want nearly seven feet of cobra in the 'fridge.

"Perhaps Mishek would like to share it with you?"

Chris shook his head, "He doesn't eat it."

He sounded vaguely surprised.

"Can I put it in the freezer?"

I relented.

"O.K., but use two carrier bags, doubled, hey?"

"Right," agreed Chris happily, "I'll have some for lunch tomorrow."

It was with real sadness that we waved Chris goodbye. Fred was going up to Harare and had offered him a lift that far, and Chris was going to hitch hike from there to Nyanga. Fred drove up to the gates in his very new, very shiny and very expensive Mercedes and Chris stuffed his sleeping bag and holdall in the boot. The top of the bag wouldn't quite do up, and I could see a very solid looking carrier wedged on top of his clothes. It sparkled with ice particles, and Chris gave me a huge wink.

"Never know when you're hitch hiking," he whispered, "Might get hungry!"

That evening the place seemed strangely empty.

John and I took the pups for a walk to the dam. Porgie had completely recovered. They tore around, fighting and growling and chasing each other over the rough ground and unexpectedly found themselves at the water's edge. Bess walked in gingerly and Porgie followed. It shelved deeply and suddenly they were swimming. They were beside themselves with excitement and began fighting in the water, pushing each other under. Then Bess struck out, swimming low in the water like a little brown and white otter, and Porgie followed less gracefully head held high, front paws splashing in a real doggie paddle. We threw sticks for them and they plunged in eagerly after them, bringing them back together, one on each end of the stick. Then they began to get too adventurous and headed out towards the middle. We called them and they immediately did a U-turn and came back to us. We stayed for a long time until the sun sank low and the mosquitoes drove us home.

CHAPTER ELEVEN

Orbit gazed at me aghast.

"Eh?"

"You can have three days off," I repeated," Tuesday, Wednesday and Thursday."

"But Madam, I have no money!"

He shook his head in dumb disbelief that fate could have dealt him such a hand.

"Friday, it is pay day?" he glanced at me for confirmation.

"Yes."

"And I come back on Friday? Ah, ah, ah!" he shook his head, "Who comes Tuesday, Wednesday and Thursday?"

"Whiskey."

"You tell him not to come; I do not want to be off with no money."

"Perhaps Whiskey doesn't want to be off with no money."

"Ah! He is OLD!" Orbit dismissed the idea with contempt, "Too old, I think - maybe sixty."

I sighed.

"Well you talk to him, and if he is happy then I am happy, as long as we have a night watchman."

"He will be happy," said Orbit flatly.

We were getting very close to the main lambing. The ewes, now one hundred and ninety five, were looking fat and productive. Their udders had developed well, promising a good supply of milk, and their overall shape was oval, each side bulging. We had started building the lambing pens in a big, shady area amongst the tall blue gums. Thirty individual pens were spaced back to back in a line across the centre making a division between a large gathering and overnight area and a smaller mothering up paddock. The ewes would be put into a pen when they lambed, stay for twenty four hours while the lambs were docked and castrated and seen to be well. Then they would move out in a small group to the mothering area, which gave the lambs a chance to get used to following mother before they were herded out on the big pastures. When lambing started we would need two night guards. Isaac had joined the sheep team some time back and was proving a very good stockman, so he was to alternate with Harrison as night shepherd, each doing a weekly shift. Neither had any lambing experience, but they were quiet and sensible with a rare feeling for the sheep. I was often told that the African has no feeling for animals, and I'm sure that in the majority of cases this is so. Certainly there is little room for sentimentality. But I was often to come across Harrison cuddling a lamb just for the pleasure of it, and still have in my mind (but unfortunately not in my camera) the picture of old Shanghazi glaring fiercely out across the bush whilst absent mindedly fondling the ears of a friendly ewe.

The nights were colder now, merely warranting a blanket on the bed at night and in no way reminiscent of the lambing weather I was used to. We had given up all hope of more rain, and winter stretched ahead of us warm and dry until the next rainy season in six months time. The small amount of rain that had fallen meant a low river and many heated discussions had taken place amongst those farmers whose land bordered the Mupfure River. Each had their own weir and dam, and normally there was water for all. This year those upstream had benefited whilst those lower down had none. Eventually people started letting water down and we all got some, but not enough for both the tobacco crop and the extensively irrigated pastures that Fred had hoped for. We were luckier than most in that we had made some 1500 big round bales of hay, which would be invaluable when the pastureland and bush turned brown and lost all nourishment.

John's mombies were looking sleek and well, and we looked forward to the first crop of calves. So with all the stock looking great and lambing just around the corner it was time for them to spring another nasty surprise on us, and they did. Someone once said to me, 'Just look at any flock of sheep, standing there with their heads together, you can see they're just dreaming up ways to die.' That man understood sheep.

The first was one of Fred's original survivors. She was only about a year old and Isaac pointed her out to me one morning, standing in the corner of the night paddock looking miserable. Another ewe had been lying down a lot, 'sleeping, sleeping, sleeping,' as Isaac put it, and it had been this one I had come to see. As we now seemed to have two invalids I decided to take them into my friend the vet and put the ball in his court.

I went off to borrow the pick-up and collect Mishek to sit in the back with them. When we got back Isaac had taken the main flock out and the 'sleeping, sleeping, sleeping' ewe had decided to go with them, so we picked up the young one and drove after them. Mishek and Isaac caught her, and in the absence of a roadside gate they threaded her, struggling and indignant, through the barbed wire fence. Once in the pick up with the other one she decided to lie down quietly, and I headed for town at a good pace, not wanting to miss the vet. Mishek, however, couldn't hold onto two sheep and his hat, and no sooner had I changed up into third gear than I heard a frantic thumping on the roof above my head and looked in the mirror to see the red-ribboned hat cart wheeling down the road in our dusty wake. Muttering, I braked and without waiting for me to come to a standstill Mishek baled out and went haring after it, leaving the sheep to do as they willed. Fortunately they weren't feeling up to doing much.

The vet was still there and he came out to look at them in the back of the truck. He examined them and then walked away wordlessly. I followed him into the surgery and out again. He had collected a bottle of cortisone and a syringe.

"What do you think it is?"

He shook his head, "I don't know."

He stood quietly, watching them for a while.

"Could be a touch of pneumonia."

"That's what I thought, so I gave the older one some terramyacin."

He nodded.

"Could it be pregnancy toxaemia?" I suggested.

"Could be, I thought that."

"Could the little one have eaten too much maize?"

"Could have," he agreed.

He gave them both a shot of cortisone.

"If one dies bring it back for a post mortem," he said encouragingly.

On the way home I called into the Farmer's Co-op and collected some of the pregnancy toxaemia treatment that I recognised, the same as the one I had used in England.

Over the next few days the small ewe lost the entire contents of her rumen, bringing up the cud and then dribbling it out of the side of her mouth, and I felt sure that she had been poisoned. She was doing the sheep equivalent of vomiting which, I reasoned, could only be a good thing. When she seemed to have stopped I gave her a warm drench of molasses for blood purification and energy. She wouldn't, or couldn't, open her mouth so I fired it carefully down the inside of her cheek with a syringe. Each morning I was fully prepared to take her for a post mortem, but each morning she was lying there, up on her chest and looking the same. I followed the molasses with a rehydration drink I had used on the other ewe, which was grazing and eating corn again, though still a little shaky on her feet. She lasted until the following Friday, standing out in the shade where I put her each morning, not grazing or moving but refusing to lie down. Then at last she went down to stay and John decided it was best to put her down. I was fairly sure she was brain damaged. Of course, being Friday, the vet was unavailable for a post mortem to be carried out. Despite protests that she had been poisoned, Sadina pleaded for the carcase and bore it away gratefully to distribute.

During the next three weeks we lost four more. Big, healthy, pregnant ewes with the same symptoms of sickness. I rang Dave in Harare again, my consolation in times of panic.

"Plant poisoning," he agreed. "And it's no good rushing out to dig things up, because some plants are only poisonous at certain times and under certain conditions. Just bad luck, I'm afraid."

We moved the whole flock nearer to the lambing area, which was on a different part of the farm and hoped that the luck would change.

Sally had sent the little black mare, who had the unlikely name of Rainbow, and the Arab stallion, Tif, had also arrived. The mare was sweet natured and so was the stallion. Mishek formed an instant bond with the little Arab, and spent many hours grooming and washing him 'til his silver coat gleamed. The mare had conveniently come into season on arrival and so we hoped for a foal early in February the following year. Meanwhile, they shared a paddock in companionable harmony. They came to Mishek's whistle each morning, the black shape of the mare moving through the gum trees and cantering before her, like moonlight and shadow, the silver stallion - tail high, floating across the rough bush land.

In an attempt to avoid the mistake we had made with the other two John suggested that Mishek should take Tif for a walk each morning on his own, leading him away from the mare. This he did, and after the first few excursions I found him one morning, watering the garden with our hoarded bathwater and looking very happy. When he saw me coming he hastily threw down the watering can, leapt the seed bed and came to meet me.

"I ride him, Medem," Mishek could scarcely contain himself, "I ride him!"

"You did?"

He burst out laughing at my open mouthed expression. It was exactly the reaction he had hoped for.

"No saddle?"

"No saddle, Medem,"

"No bridle?"

"No bridle. I take the lead rope and tie it both sides to head collar and then I jump on. We go all around the dam and back down from top of farm. He VERY good, Medem!"

Considering he had been lightly backed five years ago and not ridden since it was incredibly good. So from then on Mishek took his pride and joy for a 'walk' each morning, bareback with a head collar, ranging further and further until at last he had to be restricted to within the boundaries of the farm, so that we at least had some idea where they were.

For several weeks I had noticed a woman in the general area of Mishek's house, but as they are a very gregarious people I imagined that he had relatives staying and thought no more about it.

"Medem," said Mishek, shyly, one morning as we cleaned tack together out in the stables, "I have a new wife."

"Oh, good," I was so pleased for him, "That's really good, Mishek."

He nodded and his smile deepened.

"Yes, Medem, it is good."

"A second wife?" I was wondering what would happen to Maagi.

"Yes, Medem. That other one she doesn't come here. It is no good, so my children they go to live with my mother and I have new wife."

"Well, I'm glad Mishek, and it is good that you will see your children.

"Yes, Medem."

"And what is your new wife's name?"

Mishek peered closely at the bridle he was cleaning, gave it a hard rub then paused and stared unseeingly out across the paddock. A frown creased his forehead and at last he shook his head, annoyed with himself.

"Ah!" he admitted, at last, "I forget to ask her."

It was a while before we were introduced. I saw her in the yard beyond their little house and occasionally she passed by on the track from the village, but her eyes were cast down and she seemed very shy. She always wore what seemed to be a brown bandage around her face, as if she had toothache. Then Mishek came to me, looking at his toes and asking if I had a plaster for his wife's face.

"You see," he explained, " my wife was fighting in the village, and all this part of her lip," he traced a line from the centre of his lower lip in a semi-circle to just beyond the corner of his mouth, " it is gone."

"Gone? How is it gone?"

"The other woman, she bite it off."

"Right off?"

"Right off," Mishek assured me, his expression slightly amused, "The other woman, she eat it."

"Why was she fighting," I refused to look shocked.

"The other woman she is jealous because I choose this one," explained Mishek.

"So they were fighting over you?"

Mishek wriggled his toes coyly in the sand.

"Yes, Medem," he agreed, with a smile of barely concealed pride," it was over me."

He went to fetch her while I looked in the medical kit for a replacement lip.

We cleaned up the wound and re-plastered it; it seemed to be healing nicely. At close quarters his new wife was older than I had first thought, and even with her face intact would have lacked the charm of Maagi.

Judy's clinic continued to flourish, highest on the list being de-nailed toes and cut feet. The rural African is not the tidiest of people and although most bottles and cans are recycled and re-used until they disintegrate, even their tough feet are no match for rusty tins and broken glass.

January, Fred's house 'boy', did a one point landing off his bicycle and onto the top of his head. Aged seventy, if a day, he came with a huge jagged cut across the top of his grey peppercorn head that would have killed a healthy young European.

"Gomo, he is very sick," said Mishek, gravely, one morning before breakfast. "I have put him in my house and make a fire, Boss say you take him to hospital when he come back with the truck, or maybe try ambulance."

Being small, the Suzuki was fairly useless for taking people to hospital, and we usually used the farm truck with a mattress in the back. I dialled the ambulance number and it was answered almost immediately.

"Hello," I shouted down the crackling line to the faint voice 10 kilometres away, "We need an ambulance at Lourie Farm to collect someone who is very sick."

There was no answer, then the phone clicked down and the dialling tone cut in. I rang again. The same woman answered. I explained again, and once more she put the 'phone down.

I called Tendai.

"Maybe she doesn't speak English," I told her, "Tell her in Shona."

Tendai dialled the number and sat by the 'phone. This time five minutes passed and no-one answered at all.

"I'll take him in the Suzi," I decided, "Tendai, you come with me."

I drove the Suzi to the gate and waited for Mishek to bring Gomo. He was barely conscious. Mishek's five feet nothing frame supported Gomo's gaunt six feet carefully as he took one painful, shuffling step after another through the trees to the path. Mishek's wife asked to come too, as she needed her face checked at the hospital, so she climbed into the back with Tendai and together Mishek and I gently folded Gomo into the passenger seat. He lay limply against the door, his breathing laboured and noisy, his eyes closed.

I drove as fast and as carefully as the road would allow. In the mirror I could see Tendai, her eyes worried, and no-one said anything throughout the journey. Gomo occasionally gave a quiet, painful rattle of a cough. As we approached the hospital we could see a police block just beyond, checking vehicles. I felt a tap on my shoulder and Tendai wordlessly threaded my seat belt around me, which I had forgotten in my haste, and Mishek's wife did the same for Gomo.

To avoid the potholes and ruts of the hospital drive I drove along the grass verge and stopped under a tree in the shade. Mishek's wife went to join her inevitable queue, and I sent Tendai to find someone in authority whilst I stayed with Gomo. She arrived back with a wheelchair and a woman in a green uniform.

"We will admit him," said the nurse, "telephone later."

Two weeks later Gomo came to the gate looking incredibly well.

"I want to thank you, Madam," he smiled," For taking me to the hospital."

"Gomo, I am glad I could help, but I don't want to have to do it again, hey!"

He laughed, "No, Madam, I do not want that you should have to do it again!"

Twelve people had died whilst he was in hospital, he told me, and they had to ferry all the bodies to a hospital fifty kilometres away, because someone had stolen the motor to the cooler in the mortuary.

Some months later Gomo died of AIDS.

CHAPTER TWELVE

"Do you want to go and see your sheep?" enquired John, hopefully. "Struth, it's like being in bed with a grasshopper."

I had slept very deeply, and was suddenly awake with that excited feeling in the pit of my stomach that I always get at lambing time. It's a mixture of eagerness to see the results of seven months planning, and apprehension! Like dying, a sheep can dream up a multiplicity of ways to present a lamb, some of them quite impossible.

It was nearly dawn, for down in the village the cockerels were giving tongue, and my inner clock told me that it was time for morning tea.

"Would you like some tea?" I gave my husband a nudge in case he had managed to drop off to sleep again.

"Mmmm?"

"Tea?"

"Mmmmm!"

"It's your turn."

"I don't make tea at midnight."

He pulled the sheet over his head. "You make tea. Don't hurry."

In less than ten minutes I was back with the tray.

"Your dog," muttered John accusingly, as he struggled into a sitting position, "was making a hell of a racket last night."

"I didn't hear him."

"He must have found that tortoise again. Chasing it around barking at about ninety miles an hour."

"You can't chase a tortoise at ninety miles an hour," I reasoned, "They won't go."

"Well, he had a damned good try. If it's not the fastest tortoise in Africa it'll be the deafest."

He cheered up after two cups of tea and I left him pouring a third while I washed and dressed.

A deep crimson glow was slowly creeping across the dark sky as I backed the Suzi out of the garage and turned her in the direction of the lambing pens. As always, the first lamb born had come as a surprise. After five months gestation and a lot of planning, the first little stranger appeared out of nowhere one cool, sunny winter's morning with no warning at all. We had bought thirty five in-lamb ewes and these had begun to lamb first.

Harrison and Orbit had been on night duty, and Isaac and Shanghazi had already arrived to take over from them. They were all in a group chatting around their fire when I arrived, and I could see Harrison's broad grin glowing through the pale, first light. When I had left the previous evening I had said, 'Well, I want lots of lambs tonight, and lots of twins', pointing to the pens and counting, 'two, two, two....' They had laughed and agreed that would be good, and now they could hardly wait to show me. The first seven pens were occupied. Each had been neatly bedded down and the ewe stood with a pile of sweet hay and a bucket of fresh water, together with her lamb. Laughing they led me along the row. Single, single, single, twin, twin, twin, twin!

"Harrison! You did it!"

"Ja, Madam," agreed Harrison, delightedly.

Well, there they were. Our first planned lambs. And good, strong, stocky little lambs they were too, and their mothers bulged with milk. Considering they had never seen a lambing pen the two of them had got things remarkably well organised and I knew it was prompted by that attention to detail that I had noticed in Harrison at the beginning. Each lamb had its navel carefully sprayed with purple spray, and the white ones had a fair sprinkling of purple finger prints too. They were all colours, black, black and white, brown and white, white with brown ears and just boring old white. We all stood around staring at them as if we had never seen a lamb before, while Harrison and Orbit recounted the births in great detail for Isaac and Shanghazi. We marvelled at their size, 'makuru', their strength, 'simba', the copious milk supply, 'maninghi', and crooned over their first attempts to frisk around the pens. Eventually the other one hundred and eighty odd began protesting loudly at being ignored and the two day shepherds began feeding.

It was a short walk from the new pens to the village, but Orbit begged his usual lift, although it took him three sides of a square out of his way and landed him approximately the same distance from the village but on the opposite side.

As I stopped at the gate he opened the door and lingered.

115

"Madam," he began," I wonder....."

"You want to borrow the two dollars back that you haven't repaid yet."

"No, no," he shook his head in vigorous denial, "No, I wonder you could buy me nepis."

"Nepis?"

"Yes."

I tried not to look too blank.

"What sort of napis?"

Orbit laughed outright at my ignorance.

"Dere is only one kind of nepis," he assured me, and his hands described a good imitation of putting a nappy on himself and doing up the pin.

"Nappies!"

"Yes. My wife has two weeks to go. If you buy me napis I give you the cash."

Having waited a month for two dollars I doubted it.

"Well, if I go to Harare I will see."

"O.K.".

It obviously wasn't a satisfactory answer, but it was the best he was going to get.

John was really delighted to hear about all the new lambs, especially the twins. It was a new experience for both of us to wake up to lambs born and in the pens. Usually lambing time meant sleep snatched by the hour over the six week period, getting more and more exhausted and grumpy. In the first two weeks seventy nine ewes lambed, giving us a total of one hundred and three lambs, with twenty four sets of twins. To commemorate our first lambing all the 'sheep team' were issued with blue overalls and looked very smart and businesslike. Harrison entered into the spirit of the occasion and binned, or sold, his red T-shirt and Isaac put away his Hawaiian shorts for Sundays.

Fred made a point of calling in around seven each morning when the mothers were fed and all the lambs ganged up to run races, bucking, jumping and pelting flat out around the boundary of the pen and then turning and coming back even faster. Each morning I arrived to inspect the new arrivals before the night team left. We fed the main group and turned them out and then Harrison and I did the ringing. A small, strong elastic ring applied soon after birth to the tail and testicles of boy lambs and the tails of the girls, stops the blood supply and causes the appendage to drop off within a week or so. It is effective and bloodless and causes discomfort for only a few minutes if the lamb is newly born. The routine was that Harrison would catch the ewe and read out her ear number which I wrote down, and then he would give her a shot of wormer, catch the lamb and tell me its sex which I also wrote down. Then I would select the appropriate number of rings and apply them as he held the lamb. As we wanted to build up our flock the ewe lambs were good to have and Harrison was quick to notice that they were greeted with pleasure. After ringing a string of ram lambs his face would suddenly crease into the familiar grin.

"Baby!" he would exclaim, triumphantly, dangling a ewe lamb in front of me. So from then on it was always a boy or a baby.

My only night call came from Isaac on his first night shift. He tapped on the door at 3.00 a.m. and I was dressed and in the car almost before my eyes had opened. This was it, the one that always foxed me. The head turned back that wouldn't co-operate and stay round for me to draw it through with the front feet. Or maybe the legs of one lamb and the head of another, with the head so swollen by the time I got there that it would be almost impossible to manoeuvre. It could even be a 'foetal monster'. I had just one of those over the years, so grossly malformed that only a caesarean would deliver it. Isaac sat beside me quietly.

"What do you think the problem is, Isaac?"

"Ah," the light of the dashboard softly lit his smile," I think when we get there it is born."

And it was. No problem, just his first solo lambing.

Thanks to Blankety Blank, the teaser, all but a very few stragglers lambed in the first three weeks, and the most difficult lambing presented itself during the lunch break.

We had two casualties. One lamb made the fatal mistake of turning left when everything else turned right during the morning feed stampede and didn't regain consciousness, and one ewe gave birth to a lamb on the morning I had decided to go shopping and the lamb was dead. Fortunately the two incidents came together, and within days of two lambs - each from a twin - being rejected by their mothers. Harrison and Isaac watched in disbelief as I carefully skinned the dead lambs and held up the little jackets, complete with arm and leg holes, a navel and a tail. When I popped them over the head of each rejected little twin and threaded legs through fore and aft, they stared at each other and then fell around laughing. The two bereft ewes both viewed their resurrected babies with a certain amount of suspicion, but with a generous amount of vanilla essence applied to their noses and to the tails of the lambs to confuse their sense of smell, they accepted them as their own within three days. In Devon I had used the same trick but had used rum essence, and must have given the impression that I was a secret drinker to anyone who dropped in to see the lambs.

As we reached the end of lambing one of Fred's old survivors produced twins, much to her surprise and ours. One was a smart, black and white little boy, the other, a girl, looked at first glance to be crossed with a Boer goat. She had a long, soft, silky white coat and a reddish brown splash over one ear and her mother took an instant dislike to her. Harrison and the other night staff pinned the indignant, stamping, struggling mother into a corner every two hours over the first forty eight, so that she would get her share of colostrum, the new milk without which she would surely die. The mother, however, refused to change her mind and Harrison volunteered to feed her with a bottle so that we could let the ewe and other lamb go out with the rest of the flock.

"It must have a good Shona name," I told him.

Harrison nodded, "S'arai," he said firmly.

'S'arai,' Isaac told me, means 'remain in peace.

The pups had matured rather than grown, for although they had got bigger they would always be cuddlesome. They were quite different. Bess was half Porgie's size, a small, brown and white package of compressed energy that was constantly fully charged. On the ground she moved like a cat, bounding gracefully through the tall grass after flying ants and grasshoppers, dabbing at them with her paws, twisting, turning and leaping and often as not catching them. She was quicker than Porgie and would turn like a hare when he chased her, doubling back on her tracks and leaving him to plough straight on. At fence lines she would skim under the lowest strand of wire, just four inches from the ground, sliding on her tummy without checking speed, while Porgie inevitably cannoned into it. In the wiry, tussocky grass he could catch her as he had more ground clearance, and would mercilessly grab her stump of a tail and flip her cart wheeling onto her back from which position she fought equally well, also merciless and grabbing at whatever presented itself. In the water she was in her second element, gliding smoothly through the flat, green lilly pads with their beautiful pink and mauve flowers, easily beating Porgie to the sticks we threw.

Porgie was much more fox terrier size, a solid well-proportioned little dog who matched Bess for energy and whose masculine grace showed in more athletic ways. He leapt effortlessly into the back of the pickup while Bess stood waiting demurely to be lifted in, and he loved to climb to the top of the stacked round hay bales after mice. As a small pup I had taught him to jump into my arms, and it was now a favourite game. Suddenly turning when out for a walk, he would hurl himself at me with an unmistakable grin on his face, and no doubt at all that I would catch him. They had found out very quickly that most of the Africans were afraid of them and had a wonderful time until checked. Women would go screaming off through the bush leaving a wake of firewood and assorted bundles, and children who barked and teased them from outside the gates were quick to shin up a tree when face to face with them on the farm. No lizard dared move in the garden and Bess was often to be seen with four legs and a tail dangling from her mouth. She was every inch a hunter. In the garden was a tree with a very sloping trunk, in whose branches lived a large blue headed lizard. Porgie had discovered that by taking a run at it he could get up the trunk and onto the first long branch. It became quite common to look out of the window and see him up the tree. The lizard was a wise one though, and quite effortlessly slid round to the underside of the branch, something that Porgie couldn't quite master.

I had stuck to the natural diet advised by my herbal vet book and they were both dog shaped dogs in the peak of condition. Each evening they had their bowl of raw meat with a nice marrow bone on top for afters. Porgie had his on the back step and Bess would follow me through the house to the front veranda for hers. One evening I gave Porgie his and Bess and I went through to the front as usual. I put the dish down and a shadow nipped through the cat flap, grabbed the bone and was gone before either of us had fully realised what had happened. Porgie had left his plate untouched, belted round the outside of the house and had stolen Bess's bone from under her nose. For all of two seconds she was dumbstruck, and then she was beside herself with rage. She hurtled through the cat flap without touching the sides, and a savagely snarling bullet hit Porgie amidships. It was then that his sense of good manners returned and he trotted quickly back to his bowl with scarcely a backwards glance.

Suddenly, it seemed, they were seven months old and it was time to get Bess spayed if we were to avoid unwanted puppies and visits from all the dogs in the district. It was with some apprehension that I arranged a visit to the vet.

He met me at 7.45 a.m. at the door of his surgery with a rare, shy smile and an enquiry after the sheep. It's amazing how a warm, genuine smile can change a person. His African assistant shaved a small patch above the vein on Bess's right front leg and held her firmly but gently as the needle went in. Within a fraction of a second she had collapsed onto her side and the vet taped the syringe onto her leg to control the depth of her unconsciousness during the operation. He checked her eye reflex and I remembered sadly the last time I had held a dog for such an injection. But this wasn't a last fatal overdose. Bess would live to catch a million grasshoppers and stalk a thousand lizards through the warm brown grasses of many a tomorrow.

"Come back in half an hour," the vet was saying.

I took a last look at the tiny, helpless little bundle on the shiny operating table and left.

In half an hour, on the dot, I was back and the vet's assistant came to meet me, smiling, with an unconscious Bess in his arms. He laid her carefully on the front seat, checked the position of her tongue and gently closed the door.

"How long will she be out?"

"Oh, she will come round about lunch time," he assured me, "already she is beginning to come around."

I drove home slowly and carefully, trying not to jar her. Tendai brought the big blanket lined box we had prepared to the car and we carried her into the bedroom, covered her with another blanket against the draughts and shut her in.

Porgie was absolutely lost. He followed me around with a worried, anxious frown on his face and kept running to the passage door and looking back at me. At last I took him quietly in and let him sniff her, and he relaxed visibly and began to wag his tail. It was three in the afternoon when Bess at last opened her eyes and gave me a brief wag. Then she drifted off again until the late evening, when she began to thresh around trying to get up. I fetched some water and held her upright but her back legs crumpled beneath her and she couldn't stand. She drank, then went back to sleep. Neither John nor I voiced our thoughts, that she should be awake by now and that she looked paralysed, and what had we done to the quicksilver, brimful of fun little animal of yesterday. She stayed in our room and Porgie slept by himself on the veranda for the first time ever. It was about four in the morning when I woke to find her little face an inch from mine and her warm tongue ungluing my eyes. She was standing strongly on her back legs with her front paws planted on the bed, delighted to find herself in the usually forbidden territory of our bedroom.

Within three days she was herself again and except for the five stitches down the centre of her pink, shaven tummy, the operation was history and Porgie was more than happy to find himself being ambushed and nipped and teased as usual. Each morning after checking the sheep the pups and I went for a long walk. It was June and mid-winter. The trees flowed with the colours of an English Autumn, the golds, russets and reds contrasting vividly with the bright green new leaf already appearing on some of the smaller trees. The sky was that wonderful deep blue that sometimes follows the morning frost in England, and sometimes I could imagine that I was walking through the New Forest in Southern England where I was born. Then a big blue headed lizard would whisk up a tree, or a troupe of monkeys cross the track ahead, the early rays of sunshine slanting through the trees would bathe me in their warmth and I would feel a deeper warmth and happiness that I was, indeed, in Africa.

Across the wide brown pastures spread the ewes with what looked like a million lambs, bucking, kicking, jumping and running their endless steeplechases, until tired and thirsty they made unhesitatingly for mother. And little S'arai would detach herself from the rest and seek out Harrison. A tiny white lamb with one brown ear, whose idol in life was as dark as a noon-time shadow, and who returned her trust with a smile as broad as the blue sky above them, and as warm as the African sun.

CHAPTER THIRTEEN

John and I would be the first to admit that we are not very good employees. The desire to own our own farm had never diminished, and we found more and more that we were seeking to 'do our own thing' within the confines of our job. The wool from the sheep was almost valueless, and I had decided that it would be good to make it into a product that was saleable rather than just sell it for peanuts or bury it. To this end I went to see the African women in Nyanga who made rugs, and learned from them how they made the frames and wove the wool into the lovely African patterns. Back on the farm I experimented. John made me a frame and within no time Tendai and I were turning out quite saleable rugs. We showed them around and found that many people would be willing to buy, so I went to Fred with my plan. I would buy the wool from him and pay Tendai so that the rug making would be a project for me and the money earned I could save. To my surprise he was quite enthusiastic about the idea, but insisted that any money earned should go into the farm. It was a small disagreement and not important, but the attitude was. It meant that we would always be employees. To any sane person it shouldn't have been a problem. Our life-style was comfortable, we were doing the sort of work we wanted to do and we had a more or less open cheque book to do it. There was no logical explanation, but we needed the freedom to follow our dream. So when John got an invitation to go to Zambia and look at a job prospect he decided to go and see.

It just seemed an unfortunate co-incidence that the very weekend that we had arranged to go was the same weekend that John Valentine had decided to hold the baptisms. As a fledgling Christian I knew nothing of spiritual warfare. In fact, I had never heard of it. Of course, I was disappointed but I didn't really think that my baptism was more important than going to Zambia. After all, I could get baptized any time and if we missed this opportunity of seeing the job that was on offer then we might miss it. John Valentine was also disappointed, but agreed that I could be baptized at a future date in a friend's swimming pool. So we could do both.

We set off excitedly for Zambia early on a Friday morning, together with Richard, John's son, who was also working in Zimbabwe and had set up the interview for us. Once across the border the roads changed from the wide tar, almost empty, highways of Zimbabwe to the heavily pot-holed and dusty roads of Zambia. Some maintenance was being done on the roads, and a seven mile diversion took us over rocky tracks, through wild mango groves and all but shook our teeth loose. At one point, near a huge, unavoidable pot-hole some enterprising African had set up a car repair service. We arrived at our destination at around 7.00 p.m., in the dark, tired and hot.

The farmhouse was heavily guarded. A high security fence surrounded house and garden, and at the gate the African night-guard held a radio and a laser beamed torch. Our hosts were waiting for us and we drove inside to be instantly surrounded by a pack of dogs, all obviously selected for their size and ferocity, the most memorable being a bull-mastiff x rottweiler. The house had burglar bars on all the windows, and the two main doors had iron barred gates which closed over them with the securing clasps passing right through the wall itself to be padlocked on the inside.

Once inside and secure we enjoyed a wonderful supper and went early to bed. The next day was spent looking around the farm, at the pen-fed Boron cattle, the stables full of polo-ponies, the paddock of pedigree Dorper sheep and John talked Burley tobacco production with Ken, our host. That evening we again relaxed over supper and retired relatively early.

At around 2.00 a.m. someone switched on our bedroom light. Awakened from a deep sleep we were more than a little surprised to see a face appear around the door. It was a black face beneath a black balaclava and surrounded by a turned up jacket collar. John calmly, conversationally almost, asked the face what it wanted. The answer came in Tongan, which John didn't speak, but he continued talking quietly to the man hoping he would understand, and stalling for time as he made up his mind what to do! Meanwhile, at the other end of the corridor Ken had woken and, hearing the murmur of voices, guessed that we had got up to go to the bathroom or to get a drink. Then, in his sleepy state, he realised that his bedroom door was shut - something he never did. So he quietly got out of bed and peered down the corridor. There he saw our intruder leaning into our room. He could also see that, behind his back, the man was holding a large butcher's knife. The dog beneath Ken's bed kept very quiet and stayed where it was.

The next thing we knew was the thudding of bare feet and a banshee howl as our host flew down the corridor and grabbed the man. They both shot through the doorway and landed on the floor of our room, as I peered unbelievingly over the sheets. A short fight followed, then our would-be assailant broke free and ran back up the corridor into the lounge. There he began to throw everything he could lay hands on at his

123

captors until he was cornered and caught, and even then he managed to bite Ken.

Summoned by radio the night-guard ran in haste across the lawn and got savaged by the bull-mastiff x rottweiler. He arrived limping and consequently had little sympathy for the captive, who was trussed up with rope to await the police. The police seemed more than a little disappointed that Ken hadn't shot him and saved them the trouble of finding somewhere safe to lock him up for the night. In fact, he was found to have the keys to Ken's gun cabinet in his hand, although luckily he hadn't realised what they were. When the police had taken him away we inspected the damage. He had come unseen past the guard, negotiated the security fence and the dogs, and climbed between the burglar bars in a place that had a slightly larger gap than elsewhere. He had gone to the kitchen and found, amidst a dozen others, the keys to open the padlocks to the security gates, and both front and back doors stood wide open. On the freezer was a large branch, presumably for self-protection against the dogs. In the kitchen drawer he had found four large butcher knives (Ken was a hunter) and had left one by each open door, one by the window by which he had entered and the other he had taken with him to our bedroom. As Ken had cannoned into him in our doorway the knife had hit the door post and broken in half. He had been left with the handle.

We travelled back to Zimbabwe the next day. Why had it happened? We shall probably never know, but that day I should have been baptized. I chose to follow another route and put off my obedience to the Lord 'til another day, but He had not left me or forsaken me. Several weeks later I was baptized.

I think that experience made me begin to think about the hidden forces of good and evil. Or maybe, after my baptism, the Holy Spirit began to open my eyes more to the things around me to which I had previously been blind. It is certainly true that in Africa it is easier to see the spiritual dimension of life, because the African is a very spiritual person and his culture is inextricably bound up with the spirit world.

John Valentine told me of the time that he was warned that a woman he was about to baptize was a witch. When she was plunged beneath the water it seemed that she was being held there and it took several strong men to get her back up again. For half an hour she was in real danger of drowning. All her life she had been involved in satanic work. Spirit-mediums are chosen and trained from birth, and possessed at an early age. Satan would have preferred to have her drown than lose her to God. When, at last, she came out of the water she went straight to her young daughter and stripped her of the charms and tokens that linked her to the occult.

We know that water baptism alone doesn't save and salvation isn't dependent upon baptism, but that really isn't the point. The point is that Jesus thought it important enough to be baptized Himself and He also made it part of the Great Commission (Matthew 28 v 19, 20). I don't personally believe that Jesus would concern himself with trivia. If He says do it then the point is not even debatable. 'He who believes and is baptized will be saved.' My own feeling is that we should stop looking at baptism from the view point of 'what's in it for me?' and start wondering what's in it for Jesus. There is no doubt in my mind that having gone through that act of obedience the Holy Spirit is able to use us more, with great benefit to both ourselves and others.

It was good that Johnny and Mel were able to be present to see me baptized and it was not long afterwards that we received a 'phone call one evening from Mel. As usual the line to Juliasdale was bad, and I could only just recognise her voice amidst the crackles.

"When can you both come and see us?" She shouted.

Since lambing was over and the team were coping very successfully there didn't seem any reason not to go.

"We've had an idea," yelled Mel, mysteriously, "How about next week-end?"

Across the table John gave me the thumbs up sign.

A few days later we were sitting on Johnny and Mal's veranda, ice cold drinks in hand and mouths wide open. How would we like to join them? During the Rhodesian war Johnny hadn't been allowed to visit the far side of his ranch as the army had been in residence there. Now it was empty and unused. The 'idea' was that we could have the use of 500 acres and open it up, choosing our own enterprises. We would put some money into an account and they would match it, we would run it and share the profits. We didn't need to think twice.

JULIASDALE

1992 - 1995

'The Lord is my shepherd; I shall not want. He makes me to lie down in green pastures; He leads me beside the still waters. He restores my soul ; He leads me in the paths of righteousness for His name's sake.'

(Psalm 23 v 1-3)

'Much food is in the fallow ground of the poor, and for lack of justice there is waste.'

(Proverbs 13 v 23)

CHAPTER FOURTEEN

Fred agreed to sell us some of the sheep. We chose sixty which meant that we would have to make several trips to get all our animals and gear to the ranch. It was a six hour drive in the Suzuki, so a loaded lorry would only make two trips in three days at the most.

Harrison and his family stated flatly that they were coming with us.

"Mena hamba," said Harrison, in a tone that left no room for argument.

He wasn't the only one. Fredrikson, the Zulu handyman who helped John with the fencing, amongst other things, made it clear he was also with us. He had a wife and twin boys. Harrison had three children. Literally dozens came and asked if they could come. It never ceased to amaze me how easily any African could just leave a well paid and secure job to follow us into the unknown. We eventually chose Kenneth, who worked in the tobacco barns, Nathanial who was the son of Fred's head cattleman, and Robert who helped with both the sheep and the cattle. Wilson chose us, making it clear that when we had gone he would give notice and follow us anyway. Since none of them would make any great difference to Fred's operation by their absence he agreed.

Our final tally came to six men, five wives, eight children, five horses (Rainbow had given birth to a fine colt foal which we named Zebedee), sixty sheep, two dogs, one cat (I had been given a kitten which was half Siamese and half African Wildcat, aptly named Siwi) and half a dozen hens. Together with our own few belongings and those of our team of workers, it represented several lorry loads and a lot of driving. We took the team first, so that they could get settled in and begin to sort out their living accommodation. There had been a large farmhouse on the section we were going to develop, but the army had wrecked it and the locals had stripped it of window frames and the odd wheelbarrow load of bricks. We had reckoned that it was probably too expensive to restore as a house, but the gang decided that it would make first class 'flats', and quickly divided it up into sections. In no time at all they had made sacking curtains and utilised old pallets to make doors and window shutters.

Our last load brought the horses. I had fallen in love with a young filly called Gambler belonging to a neighbour, and had been delighted to find that her owner would have much preferred a gelding. John had suggested that I should offer a straight swap for either Anzac or Leprechaun, and to my surprise and delight she had instantly agreed. She chose Leprechaun, which was fine by my husband, as I had taken to riding Tif the Arab stallion and John was riding Anzac quite happily. So we moved with Tif, Gambler, Anzac, Rainbow and the foal, Zebedee. They travelled well on the back of the open lorry, and following them through Harare in the Suzi I was amazed how they seemed so unconcerned. The buses belched their black smoke, and with the traffic hooting and whizzing past them they just gazed peacefully around them when stopped at traffic lights and road junctions.

It was late evening when we arrived tired, hot and covered in dust. Harrison and the others came running excitedly to meet us. The previous night, they explained breathlessly, right there next to their house and where we were about to unload the horses, hyenas had killed three steers. Probably young ones learning to kill, guessed Fredrikson, as they hadn't eaten much of the carcases. Well, Johnny reasoned, he had never lost any horses to hyenas, and ours would be just as safe there as anywhere else on the ranch. So, with not a few misgivings we turned them out and prayed that they would be safe, especially the foal. Of course there was no ramp, so they had to be jumped down from the lorry onto a roadside bank, but once loose in the huge paddock they stuck together in a tight little band and Tif at once took charge.

There was an air of great excitement and adventure amongst the team. Their house was on a small hill overlooking a river, which rushed under a bridge and fell over a series of big flat rocks just below. Called the Chidya (that which eats) it kept a strong flow during the dry winters and was torrential during the summer rains. The big flat rocks provided an ideal place for the women to do their washing, and they soon met the local village women who came for the same purpose. Thus there was a constant shrill chatter of women and the shouts and whistles of small boys herding their goats and cattle along the green river banks. The river was the boundary between Johnny's ranch and the 'resettlement' farmers, who had been allocated land there by the new government after the war of independence. Here a dozen or so families scratched poor, sandy plots around their mud and thatch houses which they shared with chickens, goats and dozens of ragged, laughing children. Beyond the village were the arable lands where they raised their crops of maize each year, and near the river banks the women had fenced off a section where they could grow rape and tomatoes, carrying water from the river in big twenty litre drums. The women worked the fields and the little home plots while the men sought work elsewhere to earn real money on either Johnny's ranch or Lou's, or further away in Nyanga or Mutare. Their wealth was measured in cattle and goats, but more accurately seen in the threadbare clothes and spindly limbs of their many children.

  The government had kept its promise in giving them land, but they were miles from anywhere with little support, dumped by the side of the road with no house and no money or materials to build one. So the trees had come down and the traditional round thatched huts had gone up, in which they lived a doubtful freedom.

  Our arrival caused a great deal of interest, and with our team setting up home on the opposite side of the river bridge we had an instant introduction to our new neighbours. Opposite the ruined farmhouse was an old stone barn, and it was here that we quickly fenced off a section to house our sheep. Harrison and his wife, Emma, began to make plans for their house which was to be at the gate of the sheep pens so that they would never be left unguarded. Harrison and Emma had very definite ideas about their dream home. It materialised very quickly, with a wide thatched veranda under which Harrison intended to house his future bicycle, a grass fenced garden where Emma began to grow her precious seedlings, and a two storey chicken house with the layers and scratching hens beneath and the broody and sitting hens above. It was immediately christened Harrison's Hotel, and his grin got even broader.

  To start with we stayed in a caravan which belonged to Johnny and Mel and was sited in a sectioned off part of their garden. Johnny quickly got busy down at the river bridge and built a small header tank so that he could install a ram pump which pumped water up to an existing reservoir near the sheep house. It was while John was there one morning that he wandered off by himself and found the place that was to be our home for the next three years. After a quick breakfast he whisked me off to see what he had found. From the track leading to the sheep pen and Harrison's Hotel he led me through a sagging and rusty barbed wire fence and out across the scrub bush land. Sandy game and cattle trails led us amongst the acacias as the sun, already hot, threw black shadows across the crisp, wiry grasses. We skirted ant-bear holes and termite mounds and finally came to a granite kopje with a huge fig tree growing at its base. Beyond the fig-tree were water berry bushes and some wild guavas, and these lined one bank of a small pool which had in its midst a green, grassy mound from which bubbled a clear spring.

"What do you think?"

My husband was a little hesitant, wondering, I expect ,if I was ready yet for such un-civilization.

It was beautiful. Away in the distance stretched the Nyanga Mountains; the little kopje provided shelter and the spring a source of water. In the branches of the big fig tree doves and louries called and scolded, and around us the untouched African bush shimmered in the heat. My expression told all. Hand in hand we wandered back towards the main track which led out of the valley and joined the nearest tarred road some nine miles away. We found that we joined it exactly opposite a wide cattle trail which disappeared around a hill and back to Johnny and Mel's ranch house some four miles across country. It seemed perfect and although somewhat surprised, Johnny agreed. Within a few days he had made us a driveway with his old road grader and towed the caravan onto a flat piece of ground in the lee of the kopje. A few yards from the caravan door grew a wild gardenia tree, and round this we built a traditional African wash-room with high grass walls and open to the skies. Our well travelled stainless steel sink again came into its own as a kitchen sink/bath, and the tree obligingly held out its little twiggy branches to hold flannels, towels, tooth mugs and soap holder. I had an oval, gilt framed mirror which we hung on the grass wall, giving it a touch of glamour. A small portable and very basic toilet fitted neatly into one corner with the toilet roll inside an ice-cream container to stop it rolling away across the bush and to protect it from the damp. Water carried from the spring at mid-day stayed pleasantly warm until evening, but had to be inspected closely for tadpoles and frog spawn. Washing powder, I accidentally discovered, revved up tadpoles to unbelievable speeds.

Johnny's neighbour, Lou, who we had met previously - he of the one black eye -, was now our neighbour too, on the opposite boundary from Johnny and Mel. He often called by for a cup of tea and a chat, and was very enthusiastic about our venture. Lou provided me with my cooking stove. It came off his scrap-heap and was a big old free-standing kitchen range with six hotplates. We sited it beyond the washroom where it was sheltered by some high bushes. When first lit the smoke blotted out the whole area, but it soon settled down and was very efficient. There was a hole between the firebox and the oven which meant that anything baked came out severely kippered, but it was wonderful to use as an extension to the little gas stove in the caravan. The next luxury was hot, running water. This was provided by drilling a hole in an old calor gas bottle about half way down the side. Into the hole was inserted a metal pipe about a foot long to act as filling funnel and steam escape funnel. The gas tap was replaced by a water tap and the whole thing was placed on its side on a cradle of bricks over a small fire. Water boiled remarkably quickly, and after the first few fillings the smell of gas disappeared and eventually we were even able to make tea from it.

It was worlds away from the commercial farming atmosphere that I had come to know. At night we lay in the caravan listening to the night sounds of Africa. Millions of crickets and several varieties of frogs by the spring kept up a steady background chorus. The solos came in the form of wild, repeated screams from the larger bush-babies as they leapt through the trees of the kopje, the cries of jackals, the whooping calls of hyenas and the gentle whoo-whoo from the eagle owls. Galloping horses signalled dawn as Tif the stallion brought his herd up to the caravan each morning, not to be fed but for a pat and a brush over and general companionship.

As hyena tracks came to within twenty five metres of the caravan and the dogs slept underneath it in old tyres, fences became a priority. Again our gear from our Devon smallholding came into play, and some very professional, battery powered electric fences went up around us. The dogs soon learned about the fences and we have seen Bess, in hot pursuit of a mongoose, come to a violent emergency halt inches from the bottom strand as her quarry ducked through. It also took them no time at all to realise that the gates didn't sting, and they joyously absconded for a twenty four hour hunt during which we doubted ever seeing them again. When they did finally return, crawling ashamedly on their bellies in contrition but unable to conceal the huge grins on their faces, we decided that the only solution was going to be to keep one tied at all times and to change them regularly, as they would only go off to hunt as a pair. This was to prove to be life saving training for them, as later they both became caught in snares several times and as they were used to being tethered they didn't panic and strangle themselves. They still gave us the slip a few times, and we learned that if we didn't secure the second one before we loosened the first one it took only a second for them to be gone. One would look at the other and that was it, we could bellow at their retreating little forms till blue in the face. Although now full grown they were still small, but they never gave that a thought. Anything was huntable - hares, mongoose, jackals, serval cats, kudu, baboon, leopard, bush-buck. Some way beyond the spring was a stream which flowed back to the Chidya, and near its banks an aardwolf had set up its burrows. The maze of underground tunnels was irresistible to the two dogs, and if either of them was missing it was the first place to look. On the occasions that they did get away from us Porgie once came back without Bess, and she later came limping home at dusk dragging a snare with part of a branch still attached. Porgie was caught several times, but on finding himself immobilised he would just sit down and bark for help. This was fine unless some predator got to him before we did. He also had the annoying habit of keeping quiet when he thought we had found him, so although we knew he was somewhere close by in the thick bush we had to physically search every square foot of it before we found him sitting there grinning at us.

Once the home base was set up and running to a regular routine we had to think of something to make us a regular income. The sheep would produce lambs in season, but short term we needed something that would produce a quicker profit. Broiler chickens seemed a good idea as they took only six weeks to mature, would be inside away from predators and seemed to be in demand. Harrison assured us that people would come from over the river to buy, so John and his team set to work building our first chicken house from clay bricks and locally gathered grass thatch. Soon our day-olds were ready to be collected from Rusape, a two hour drive away. The roof wasn't quite finished, but with the team in charge and a good five hours to finish it we drove away confidently to collect our chicks. We arrived back to find the roof in exactly the same state as we had left it. There had been a local storm with torrential rain and the whole place was soaked. Our precious chicks were desperately needing water after their hot, lurching journey down the nine mile sand and gravel road from the main tar, so knowing nothing at all about chicks we put a shallow bowl of water near them and they all dived in. In seconds we had a heap of bedraggled, miserable, half-drowned little bodies. It was now dark and cold and we had no way of drying them, so back they went in their box and we made a dash for Johnny and Mel's farmhouse and an electricity supply. An hour later Mel's kitchen was transformed into a broiler pen, complete with infra-red lamp and proper chicken drinkers, and our small, scraggy wet bundles had miraculously fluffed out into bright little chicks again. Next day they were transferred to the veranda where they stayed until the roof was secure on their shed.

Despite their unfortunate start they grew well, as book in one hand I measured out their rations and John tended the paraffin hurricane lamp which kept them warm. I felt quite guilty about how trusting they were. When they reached six weeks I was able to take my kitchen scales down to their house and sit them on to see how they were progressing. At six weeks they weighed between 1.5 -2 kg, and we sent out word that we had chickens for sale.

The response was remarkable, and was my first real experience of bush-telegraph. Chickens went off in shopping bags, in boxes on the carriers of ramshackle bikes, and perched side by side on the spare seats in cars. The police called for them in their landrover, teachers from the little school across the river sent their pupils to collect them. Our own workers, who were allowed one each at half price, enthusiastically broadcast their size and quality to all they met and in no time at all we were chicken- less, and still the buyers came. So the next house was built and we ordered day-old layers as well as broilers.

The locals were fascinated and many called in just to see what we were doing and how we were doing it. At least two went away to copy our success, but inattention to detail caused one to burn his kitchen down because he hadn't secured the hurricane lamp, and another allowed his more agile 'outside hens' to fly in and out over the door, thus introducing disease. We were happy to help with advice when needed, and also collected day-olds and chicken feed for them when we went to town. Help travelled both ways, and when Johnny loaned us two young bullocks to train as oxen the villagers were mightily enthusiastic. We paid them to make the necessary yokes, and when we began to clear a patch of ground to grow a fodder crop for the sheep they came with their own teams of oxen and helped unasked.

Our greatest friend across the river was Peter Grant. He was a very elderly but very spry farmer, who loved his mombies and he and John soon became firm friends. My first recollection of him takes the form of two disembodied white eyeballs and a single white tooth in the dark interior of a hut. As a strict' Apostori', an African religious sect who shave their heads, grow beards and wear white robes on Sundays, he was a firm believer in women being subordinate beings, but was always very polite to me and very willing to help John. He regularly called in to see us, and often I would find him waiting patiently under the trees near the caravan when we rose at dawn, having already walked four kilometres.

Always outspoken, we learned from him the reason for some of the attitudes of the African towards the white person. We knew that in the African's mind, to be white was to be rich. Rich we were not, but we did still have the Suzuki which we used quite frequently to bring back supplies for our neighbours and to give them lifts up out of the valley. Apart from that we probably had less money than they did since we had no cattle or goats of our own. John tried to explain our poverty to Peter one day, who dismissed the idea with a lofty wave of his arm.

"When you were born," he told my husband, emphatically, "Your father opened a bank account for you. From the time you left school you have been able to live on the interest of this bank account, and the money is still there. Also," he added, "He bought you the car."

And that was the end of the matter.

We planted ranks of lukaena trees, bana grass and comfrey and the kudu loved them, reducing them to stalks overnight.

"I've got a house cow," said Lou one morning, as we sat out in front of the caravan in the sun having a leisurely cup of coffee. "I don't really need her. She's going to calve any time now, so when she does I'll send her over and you can have the milk."

Good as his word, Susan the Brahman x Jersey came walking down the drive a few weeks later followed by the most beautiful little Brahman heifer calf I had ever seen. Susan had a formidable pair of horns, and that way of looking down her nose at you that Brahmans have, but she was very sweet natured and bulging with milk. We called the calf Nyuchi, which means honey and described her lovely golden brown coat. They stayed in a small paddock next to the caravan during the night, with Nyuchi safely tucked up in a small wooden pen so that there would be milk for us in the mornings. Then, after milking, they would wander off over the huge paddock where the horses grazed for the rest of the day. We put out the word that we had milk to sell, and soon a procession of children and women arrived each morning carrying old cooking oil bottles, chipped tea pots and jugs to collect a pint of milk for a few cents. They came for many miles, and I soon ran out of spare bottles and began to sell it in tightly knotted plastic bags, which seemed to work quite well. One of my most vivid memories is that of two young children, hessian sacks pinned around their shoulders for protection, arriving in the midst of a violent thunderstorm and torrential rain, having walked four miles for two pints of milk.

The day-old layer chicks blossomed into smart black hens, and the team put up a chicken run and added laying boxes to our first chicken house. Soon the odd brown egg arrived, and not long after that I was collecting a basket of brown eggs every morning. I loved collecting the eggs, and again there was a very ready market. Those who couldn't afford a chicken could feed a family with a dozen eggs. The sheep were looking happy, out with Harrison each day roaming over the sparse bush land but getting good pickings where no sheep had roamed before. Harrison was now a hero. He had gone out as usual at six one morning and had noticed that a few of the sheep were bunching together and looking nervously at something in a ditch, so he went to investigate. All the Africans carried a 'demo', a small axe usually fashioned from a car-spring, and this was their only weapon. On reaching the sheep Harrison suddenly found himself staring into the eyes of a leopard just five metres away, crouched in the tall grass lining the ditch. Five metres equals one bound for a leopard and without thinking Harrison hurled his demo straight at it. In one smooth action he infuriated the leopard and threw away his only form of defence. Why it didn't attack we shall never know. The demo glanced off its shoulder, and according to our hero, its eyes blazed red and then with a snarl it turned and fled. For weeks Harrison basked in the afterglow, the flames being fanned each day as the story was recounted to the many who came to hear. It was decided then, that he should have a dog with him which would give him some warning if the sheep were threatened in any way. Johnny and Mel had a young bitch named Jackie, a bull terrier cross with nothing to do all day but get into mischief, so she was promoted to sheep dog and went to live at Harrison's Hotel. They soon became firm friends, and Jackie took her job very seriously. Too seriously one day, when she chased and caught a baboon bigger than me and killed it. Baboons will take young lambs if given the chance and this one had come too close in Jackie's opinion. It hadn't given up without a fight, however, and the vet put over forty stitches into Jackie's wounds. She made a complete recovery.

Our accident prone friend, Chris, was also an occasional visitor to the caravan. He was always busy, either herding cattle to the dip tanks on horse-back, or patrolling the farm in sections, discouraging poachers and searching for snares. His declared enemies were the bush-pigs, and he was often out at night on his own, laying in wait for them. The meat was dark and gamey and much sought after by the locals. Leopards were also a great problem, and Lou told me that one year he had lost fifty calves to leopards. The problem was that even if an animal got away, the wounds left by a leopard are so infected that the animal will die anyway. So Chris sometimes sat up by a kill waiting for leopard as well. All by himself, miles from anywhere and as prone to mishaps as he was, it seemed nothing short of a miracle to me that he should survive.

One morning Johnny and Mal came sweeping into the drive in their pick-up with Chris sitting in the back with his gun, and at his feet a dead leopard. It was the nearest I had ever been to one, and although I knew that it had killed and wounded many mombies it was really sad to see it dead. The coat was beautifully marked, and the strength in the muscular forelegs was incredible. Chris must have had the protection of the Almighty, however, as he had sat by the kill during the night. The leopard had seen him just before he was aware of its presence, and his one shot as their eyes met had been the only one needed.

So with the sheep doing well, the chickens selling as fast as we could produce them, and milk and eggs in abundance it seemed time to look for the next venture. It came via Mel, who took us one day to see a friend who had a few animals but had to sell them. Amongst them were two young sows, due to farrow within a few weeks. Of course, John didn't need much time to think. He loved pigs and these were an exceptionally good looking pair, a fact that even I had to admit. Personally I can find no amity with pigs except in the form of pork and bacon, in fact I am more than a little scared of them. I was quite happy to peer over the wall whilst John and Mel's friend, Liz, scratched their backs and tickled their ears. So it was agreed that we should take them after they had farrowed, as it seemed unkind to move them when they were so very heavy in pig. The team set to work again, and soon part of the stone sheep house had two large pig-proof pens installed, a supply of pig meal was obtained and we were ready to plunge into pig production.

Although our new projects were going well, with a team of Africans to pay and food to buy for the livestock we were finding real problems with the financial side of things. As always we came last on the list of those to be provided for and our food became very basic. Eggs and vegetables were a mainstay, and we were able to keep our freezer at Mel's house so we could keep some meat in reserve, but usually it was full of chickens which we rarely ate as we needed to sell them. We slaughtered at six weeks any that didn't get sold, reasoning that it was cheaper to keep them in the freezer than in the pens. We had orders from various people for frozen chickens, and sold to the bank, the electricity company, the council offices and several private families in Nyanga. We delivered these when we went to the bank or had other business in town and it worked very well, everything being sold for cash. Our break came when I managed to negotiate a deal with a large supermarket in Rusape. We delivered weekly and were paid cash which we then took to the agricultural feeds merchant and converted it to stock feeds. Any left over we could spend on ourselves, but that didn't happen very often as we also had to pay regularly for new batches of day old chicks. At one time we got to the stage of having nothing in the caravan to eat, but the Lord always provides. Along came an African woman to see what we were doing, and with her as a present she brought a basket of tomatoes. Tomato soup went down very well that evening. As tomatoes were grown by all the women they were very cheap to buy, so blended together with our rich fresh milk and a handful of fresh herbs it was a meal that was more than welcome and oft repeated.

To help out a little with the finances, I put the very moderate skills I had learned whilst at Chegutu into making woollen rugs from our sheep's' wool. Mel had got me an order from an hotel for a wall hanging and the subject chosen was, to me, both boring and uninspiring. Under the old patched awning fronting the caravan it was hot. Still early morning, before nine, the sky blazed blue, the sun throwing deep pools of shadow beside the mountain acacias and thorn bushes that studded the brown, dry bush land surrounding us. John was off checking the pigs and horses, and I was seated reluctantly before the wooden frame propped against the caravan wall working on the tapestry. My eyes kept drifting away to the nearby mountains, to the eagles soaring above, to the little jewel-like honey-suckers that fluttered busily from one blossom to another. Close by in the bushes partridges were calling, sounding just as my husband said, like someone pushing a squeaky wheel-barrow. Above them came the shouted conversation between Fredrikson and Wilson, working with the broilers on the other side of the kopje. They were all of three metres apart and their voices reached me clearly!

Suddenly I was conscious of another noise. Down by the stream behind the caravan, which flowed back to the Chidya, in the thick bush lining its banks, a dog was barking. As I listened I became convinced it was Porgie, and as it didn't seem to be moving I guessed he had become caught in a snare and was yelling for help. I knew John would be away for most of the morning, and I also knew that he would take a dim view of me going off by myself to look for my dog. The barking became more frantic and I could ignore it no longer. I would take Fredrikson, I decided, he had spent a lifetime in the bush and I would be safe with him. I found him washing chicken drinkers down by the spring. Fredrikson and I communicated by a mixture of sign language and the odd word in Shona.

"Endai (Lets go)," I pointed towards the stream," Porgie, maybe....." I put my two hands round my throat to illustrate a snare.

Fredrikson nodded eagerly, left the chores to Wilson and quickly ducked through the fence, holding the strands apart for me to follow. Almost jogging to keep up with his walk, I followed him along the narrow, sandy, bush trail down to where the stream trickled over big flat rocks. We crossed over, ankle deep in the warm, clear, amber water and hurried along the banks until we reached the spot where the barking had been, but it had stopped. Fredrikson seemed to know where he was going though and was off again, dodging through the water bushes and the buffalo thorns that skirted the water.

Ahead we heard a yelp, and Fredrikson turned and gave a knowing, gappy grin. We must have been wrong, he was further along. Tall, beautiful aloes, like red candelabra grew down the banks, and reaching a natural rocky causeway we re-crossed the stream. Everything had gone quiet again, except for the cicadas in the m'sasa trees and the hornbills arguing with each other over the wild figs. Fredrikson suddenly stopped and pointed. From the reeds and into the bush he indicated the long curving mark in the sand, showing the passage of an enormous snake.

"Nyoka - Shato," whispered my guide, snake- python.

I stared at it. That last sound had been a yelp, not a bark. Was that really the end of my Porgie? Surely it couldn't happen that quickly.

"Eat, then sleep," said Fredrikson confidently, casting bush-trained eyes around the sparse undergrowth. The reeds, however, were high and thick and I wondered how he knew which way the snake was going. Maybe it was in the reeds, right next to us. I had seen such a python, sixteen feet long if it was an inch. We wandered around for a while, but no snake. Then, to my great relief, I heard another bark. Fredrikson jumped back into action.

"Endai," he ordered.

We left the cool shade of the riverine forest and emerged into hot sunshine, the brown coarse grasses rising tall above my head. I began to whistle, willing Porgie to answer me. I could picture him in my mind's eye, a snare around his neck, sitting patiently under some dark bush. The poachers were clever in siting their traps; they were usually in the deepest thicket so that anything caught was well out of sight. He would be listening to us coming, knowing that we would find him. Why couldn't the stupid little thing bark! In front of me I saw Fredrikson stop and examine the ground.

"Look," he said.

Where two game trails met a set of Porgie like paw prints were clearly visible. Behind a bush at the intersection, where the sand was deepest, was the single pad mark of a large cat. The Porgie prints ended in a long skid - then nothing.

"Leopard?"

My mind went back to that last yelp.

Fredrikson nodded.

"Endai!"

Suddenly he had stopped looking on the ground and was gazing up at trees.

"Sometime," he explained," this kind put in tree."

I didn't want to find my dog up a tree, any more than I wanted to find a python with a Porgie shaped middle, but I bravely peered up into the cool, green branches as we followed the river bank towards home. The thought of a leopard being in the vicinity was hardly reassuring either, and I marvelled at the brave way Fredrikson was striding ahead. I stole many a look over my shoulder as I followed him.

Ahead of us, down by the stream banks, we could hear baboons coming down for their morning drink. The big males were much bigger than me, and I knew that they were a real danger to dogs as well. The fact didn't escape my guide and protector.

"Sometime...." Fredrikson inclined his head, sorrowfully, towards the scolding and bickering ahead. He left the rest unsaid, but continued to shake his head doubtfully as we continued on our way.

It wasn't far from there that we found the ant-bear hole. In fact it was roughly where we had seen the python trail, but on the opposite bank of the river. The hole had been enlarged, the newly dug earth was fresh, and there in the middle was a very big, squarish, dog-like print. Fredrikson pointed.

"Fisi," he whispered, hyena, "Sleep when hot."

He inclined his head towards the climbing sun,

"Kabanga (maybe)," he added thoughtfully," Eat, then sleep."

We made slowly for home, my heart so heavy. Porgie, my happy little extrovert of a dog had been very special. He had been my constant companion, out with the horses, leaning over the back of the passenger seat when I was driving, watching the road ahead. Whatever I was doing, from baking a cake to filling a bucket, Porgie was always watching in joyful anticipation, his eyes alight with the sheer fun of being just Porgie. How could I have let him go off by himself? What match was a little dog like him against the wild animals around us, who lived and survived by tooth and claw?

John was waiting anxiously by the caravan when we crawled back through the fence, hot and dejected.

"Where have you been? No note, no hat! I didn't know where you were."

My husband was both relieved and exasperated.

"Porgie ..." I began, not knowing quite what to say.

"Porgie? Porgie came with me, in the truck. There he is."

In the shade of a deep red bougainvillaea, Porgie lay side by side with Bess, tongue lolling, an expression of deep contentment on his face.

"But," I reasoned, "I heard him, by the river...."

"So he chased a rabbit," answered my husband reasonably," dogs do."

He disappeared expectantly into the caravan.

"What did you cook for lunch?"

Despite his failings as a bush tracker, Fredrikson was a wonderful person to have around. His unfailing optimism and his ability always to 'do a plan' when problems arose made him an indispensable member of the team. He was usually in charge when we had to go away, and again whatever happened his enthusiasm and his natural talent for looking on the bright side carried him through all situations. I was so amazed at his summing up of events when we had to go to town and stay over a couple of nights, that I wrote them down. He had met us at the gate on our return with a broad grin and (translated by John from Chilapalapa) answered our queries as to how things were, like this:-

"Everything is alright.

One of the little, little chicks died, but the rest are fine.

There was a sheep that lambed. It had twins born backwards but they were both dead. Harrison skinned one and put the skin on an orphan, so that's fine.

Porgie got away from me and then Bess went as well. They went to the river but we got them back. Porgie was spat in the eye by a cobra, but I washed it out with milk, so that's fine."

Robert attempted the same philosophy when he came to report on the sheep.

> "One ewe got mastitis when you were away and it is dead. The ewe we gave the orphan to has taken it, so that is good. There is a ewe lambing now and the water she has brought out does not look good."

The ewe in question had a dead lamb coming backwards. She recovered well from her ordeal and we gave her the lamb from the dead mastitis ewe. The latter was cheerfully cut up by Fredrikson and distributed. Robert pointed out another lamb, one of a twin, who was looking in need of a bottle. An hour later it was dead and another good lamb was looking sick. I gave it an anti-biotic and tucked it up in a bed of straw. No ewe wanted to claim it. The next morning it was dead and the mother was standing outside the pen.

Back at the caravan, the senior cockerel of the 'Thunderbirds' was looking sick. We had fallen for a pair of Sumatran Game birds at Harare Agricultural Show and they had interbred with our locally purchased 'village vultures' to produce beautiful fowls whose seemingly black plumage turned to a wonderful, iridescent jade green as it caught the sunlight. They spent their lives eating bugs, spiders and even small snakes around the caravan. As one of the 'little, little chicks' had died and we had more cockerels growing on, we decided that for the sake of the broiler project the sick cockerel would have to go. Two more of the little chicks were looking below par, so that clinched the decision. Ten minutes after knocking off the cockerel the chicks perked up and started fighting over beetles. Sometimes, one felt, it was hardly worth going away.

It was as we sat down to our meal one evening that we saw twin headlights making their way down the long road through the valley. Cars were very few and when it turned into our driveway John went out to meet it. He came back with Liz, owner of our future pig project, who was looking flustered and anxious. One of the sows was farrowing, she had produced eight babies and there was another one that seemed to be stuck. She had been trying to give birth to it for some time, and now Liz was getting worried. As it was going to be our pig she wondered if we could go and help.

"No problem," I was horrified to hear my husband say. "Judy's very experienced in lambing and I'm sure we can sort it out."

The fact that Judy was terrified of pigs obviously hadn't entered my husband's mind. I could think of little else that I would rather not do than be in a small pen with a large pig, with my hand in what she might well consider a liberty taking position. However, nobody actually asked me what I thought and I was soon in the passenger seat of the Suzuki with my usual emergency lambing gear of Dettol soap, binder twine and a bucket, following Liz's speeding tail-lights up out of the valley.

We arrived at her home to find her stockman standing in the pen with the sow as she walked round and round, stopping occasionally to strain half-heartedly. It was agreed by the rest of the group that they would stand by her head and talk soothing baby talk whilst I attended to the business end, and it was with a thumping heart that I edged into the pen and gave her a timid pat. She was, Liz assured me, a very tame and placid pig, so I soaped up my hands bravely and began to gently explore the situation. The piglet that was stuck and causing all the problems was, indeed, very large. It was also very dead and as I worked my fingers around the little body I came across what felt like sharp bone. The stockman told me that he had actually pulled away part of the piglet when he was trying to dislodge it, and I wondered gloomily what damage he had done to the mother in the process. I could cover the sharp pieces with my hand to prevent more damage, but the rest of it was still too big to draw through.

"I'm afraid it's a job for the vet," I told Liz, "I think the only way would be a caesarean."

"Right," said Liz, "I'll phone the vet in Mutare and let him know we are coming."

By this time it was nearly mid-night and Mutare was a two hour drive away. After phoning, Liz backed her covered pickup up to the pen and we began to search around for a ramp. An old door was found, and without the slightest fuss or hesitation the sow walked straight up the makeshift ramp and into the truck.

"You see," smiled Liz, "She knows we are trying to help her."

When we reached Mutare we found that the vet's surgery was in the middle of a rather nice residential area, with large houses, lovely gardens and green lawns on either side. The vet himself was a strong, capable looking young man who, together with a friend who had been roped in to help, had set up a pig surgery on his lawn with flood-lighting and instrument table. Having got to this strange destination the pig began to object strongly to being examined again by total strangers and set up an ear-splitting, shrieking argument that must have woken half of Mutare and sent the vet's friend running to shut all the gates lest we lose her. A thorough examination confirmed my suspicions, and I must confess to a feeling of relief having instigated the proceedings. The sow was sedated and silence suddenly enveloped us. The vet worked quickly and with great expertise and soon the unfortunate little piglet lay on the lawn and Mum was being stitched up again. Back in Liz's truck, she settled down to sleep through the journey home and to be re-united with her other eight babies. On the way home we were amazed to see a lioness cross the road in our headlights. The Eastern Highlands is not an area where lions are encountered very often but can be seen very occasionally when passing through from Mozambique. We arrived home well after daylight.

Sadly the sow didn't survive the ordeal, and we got a message from Liz to say that she would like to give us the litter of orphan piglets. We picked them up that day, still looking remarkably bright considering the lack of milk and we just hoped that they had managed to get an adequate supply of colostrum in their first feed. My vet book was again consulted, and it seemed that a mixture of cows milk with an egg added was the thing to offer them, and since we had an abundance of both it posed no problem. Actually getting it into the piglets wasn't quite so easy though. Piglets are born with very sharp little teeth, and whereas you simply open a lamb's mouth, shove in the teat and clamp the mouth shut again until it gives in and sucks, the same method used on a piglet reduces your fingers to tatters. It took an average of half an hour to feed each piglet to start with, and as there were eight piglets and they had to be fed every four hours it doesn't take a mathematician to see that they took up most of my time, day and night. They slept in a box beneath the awning of the caravan, so at night I could just slip outside and feed them sitting on the steps. The dogs thought this was wonderful and came to sit with me, staring out into the darkness and growling menacingly at things I couldn't see. While I struggled to feed one baby the seven others would keep up an incredibly loud screaming for attention, which I felt must surely draw every predator in the vicinity.

Despite their bad start, however, they grew rapidly and soon I was feeding two at a time and life returned to some sort of routine beyond raising piglets. They moved into the new pig-quarters as soon as I was able to give up the night feeds, the other sow arrived with her family and John's new project was up and running.

I missed the little church at Chegutu, but Sundays now came to be a time when John and I could relax together and explore our new surroundings on horseback. Born and raised in the country, John had a wonderful sense of direction in the bush and we spent many hours off the trails pushing our way through acacia thickets and head-high brown grass in search of the abundance of game that dwelt around us. We discovered the Seven Brothers, huge kudu bulls with magnificent spiralling horns in a bachelor herd who, without fear, stood with heads raised high watching us watching them. A herd of black, scimitar horned sable could sometimes be seen at a distance, but we were never able to get close. Once we came across a sable bull that had become separated from the rest by a fence and had the rare opportunity of watching him as he ran up and down searching for a way through. Eventually, with some reluctance, he jumped and cleared it effortlessly.

Tif was wonderful in the bush, very sure footed and very aware of everything around us. If Tif refused to go along a certain path or past a particular place then I knew better than to argue, for one thing we tend to forget about a horse is that it had a sense of smell. Near one of the trails away from our caravan was an area of old termite mounds where there lived a large banded cobra. John and I had both seen it on several occasions, but Tif could smell it. Most days he would just walk past, but some days he would come to an abrupt halt and make a wide detour and it was this that encouraged me to trust his senses over mine every time. Through watching his ears and feeling his reactions when riding through the bush I came to see many things that I would have missed. One day, whilst riding past a dense thicket of young acacias, Tif stopped and stared into the trees. I couldn't see a thing, and neither could John, until suddenly a large section of the spindly tree-trunks moved and were transformed into the legs of a huge herd of kudu.

Anzac however, being a real nutty cookie, usually had the typical thoroughbred reaction of run first and reason later. Thus John missed many of the things that I saw due to the fact that within seconds of it appearing he was sitting on the ground and Anzac was gone. When I rode Anzac I used my 'geriatric, vertical hold' saddle, which helped no end because, when startled, Anzac would go down in front, a bit like a dog inviting you to play, and then spin. With my saddle that initial reaction just served to push me deeper behind the leg flaps and I was ready for the spin, with John's English saddle he was thrown off balance and the spin just finished him off! So sometimes our rides were punctuated with

"Oh look, there's a green woodpigeon!"

Thump!

"Wow, did you see that bush pig?"

Thump!

Luckily Anzac only retreated a few yards and John was never hurt, because I would never have found my own way home to get help. It wasn't long before we got Gambler, the young filly, under saddle too, and she became a lovely ride and John got to see more game!

So, although I missed going to the little church and I missed the singing, riding Tif through that beautiful country with God's unspoilt creation on all sides brought us closer to Him in many ways. John had always said that on a horse was where he felt close to God and, whilst my husband had never come to church with me, in sharing these wonderful Sunday rides we were close to Him together. Looking back at our time in the Valley I realise that it was a time of learning. Together we learned to live without security of any kind, except our security of being in Him. Without the 'security' of money in the bank we learned to rely on Him to answer prayers for all we needed, and we were never let down. Without the 'security' of locked doors, high fences and barred windows we learned to trust Him to protect us. When we could see no way out of a situation we prayed, and we learned that prayers are most often answered at the very, very last moment. God knows the future, He has no reason to provide anything before it is actually needed; it is our lack of faith that wants to see the answer arrive well ahead of the looming problem. It was a time that was both idyllic and stressful as we learned to trust God the hard way.

CHAPTER FIFTEEN

Pigs are as prolific as rabbits, and having purchased a young boar from a farm near Rusape, John found his project expanding very rapidly. A larger section of the sheep house was taken over and fattening pens were built. Before long we had to consider where we were going to sell and a visit to Mutare secured an arrangement with Colcom, suppliers of pork and bacon to the major retail outlets in Zimbabwe. The biggest problem in this was that we had to get them to their slaughterhouse. When we left Devon, however, one of the essentials that John had stowed away in the container was the axle of his old caravan and the materials to build a trailer. Together with Fredrikson, who could literally turn his hand to anything, the heap of metal, timber and wire netting was transformed into a quite substantial livestock trailer to pull behind the Suzie. It was estimated that we could carry a maximum of four baconer sized pigs at a time, and before long a regular run was established. When I say 'run' I use the term loosely. It took over an hour to pull up out of the valley and onto the tar. The gradient wasn't particularly steep but it was continuous, so a missed gear could get one seriously stuck without the power to pull away again. Nine miles in second gear is a frustrating way to travel. We also had to secure a livestock movement permit each time, which meant a trip into Nyanga to the Government Vet. One day we quite truthfully forgot to get one and met the inevitable police road block just outside Mutare. Ten minutes later we were sitting in the police station while they considered what they would do with us and four pigs. A 'phone call to the Nyanga Government Vet would have cleared the matter in a few minutes as we had come to know him quite well, but as a matter of principle they let us stew whilst muttering dark comments about what could possibly happen to us. Consequently both we and the pigs became hotter and hotter and it was a great relief when we were finally given our freedom and arrived at the slaughterhouse. We never again forgot to get a permit.

The grading received for our pigs from Colcom was excellent and gave John a great deal of satisfaction, which outweighed the hassles. Again, our neighbours were fascinated by the project and several would dearly loved to have tried it. Water was the limiting factor, however, as pigs need a great deal of it and over the river it all had to be carried up the hill from the river banks or pumped up from the various government dug wells that were scattered around. They became our partners in other ways though, as we put out the word that we would buy maize and pumpkins from them for stock feed. Soon we had a heap of pumpkins and a good store of maize, and then someone left the door of the feed store open and the sheep got in. It doesn't take long for a sheep to literally eat itself to death on whole grain, and ten ewes were affected. We lost two or three, to the advantage of the team as usual, but the others were gradually nursed back to health.

The nastiest problem we had with the sheep was the spear-grass. This is a local grass that has a seed at the end of a shaft of grass which is programmed to detach easily from the seed when it is in place. So the sheep would brush against the grass, the seed would be deposited in the wool with the shaft sticking out, and when the animal rubbed itself or one attempted to pull the shaft out the seed was left behind. The seed is affected by moisture, when wet it rotates one way and when dry it rotates the other way, thus boring its way through wool, hide, skin and fat layers into the deepest tissues of the body. All animals and humans could pick up the sharp little seeds, and as they also had a hook on the end they couldn't be pulled out. The only way to get them out of one's clothing was to pull them right through. Once embedded in the skin they were almost impossible to remove, so when John rushed into the caravan one morning to say that Anzac had spear grass in his eye and please come help, I heard the news with mixed feelings of dismay and inadequacy. I had no idea what I could do.

Anzac stood with his head down, both eyes shut and one eye shut tightly and twitching as the tears rolled from under his lashes. I dampened a piece of cotton wool and carefully prized open the affected eye as John and Nathanial held him. In the split second it was open I saw the seed and dabbed at it with the cotton wool. I cannot describe my feelings when I looked down and saw the seed sticking to it!

Nathanial hadn't been a good choice as a team member. His father, Shadrak, was a wonderful man with the mombies and I remember seeing him one day at Fred's farm when we had driven out into the bush to bring in a newly calved cow. The distance was too great for the calf to walk, so Shadrak picked it up and put it in the back of the truck, and the mother charged him. He stood his ground and threw dust in her face, which checked the charge long enough for him to reach the safety of the pick-up. He was devoted to the cattle and we had great respect for him.

One day he had come to greet us with tears of joy. His son had been abducted from school during the war by the 'freedom fighters ' to be trained as a child soldier. That had been more than ten years ago and they had given him up for dead. Now as a grown man of nineteen he had just walked onto the farm. Shadrak was overjoyed, and when Nathaniel had asked to come with us we had agreed for Shadrak's sake.

He was always quiet, withdrawn and a little surly, but when one considered the kind of life he must have led from the age of eight or nine it was easy to forgive. Nathaniel had gone back to Chegutu for a few days holiday and returned with Shadrak's littlest child, a lovely, friendly little boy that we had known well and christened Mini-Mof - Shadrak's family name being Mof (cloud). He was aged around five or six and he fitted in well with Harrison's young children.

Fredrikson's wife had left not long after we were settled in the valley. She was going, she had told us, to stay with her father for a while in Kadoma. She had insisted on taking the children with her, however, and Nicholas - Johnny's cattleman - whose wife had become very friendly with her, shook his head sadly. If the children were going with her, he told us, she would not be coming back. He was to be proven right. I remembered seeing her in her garden just before she left, she had worked hard and her tomatoes and maize were growing well. Then someone trashed it. We never knew who it was, but we were to learn that it could happen quite often. Jealousy, spite, just the very fact that someone was doing a little better than the neighbours. She was a hard working, honest, and upright woman and I can quite understand that she would have found it impossible to live amongst people who could do such a thing.

So little by little rifts were beginning to appear amongst the team. The first came between Nathaniel and Kenneth. Kenneth's wife had a child by a previous marriage, and one day Mini-Mof told him that Nathaniel had a knife in his bed. It was a very lovely sheath knife and exactly fitted the description of one that had been stolen from John. Kenneth had accused him of stealing it and together they had come to us. It was stale-mate. Kenneth accused Nathaniel; Nathaniel said that the one who knew it was in his bed (Kenneth) was the one who had put it there. Peter Grant and Nicholas came as elders and together with John a 'court' was held under the M'sasa trees beyond the caravan. The knife came back to us and the matter was put to the back of our minds.

Next arose an argument between Kenneth and Wilson's wife, Lucinda. In the chicken houses one day I heard such a shrill screaming and shouting going on that I rushed to see what was happening. Kenneth was standing over Wilson's wife with a face like thunder and she was screaming at him in such an insolent way that I was sure he was about to kill her. Pushing between them I told her to be quiet and go and sit down and she backed away still hurling insults. Kenneth stood there, eyes burning and fists clenched, and I suggested that he had no right to disturb my peace this way and that he must settle his quarrels at his own house. To my relief, after staring at me for a few minutes he nodded briefly and turned away. Having seen them both back to their work I went into the caravan and made a large pot of tea and took it out to them.

"In England," I told them," When you have a problem you sit down and talk about it with a nice cup of tea."

The rest of the team began to laugh and at last a smile spread over Kenneth's face as he helped himself to more sugar. Later he came to see John, and as he began to explain the problem I was amazed to see this big, strong young man begin to cry. The tears poured down his face and he sobbed his way through a long discourse in Shona. At last he went away, consoled, and my husband told me the story.

It seemed that when Lucinda had gone back to Chegutu for a few days to see her parents, she had given a glowing report on what was happening with us all in Nyanga. She went on to explain, quite untruthfully, that her husband Wilson was now foreman of this great enterprise but that Kenneth had not been so successful. In fact, she went on to elaborate, Kenneth was so unsuccessful that he only had one shirt to wear. It was this great shame that had been brought upon his reputation that had reduced him to tears. The mystery solved, Kenneth was dispatched to Chegutu for a short holiday with several shirts and Lucinda was severely reprimanded.

The next drama involved Mini-Mof. He began to go missing. Members of the team spent many hours over a period of some weeks searching the bush for him and bringing him back. No-one knew what the problem was, but the whole thing came to a head when he was missing all night. It was mid-winter and the temperature could fall below freezing at night, and in the wild country surrounding us there was very real danger from leopard and hyena. The whole team, led by John, left work to search for him. Just after breakfast my husband arrived with a frozen Mini-Mof sitting in the front of the Suzi. He had been hiding under the river bridge, just about the coldest place he could have chosen. We took him into the caravan and I made him a plate of porridge and a big mug of hot, milky cocoa which disappeared in no time. Later, Fredrikson and Lucinda were talking to him and Fredrikson beckoned us over. He took off Mini-Mof's thin T-shirt, and there on his back were the unmistakable signs of belt marks. We never knew why, but it had obviously been happening over a long period, and the poor child had decided that he would rather face the animals in the bush than his elder brother. Nathaniel was sent for and told that we were taking his young brother back to his father, Shadrak, and that he would stay with us until the trip had been arranged. He had no warm clothes, so I drove up to the African store on the tar road where I found a hand knitted sweater and a few other essentials. From there we put him on a bus with Lucinda to look after him and back he went to his parents. The Africans are incredibly resilient people, and for a while it seemed that we were back to a normal, happy little community and Nathaniel was accepted back into the team as if the whole thing hadn't happened.

Wilson's young son was by a previous marriage also, and Lucinda seemed to be unable to have children which is a source of great shame to an African woman. Wilson came to me and discussed his problem in great depth, but apart from making an appointment for her with a doctor to see if there was any physical problem for her inability to conceive, there was little I could do. They seemed to remain a cheerful and close-knit family, but one day Wilson brought his son to me. He was a quiet boy of about six or seven, and as he stood before me it was obvious that his face was very swollen, his eye almost closed. I thought, at first, that it must be an allergic reaction to something, but Wilson hesitantly told me the truth. The previous evening Lucinda had beaten him until he was almost unconscious. The reason was so paltry that Wilson couldn't remember what he was supposed to have done, but obviously the burden of caring for a step son while she was unable to have her own children had finally made her snap. The child had slept all night, and Wilson told me that Lucinda had been up early to examine him as she was worried that he may have died during the night.

"So how could you stand by and let her do this to your son?" I asked Wilson in disbelief.

"Ah, Madam. Her grandmother, she is a witch doctor. I know that if she wants she can put poison in my food any time."

"But, Wilson," I reasoned," This is your own son. He is a small child; he looks to you his father for protection."

Wilson shook his head, "She has rages, she can kill us both. Each time I eat I wonder if I will die."

"Then she must go," decided John, when I told him. "He's got to make the decision, either he stays here with his son and does his job or they all go, we cannot have this problem."

When he saw the child it was my husband who made the decision. Lucinda was told to leave; Wilson walked the nine miles to the bus-stop with her and came back. We never saw her again.

Once more we settled down to a routine and it was a happy team again, but I had been given a glimpse of the savage emotions that could lie just below the surface laughter and friendship. I had also seen the real fear in Wilson's face of witchcraft and the hold this fear had. Nyanga means 'horns' and N'anga, the same word, means witch-doctor. Later I was to find that the area was known to be a witchcraft stronghold.

The African store where we had got clothes for Mini-Mof was very successful. It was actually a string of enterprises owned by the same African family, comprising a petrol station, grocery store, fast food kiosk, butchery, restaurant and beer hall. The long distance buses always pulled in there and it was teeming with people day and night, and behind the complex lived a number of young women who added to the attractions. It was unusual to see such success, but I learned that a close relative of the proprietor was serving time in prison for his part of the success story. He had killed a man and taken certain parts of his body to a witch-doctor to make extra strong medicine to ensure prosperity. It had worked, I was assured, but it would only work for this generation. When the next generation came to take over then more magic would be required.

For Christmas Johnny and Mel had given us a little Jersey cow. She was very small compared to Susan, but gave a wonderful supply of rich milk. Nathanial milked her and was responsible for her well-being, together with the horses. One morning we noticed that she had a large, hard lump on her jaw and a few days later Harrison came to us with the explanation. He had seen Nathanial throwing stones at her, and he had also seen him throwing stones at the young colt, Zebedee, until he panicked and pushed through an electric fence. Harrison was enraged. Never had we met an African with such a real, deep sympathy for any animal and against all the laws of the African culture, which keeps a code of silence about the misconduct of fellow Africans, he had come to us. John was also enraged. Again Nathaniel was called and this time given an ultimatum. We were digging a ditch for a water pipe to save us carrying water for the chickens from the river. Nathaniel could, if he wished, stay and dig the trench or he could go. Either way, he would never be employed with us as a stockman again. He stood there, sullenly, for a few minutes before speaking.

"I will go," he said slowly, " But one day I will find you. Wherever you go, I will find you."

And with that threat hanging in the air he turned and left.

CHAPTER SIXTEEN

It was the spear grass that put an end to the sheep operation. It was indigenous to the area and it wasn't fair on the sheep. We sold them to an aid agency working along the border of Mozambique, just beyond Nyanga, who wanted to use the wool for local crafts. That left the way clear for the pigs, Robert became pig-man and Harrison took Nathaniel's place with the horses and milk-cows. On Sundays I did the milking, tying Susan's horns to a branch and tying her back legs together as well, to keep them out of the bucket.

Without the sheep I became a little lost. The chicken business had expanded to the stage where we could have easily sold five hundred a week and some of the team had taken over the day to day running of it. John was busy with his pigs and various other things, like fencing and building. So I began to wonder just what I could do that would be useful and a seed of an idea came into my mind. Having now shown we could do all these projects successfully with no more resources than the average peasant farmer, perhaps we could teach the skills that we had learned to those who were wanting to learn. We had many visitors, sometimes groups of school children, and sometimes teachers, as well as the locals. I suggested the idea to John, who agreed that we did probably have something to offer. Just how to do it, however, wasn't very clear.

As we moved into our third year in the Valley things began to change. Again, looking back we can see that at almost every step of the way this is how the Lord has guided us. The end of an era has come, a move is near.

We had such high hopes on our Devon smallholding, but it all went very wrong and we found ourselves in Zimbabwe. At Chegutu all had been well, until we began to yearn for more independence, and suddenly there was the offer from Johnny. This time it was different. Walking round the pig pens one afternoon John suddenly said,

"There's something not quite right about my left side."

"How do you mean?"

"Well, it doesn't respond."

And it was Liz who put her finger on the trouble. Being a nurse she had been quietly noticing signs that neither John nor I knew existed.

"I think you should go for tests," she told John, "See a neurologist, I think it may be Parkinsons."

I don't think John knew anything more about the condition than me, for he decided that it was probably some muscular problem and made an appointment with a chiropractor, who refused to treat him and very quickly made an appointment with the neurologist. Parkinsons was confirmed.

We didn't go rushing around finding out all we could. I have always had the opinion that things will only get as bad as God allows them to be and that we have to pray, trust, and really believe that He is in control. John also took it very calmly and life continued much as before.

It was then that we had a visit from the bank manager. To enable expansion we had been advised by Mel's brother, who was officially financial advisor to our little joint project, to get an overdraft facility, and this had been done. The bank manager came to inspect his investment, loved everything he saw, went away smiling and wrote us a letter calling in his money. We just could not believe it. A furious little deputation went to the bank to demand an explanation, only to be told that it was no longer the bank's policy to support small farmers. Since a good 90 per cent of Zimbabwe is made up of small farmers this seemed even more unbelievable. We had no money, just a very successful and rapidly expanding little holding. Ah, the locals told us wisely, when you sell - watch out, that manager he will have friends just waiting to buy. Well, he would be unlucky because it wasn't ours to sell. The only thing we could sell was the livestock. Then what would we do?

Johnny and Mel were very supportive. As Johnny said, he could sell a few mombies and clear the overdraft, that wasn't a problem. The main problem was that we didn't know how quickly John's health would deteriorate, and without working capital it would be almost impossible to continue to feed the stock we had and to pay the wages of the team.

John's son, Richard, had recently gone to work for a large commercial farm north of Harare, and when he came to stay for a few days, pitching his tent beneath the trees beside the spring, we put the problem to him. We knew that the manager of the farm he had joined was heading up an outreach project to the rural African, teaching the advantages of 'zero tillage'. This was a method of 'no plough' cultivation more suited to the African soils than conventional western methods. We also knew that his outreach was purely arable and that no African was without his livestock, perhaps this would be where the seed of our idea came in. Perhaps we could teach what we had learned alongside the arable.

Not many weeks later we had a message from Richard. Brian, the farm manager, Stuart the owner of the farm, and Alan the outreach co-ordinator would be coming to see us to discuss our projects. And so it was that around mid-morning, some days later, a gleaming 4x4 Land Cruiser containing three very well dressed, high powered business men holding clip-boards descended upon our little caravan, bringing with them an air of wealth and enthusiasm that was a little overwhelming. We were soon put at ease, however, for the friendship was sincere and their interest real as we went around the chicken houses and pig pens. We had a lunch of quiche and salads under the trees, and they went away still enthusiastic and promising to get in touch.

We had actually met Brian some years previously, and had been impressed by his story. He had been a very successful and award winning tobacco farmer, then he and his wife Cathy had become Christians. One day, whilst telling his children that they shouldn't smoke, one of them had asked why, then, was he growing tobacco? The point went home, and they decided that they would no longer grow the crop. His farm, however, was suited most to tobacco and his attempts at maize and other crops were so unsuccessful that his bank manager would only continue his overdraft facility if he reverted to tobacco. This he refused to do and he lost his farm. He went to manage for Stuart's mother, worked incredibly hard and prayed hard and began to make a success of what had been an almost bankrupt farm. He had then discovered the method of zero tillage, and gradually introduced it until the whole of the farm was cropping twice a year on a no-plough basis and producing consistently high yields. In fact over the fourteen years he had managed the farm the profits had increased each year.

Across the river which formed the boundary of Stuart's farm were vast communal lands with the same soil and, of course, the same weather conditions but producing very, very poor yields. Brian felt that the Lord had shown him this method of farming because it was successful for Africa, and he made it his goal to take the method to the poor African farmer in order to increase his yields and make him more prosperous.

At last the answer came.

"Come," said Brian, "Come and join the team."

BINDURA

1995 - 1998

'...Repent, and let every one of you be baptized in the name of Jesus Christ for the remission of sins; and you shall receive the gift of the Holy Spirit. For the promise is to you and to your children, and to all who are afar off, as many as the Lord our God will call.'
(Acts 2 v 38-39

CHAPTER SEVENTEEN

This time our move should have been easier. We no longer had the sheep and only had the horses and the Jersey cow to transport besides our six families, now somewhat re-arranged, and the dogs and Siwi. Mel's young nephew had been looking for a project and had stepped into our place down in the Valley. He had taken over the chickens and the pigs, and it was good to know that the work we had put in would not be wasted.

The farm at Bindura had offered to send a lorry to pick everything up, so we just collected together a few personal things into our livestock trailer and took them with us each time we visited Richard. Brian had ideas of starting up a game-park, and he felt that it would be a good thing for us to do until our side of the Outreach project was up and running. The idea of organising a game-park was really exciting.

We set off early one morning at the beginning of December for a week-end's stay with Richard, taking with us the trailer and a few bits and pieces, and also Fredrikson and Lovemore, a builder who had joined us when Nathaniel left and was now part of the team. It was during the rainy season, we had a heavy shower of rain that morning and a thick mist was hanging over the highlands. We know now that spiritual warfare is not all spiritual, it often touches our lives physically in very dramatic ways, but at the time we were blissfully unaware that Satan and his forces are very active in blocking the way of Christians as they move closer to the Lord.

We were going to join a Christian farm and a Christian Outreach team, and over the next few years we were going to come much closer to the Lord and, hopefully, we would be helping others to do the same. No-one thought to pray for a safe journey.

As we approached Rusape the fog became thicker, and we were crawling along in second gear with John driving. Suddenly, just a few yards ahead we saw a solid wall of animals crossing the road. An old African was driving his herd of oxen, sheep and goats straight across the main road, in almost nil visibility on the brow of a hill. There was nowhere to go. John braked immediately but we had a heavily loaded trailer behind and we had practically no braking distance anyway. John steered for the sheep, hoping that being more nimble they would jump out of the way, but the oxen kept going and collision was inevitable.

The thing that I remember most is the silence. It was like a silent film. No-one shouted, the thick mist enveloped us, and I remember one loud bang and a large black oxen coming up over the bonnet towards me. It slid over the bonnet and fell at the side of the road, and then the silence was broken by a woman shouting in a high voice, "Sekuru, Sekuru....." (Grandfather, grandfather), as she ran towards the road from a group of huts. The old man was fine, but three oxen had gone down. Two got up again. Then we heard another car coming behind us, much too fast for the conditions, and we hurriedly pushed the Suzi and trailer off the road and down a bank out of the way, before it could plough into the back of us. The car stopped and so did the next one. The driver of the first stayed with Fredrikson and Lovemore, whilst the second took us into Rusape and to alert the police. We were very pleasantly surprised with the help and care we received from the police at Rusape. They were genuinely concerned about our well-being, and helped us find a breakdown lorry to tow the Suzi to a safe place in town. By the time we got back to the scene of the crash the local butchery was loading the casualty ox onto a trailer and the old man was being paid his money. Would be our troubles could have been sorted out so quickly! Our good Samaritan then took us to our Insurance agent to get that sorted. Doubtless our insurance would have to pay for everything, as the old African would have had neither money nor insurance. Our new friend then took us back to his home for a cup of tea and a sandwich and we telephoned Richard with the news.

The whole sorry incident accelerated our move, for without a vehicle it was now impossible for us to travel at will between the Valley and Bindura. We had also had no time to arrange living accommodation for either us or our team on the new farm. The Suzi had been badly damaged, but wasn't a write off. She had been transferred to a body repair yard in Harare and we would have to wait for replacement parts to be sent up from South Africa as they weren't available in Zimbabwe. Meanwhile, Richard loaned us his farm truck to go back to the Valley and make final arrangements for the transport of the livestock and the rest of our things. Enoch, one of Stuart's drivers, came down with a huge 30 ton lorry and stayed overnight with the team so that we could load and move early in the morning. Our last night in the caravan in the Valley was a very sad one. We had truly loved it there and would never have left if things had gone according to plan. Which was probably why! Often the Lord allows drastic things to happen in our lives as a means of moving us out of our comfort zones and on to the next stage. We tend to be a comfort loving race, us humans. Often I look around and see people who are comfortable, well-off, and doing all the things that they had planned to do. They seem so settled and happy, and I think ' Why can't we be like that?' And I suppose the answer is, in many cases, that those who have no inclination to serve anyone but themselves are allowed to gather together riches on this earth. We are told that our reward will be in Heaven and God's not going to damage His reputation by lying to me.

   The long haul out of the Valley was a test of Enoch's patience and driving skills, the temptation to change up a gear when the road momentarily levelled out in a few places was resisted and we all got to the top safely. We stopped a couple of times for a rest and a cold drink, and arrived at Bindura in bright moonlight. The horses found themselves transported from the dry brown lands of the Eastern Highlands to the deep, lush grass of the pecan orchards, and their heads were down before we could get their head collars off. The next stage of our training was about to begin.

CHAPTER EIGHTEEN

My only experience of a large Zimbabwean commercial farm had been on Fred's tobacco farm, which was smaller and much less intensive. Here on Stuart's farm the land was always productive, the crops always immaculate and the yields consistently amongst the highest in the country.

Through Brian we were to learn a few frightening facts about conventional western farming methods in Africa. Rainfall, when it comes, is over just a few weeks and is therefore heavy. When it comes into contact with soils which have been ploughed and tilled under western methods the soil loss is devastating. It has been estimated that from the communal lands alone enough soil is being washed away each year to fill a goods train that will stretch twice around the circumference of the world. Soil is being formed at the rate of 1 mm every 100 years! Maize is the staple diet in Zimbabwe, and yields of dry land maize (no irrigation) on Stuart's farm averaged 6.5t/ha. Just across the river, under the same conditions, traditional farming gave often less than 2t/ha. It was because of this direct comparison that Brian had formed his 'Outreach' programme, sending staff out to teach the method of zero tillage. Under his guidance some people had trebled their yields.

But then, Brian told us, they hit the 'African Phenomenon'. When supervision was withdrawn the projects collapsed and many of those who had experienced high yields had next to nothing to harvest once more. He realised then that the problem was a spiritual one. It seemed to be that if an African succeeded and did better than his neighbours, the tendency is to pull him down to the level of the rest. This is usually done through the fear of spirits and witchcraft. Good crops produced under the guidance of the Outreach were abandoned because the farmer had been frightened from entering his fields. To us it may just be a few seeds in a twist of paper in the gateway, but to him it is a very powerful warning and he is literally likely to be killed or injured if he ignores it. The African, generally, seeks guidance from the ancestral spirits, through spirit mediums. In every walk of life they are subject to the guidance and control of these spirits, and they are very real.

The Bible tells us that we must not try and communicate with the dead, and this is for the simple reason that we cannot, but if we believe that we can then we open our minds to the occult and satanic influence. Poverty in Africa is, in most cases, due to this bondage, for the people themselves are intelligent, eager to learn and potentially good farmers.

The 'cultural religion' teaches people to pray through their ancestors. We all believe in God, there is no difference there. The difference is in the mediator. As Christians we know that the Bible tells us absolutely clearly that Jesus is the Person through whom we pray to God. He is the only way. The African believes that Jesus is for the white man, they pray through their ancestors. If he prays to his dead grandfather, say, then his dead grandfather's spirit will pass the prayer to his father's spirit, who will pass it to his father's spirit, and so on and so on up the chain until it reaches God. Then, they believe, God's answer then comes back down the chain and is delivered through a spirit-medium or sometimes a 'prophet'. We know, through the Bible, that the subsequent answer comes from a 'familiar spirit', a demon. The prayer has been effectively side-tracked.

The Outreach team had realised that it was pointless to just teach a skill. Man consists of mind, body and spirit. They could train the mind to nourish the body, but the spirit had to be free from satanic influence. A man had to know that, in Christ, evil spirits could not harm him. To succeed, the farming methods had to be taught alongside the Gospel.

I found it all absolutely fascinating. Our time in the Valley had brought us in very close contact with the rural poor, and I knew their problems. To understand why they had the problems suddenly brought it all into focus, and we just couldn't wait to be a part of it all. Soon after we arrived on Stuart's farm there was an outbreak of army worm. This is like a small black caterpillar that suddenly appears by the million and eats everything in its path. The only way to stop it is to spray. As soon as they heard of the outbreak, the Outreach team went out to the communal lands with sprays and equipment, but the spirit-mediums had warned the people not to spray. Those who listened to them had nothing left to harvest, those who sprayed had food. It was a vivid illustration of the power that the spirit-mediums wielded.

For a while John and I were a bit lost again. It was a very busy farm, and having come to run a hypothetical game farm we soon found that it was unlikely to become any more than that. It was a long standing dream for Brian but unfortunately Stuart didn't share his enthusiasm. Since the farm employed nearly 1200 workers, our little team of six were soon absorbed into the workforce, and the wives got part time jobs too in the fields. This relieved us of the wages problem, and then John found himself in charge of building works on the farm, as there was an extensive programme of staff housing in progress, carried out by a team of contractors who needed supervision and co-ordination. It wasn't at all the sort of thing he enjoyed doing, but he borrowed a bicycle and spent his time cycling from one project to another which kept him fit and out in the fresh air.

Brian then decided that Stuart needed a personal assistant in the office and that I would be just the person. I had spent my life bolstering up our farming enterprises by taking part-time secretarial positions, so I was well able to do the job. Stuart, however, wasn't the slightest bit sure that he needed an assistant and I found myself under-employed rather than unemployed.

The dogs took to their new surroundings with terrier type enthusiasm, and we had been there only a short while when Porgie distinguished himself by killing a rabid jackal all on his own. Whenever a dog has such a close encounter with rabies it has to go and have a vaccination and a tattoo in the ear at the Government Vet's office. By the end of our first year at Bindura Porgie had no more space for tattoos and had killed another two jackals. Although it was reassuring to have him with me when I was walking alone, for I knew he would attack absolutely anything that was likely to harm me, I was sad that he had got the taste for killing. I really didn't want him to hurt any of the buck and other harmless game that lived in the wooded outskirts of the farm.

It was whilst walking the dogs early one morning, over the lovely tree covered kopje that bordered the coffee plantation, that the Lord gave me the picture. Just how our livestock teaching programme would be incorporated in the main Outreach work had yet to be decided, but as I was about to duck through a wire fence this picture came suddenly into my mind's eye. I saw a small church and surrounding it were huts, each one housing a family. I'm really not sure now if I saw more than this or if my own imagination then took over, but by the time I got back to Richard's house I had a clear idea in my mind and I searched hastily for pencil and paper to write it down.

The idea was for a Christian village. The centre would be the Church, both physically and spiritually, and in the huts surrounding the Church would live the families responsible for the various livestock enterprises. At the next Outreach meeting John and I presented the plan and it was enthusiastically accepted and enlarged upon. Our project would be a Christian Farm Village, situated directly across the river from the communal lands. Central to the village of eight families would be the church, not a building but a peaceful garden where an African pastor would live, and he would be available to provide counsel in an environment free from satanic oppression. This way people would not feel they were forsaking their own church or cult, of which there are many, in seeking advice there. In the huts surrounding the garden church the family units would emphasise the importance of the family business, demonstrating that it was unnecessary for the husband to work in town while the wife remained on the farm. Split families rapidly fuel the AIDS epidemic. Across the river on the communal lands were over 60,000 people. If we could site the project in an easily accessible place we could expect many of them to visit just as our neighbours in the Valley had. They could come and buy produce or just come to see the projects. Teaching would be there for those who wanted to learn, but the farming would be taught side by side with the Gospel. When they took their expertise home then the Outreach would follow up and their own local churches would be encouraged to support them. The beauty of the idea was that it was a capsule which, like churches, could be planted anywhere. It was very exciting.

CHAPTER NINETEEN

We still had time for our horses. Rainbow was in foal once more and Anzac had been in the wars, literally. Just before we left the valley we had been going out for a ride one Sunday and Harrison was helping us get the horses ready. Usually we tied them to a piece of binder twine which was in turn tied to a tree. In this way they were able to snap the string if something frightened them without doing themselves an injury. However, on this particular morning the string was missing, so Harrison decided to tie Anzac straight onto a branch. I don't know what spooked him, we were grooming Tif and Gambler near the caravan, but we suddenly heard a commotion and turned to see Anzac in a half rear, fighting to get his head free from the head collar. The branch remained firm, but the halter rope snapped. It gave way so suddenly and Anzac had been pulling so strongly that we saw him catapulted straight over onto his back, like a tree being felled. He got up, dazed and obviously hurt. He had landed on his withers, but apart from a graze there was nothing to see. We gave him the run of the paddock so that he could move around at will and hoped that he would keep himself moving and be OK. This he did. Over the next few days he grazed and wandered and gradually the stiffness began to wear off and he seemed to recover. Then Tif attacked him. They had all grazed together for over two years, but suddenly Tif flew at him and John bravely stepped in and managed to separate them. It had happened just before our move, and Anzac was still on sick-leave. Zebedee, our first foal from Rainbow and Tif, was now four years old and we were beginning to work him. He had outgrown both his parents, and had developed into a very handsome iron grey colt of about fifteen hands, with a good temperament. Both John and I had been up on him, and I had spent many an hour long-reining him, so now John decided that we must start his education in earnest.

So given a free afternoon, on a Wednesday, we collected Harrison and his young son Knowledge, and had just finished tacking up Zebedee when a message came from Brian asking if John could go and help him. He was trying to sort out a staircase in the new office block and needed a hand. We had intended to ride Zebs out through the coffee plantation, with me on top and John and Harrison as 'anchors', so my husband suggested that we go ahead and he would join us later.

I had a really bad feeling about this. I couldn't quite put my finger on it, but for some reason I was worried so I prayed for safety. I decided we would long-rein him out to the coffee and then I would get on, so I gathered up the reins and moved him on ahead of me. When we reached the gate he stopped. He tended to be a bit sulky and this was nothing unusual. I did something I had done dozens of times before, I gave him a slap across the rump and told him to move on. I think my sixth sense must have heard the grunt before I did and I moved back fractionally. The grunt accompanied the two back legs as they lashed out at me, one hoof catching me squarely in the middle of my face. An inch higher and I would have been history, an inch lower and he could have broken my neck.

Harrison took one look at me holding my face in both hands and streaming blood, threw the lead rope he was holding to Knowledge, and ran like a hare to fetch John. My husband and Brian arrived almost instantaneously, I was piled into Brian's Land Cruiser and we headed for the town of Bindura and a doctor. The blood, we found, was coming from a cut on my lower lip where the force of the blow had knocked my bottom teeth through it. I still had my teeth! My nose was swollen as well as my lips and I looked quite ethnic.

When we arrived at the surgery we found it closed. The doctor played golf on Wednesdays, a neighbour told us, and he suggested that we should go and find Sister Badza, the African sister in charge of the surgery. We followed his directions, along shady tree lined streets to a block of flats and found that Sister Badza was also off on Wednesdays, but another nursing sister was there. This very enthusiastic lady took one look at my injuries and almost hugged me with joy. It would definitely need stitching, she told me, and with both the doctor and Sister Badza away this was her big chance. Her excitement was far from infectious, but she bustled us back to the surgery and telephoned someone at the hospital to get permission to stitch me up. Permission granted without much debate, she sat my anxious husband down in the waiting room and trundled me hastily through to the treatment room. There was much banging of cupboard doors and drawers as she searched for all the equipment she would need and I wondered gloomily whether anaesthetic would be part of her plan. She was looking for a particular sized needle. The needles were already threaded with suture and packed in sterile packs, but each one she found was the wrong size. She was getting more and more frustrated.

"Oh, no," she exclaimed, as she searched, "Oh, no. Oh, no. Oh, my God."

John, following proceedings by sound only, came skidding into the treatment room to see what she had done to me. I reassured him as best I could, and he reluctantly allowed himself to be driven back to the waiting room. At last she found all she needed and I was a little relieved to see her drawing anaesthetic into a syringe, and tried not to think about whether she knew how much to give me and where. Once numbed she proceeded to put six stitches below my lip, three inside and three outside. She did a wonderful job and today you would have to look very, very closely to see the scar.

It was, however, the beginning of a new kind of spiritual attack. Having spent most of my life with horses and rarely been hurt, it suddenly seemed that I only had to go near them to be an accident waiting to happen. Mostly it happened on the ground, once I was on board I felt safe. When I was vaccinating them against horse sickness I got knocked and the needle got me, when I was leading them I would get barged over. The last straw came when Rainbow kicked me into a swamp. Rainbow, our old brood mare who had the gentlest disposition, actually swung around lined up and kicked me from behind when I was leading Gambler down a narrow path. I had the perfect black imprint of a hoof on my backside for weeks, the cause of much mirth and little sympathy from my husband.

It was actually quite serious, because I completely lost my nerve in handling the horses and they had always been something that John and I had shared together. Our best relaxation became a source of anxiety to me.

CHAPTER TWENTY

We found what we felt would be the perfect site for the Christian Farm Village. It was right on the edge of the farm, near the river and overlooking the communal lands. Tracks ran past it on two sides, one was used often by the people across the river as a route to the tar road to Bindura, and the other met with a footpath used by people from the adjoining farm. It was a wooded hill which rose gently and then flattened out into a plateau and then rose again to a high point from which one could see for miles. The lower part was flat enough to contain the livestock units, the plateau perfect for the Garden Church and the pastor's house, and the high point could be utilised to build a water reservoir from which we could gravity feed water to the rest of the site. On the plateau was a big rock formation which I could just see being used by the pastor as a platform from which to address his congregation seated around the garden. John and I felt it was right, so we went to see Stuart and later he came with me to see it. Sitting there on the ground, drawing ideas in the sand he really seemed to catch the vision and agreed to the site.

Carried along on a wave of enthusiasm, we were suddenly brought up short as our wave dumped us into the cold water of realism. If our site was to be free of satanic oppression, then those people living there and demonstrating the livestock enterprises must also be free. In other words we had to find eight born again African families. There were plenty of volunteers, of course. Just as we had plenty of people begging us to take them to Juliasdale from Fred's farm, many working on Stuart's farm saw our project as an opportunity to be involved in something that would probably give them status as well as being heavily subsidised. On a 'Christian' farm of 1200 workers I began to doubt if we would find even one family. Everyone we spoke to professed to be Christian. On the farm there were two African churches and many religious cults. The problem was that it was advantageous to be 'Christian' where the management was Christian, and a few 'Praise the Lord's and ' May God bless you's' liberally sprinkled throughout a conversation never came amiss. When I really thought about it I realised that from the African's point of view there was nothing wrong in this. The Bible and the commandments are only important to a Christian. Their culture had no such commandments, so why should I be surprised because they didn't behave like black Europeans. Almost without exception the people around us gave lip service to being Christian but then went back and practised ancestral worship in their home lives. I heard it described very accurately as 'riding two horses'.

The bondage of their cultural religion was very strong, and they were too frightened to completely break free of it. I learned that it wasn't simply a matter of a person deciding to follow the Lord and renouncing his former ties to satanic influences. Their religion is taught from the age of three, and they live in fear of upsetting the 'ancestral spirits'. If, say, a woman wants to become a Christian she will anger the ancestral spirits by doing so. So if someone in her family, maybe a child, becomes ill or even dies then the blame will be upon her because she angered the ancestral spirits. To be a true Christian she would also have to be willing to accept separation from her family. The African family is very male dominated, as it should be for that is the way God planned it, but he also expected love and respect to be part of it and in many of the poor families I knew the woman had a very hard time. It was probably this basic need for love and understanding that made the women more open to the Gospel, but they were in every way dominated by a husband who followed a cultural religion.

I realised that I had only scratched the surface of the problems involved and we needed someone who knew the culture, knew the people and their problems and was truly born again. We would need an African pastor for our Christian Village, so it looked as if he might be the answer to our problems. If we found him first then he could select the families we needed from his cultural vantage point, he would know the real born again from the pseudo ones. This step agreed, we telephoned John Valentine at Chegutu Bible College.

John felt he had just the right person, and invited us down for the weekend to meet him. We were delighted to go, and I really looked forward to going to Church again in that little wooden hut, joining in with that marvellous singing that I remembered so well.

On the Saturday we met the candidate put forward by John Val and, frankly, were quite disappointed. He seemed a very self-assured young man and gave the impression that we were keeping him from something more important. The third time he looked at his watch we ended the interview, feeling that we were unlikely to get the commitment we needed from him. John Val was undaunted however, and suggested that he did have one other man, a mature student, who might be suitable. We arranged to see him next day, Sunday, after church.

Next morning, for me, was the best bit as we joined the congregation for two hours of praise, worship, prayer and teaching. The service had hardly got going, however, when I suddenly became aware of a dull pain in my left side. I tried to ignore it, joining in the well known choruses that I had been looking forward to singing so much, but it became worse and soon I could sit there no longer and went outside. I walked around the garden and paused in the shade, wondering what it could be. At last the service was over and I had missed it all. My husband joined me and we were then formally introduced to the new candidate, Anderson. We drove back to the Bible School and then went to sit with him in the garden for a chat before lunch. But I couldn't sit. I excused myself and went to lie down. But I couldn't lie down either. I had never known such pain, sitting, standing, lying, walking, it just got relentlessly worse. John was worried and John Val rang his doctor in Kadoma, an hour away, to see if she would examine me, while my husband packed a few things in a bag for me in case I was admitted to hospital. The appointment was made with the doctor for 2.00 p.m. and it was then 11.00 a.m. I had three hours to wait.

It was suggested then that as all the church elders were in the house - they had come to lunch because we were there - the elders would come and pray for me. This they did but, although I was grateful, my mind was fixed on 2.00 p.m. At 2.00 p.m. I would see the doctor and then I would know what was wrong. When I got to the doctor she would know how to take the pain away. I had started to vomit and when the time came to leave I climbed into the car with a large plastic bowl on my lap and closed my eyes. The road was good and we made excellent time. Every now and again I would open my eyes to see how much further it was to Kadoma and the waiting doctor. At last we arrived and I must have been a sorry sight clutching my plastic bowl as I was received by a pretty Indian doctor and shown into a deeply carpeted lounge. I remember the upholstery was a dark red and the cushions snowy white. I sat down on the very edge of the settee, and the pain vanished. It was as if someone had flicked off a switch, it was just gone, not even an ache left.

Jesus had met me where my faith was. The Elders had prayed for me to be healed, I had been sure everything would be fine when I got to the doctor. So it was.

Once back at Bindura, John insisted I have a check up and our doctor sent me for a scan. I well remember Sister Badza's words as she met me with the result.

"There is nothing," she told me, "You are perfect."

Then looking me solemnly in the eye she said, matter of factly,

"You were bewitched."

I was to meet many others stricken ill by witchcraft. We came from different beliefs, but the result was the same. They believed in the anger of the ancestors and had no doubt at all that a spell had been put upon them which could result in death, I had believed that a doctor was a better bet than a prayer. We are told to pray ' believing that we have received'. When I had got to the place that I believed I would receive, I did!

The positive side of this episode was that I learned from the inside out that Jesus heals, and later when I had cause to pray for others I really could pray a believing prayer. Also, I learned that Christians are not immune from physical spiritual attack. In fact the closer you get to doing the Lord's will the stronger the attack can be and the more we need to realise that a prayer is not just a better bet than a doctor but an essential back-up.

The negative side was that I had completely missed the wonderful, uplifting week-end I had looked forward to, and we really hadn't had time to interview Anderson. So we called the Bible College again, and arranged that he should come and stay for a few days, see the place and we could get to know each other at the same time. In many ways it was better to have an older person, as he had experienced a good selection of the problems of life and we also felt that he would have more respect and credibility amongst the younger people. He was a very personable man, with an air of enthusiasm and determination about him that was very attractive. He was, one of the Bible College lecturers told me, the 'crème de la crème' of those graduating that year.

We visited the proposed site where we discussed the project, and unprompted he immediately led us in prayer for both success and for the provision of the many practical things we were going to need before we could physically build. He seemed quite happy with the thought of living in a mud hut again with his small flock, having spent the last three years in student accommodation. We suggested that he should consult his wife first and he went away promising to give a decision soon. A few days later we received his letter.

"We will come. Let us go and do the Lord's work together."

CHAPTER TWENTY ONE

It was becoming more and more obvious to me that I really would have to pass my Zimbabwean driving test. For one thing John's reaction time was getting longer, due to the Parkinsons, and for another I was technically driving illegally. I had held a clean British driving licence for thirty years, but it wasn't recognised in Zimbabwe and police road blocks always made me a bit anxious. It wasn't through choice that I didn't have the proper licence, I just seemed unable to pass the learner's test!

I had taken it twice at Rusape, both with the same examiner. He had been a very officious and unpleasant man towards all of us hopeful entrants. Thirty or so eager would-be drivers in a hot little room, squashed side by side on wooden benches balancing our multiple choice test papers on our knees. Me, the only white person there, and probably twice the age of the others, concentrating hard on the questions, fired at us in English with such a thick, African accent that I had no advantage over those for whom it was a second language. We were allowed three wrong and then we were out. Then another six months to wait for an appointment, another six months of frustration because I knew I could drive as well as others on the road (many of whom had bought their licences) and probably as well as the examiner.

Now, in Bindura, I was in a different area and could take the test again under a different examiner. In fact I could take it at the police station. Waiting for my third test I sat on the wall of the police-station car park with a group of others, all with their Highway Codes open, swotting up on the answers to possible questions. I felt the exam stretching in front of me like a black, gaping chasm. One of the first questions one of my friends had been asked was 'What is Zimbabwe?' The right answer had been 'cattle country', because this is a statement made in the introduction to the Highway Code! Only two more like that, I mused, and I would be out again. And then it struck me, sitting there amidst fallen flame tree blossoms, drying up puddles and old sweet papers, how wonderful it was that there is no entrance exam for Heaven. No swotting up, no trick questions, no officious, condescending scrutiniser. All you had to do was say from your heart 'Yes, Lord.'

Yes, I believe You came to save little, old me. Yes, I believe You are alive now. Yes, I'm sorry for the things I did that I knew were wrong. Yes please, Lord, I want eternal life. And if you are truthful and your heart sincere, you are in!

That day I passed the exam. Once I had the precious piece of paper with my photograph stuck to it and the official stamp, I applied for the driven test and passed first time. I was a little concerned about parallel parking, but in Bindura there were only two spaces where you could do this and happily both were occupied as I drove past. The examiner was obviously impressed with the Suzuki which we had back at last, and was more interested in her performance than mine.

The next great event was John's baptism. It was three years since I had been baptized, and the Christian Fellowship we had now joined with Brian and the rest of the Outreach team held their baptismal service at sunrise on Easter Sunday, and John was going to join them. We went to a farm just outside Bindura owned by Ken and Margaret, long standing members of the Fellowship. The farmhouse stood on a hill with wonderful views out across the bush land and the swimming pool was between the house and the view. We started the Service before dawn by torchlight, singing to guitars and the Baptism was performed as the sun rose over the hills. Four people were baptized, including Brian's youngest son who was 18 and badly epileptic. Everyone cried! It was just such a wonderful atmosphere, about 70 people with tears of joy in their eyes. Then afterwards we all had hot mealie meal porridge, hot cross buns and coffee, and then went on to our usual Church service in Bindura. Brian and Cath asked us back for the rest of the day, which we spent out on their huge lawn under enormous shady trees tucking into a prolonged Sunday lunch of roast lamb.

With everything going so well it was, I suppose, time for something nasty to strike again, and this time I got malaria.

I had just come back from a shopping trip to Harare and suddenly felt so strange that I just had to go and lie down. This was followed by a week of violent headaches and freezing cold shivers followed by high fevers which left the sheets soaking and me shaking with cold again. It was impossible to keep food down (or up, if you see what I mean) and after ten days it was decided that I must have a drug resistant strain and the doctor prescribed good old quinine. Within a few days I was better and longing, more than anything, for a hot, meaty soup. Phineous, Richard's cook, made me a wonderful soup that I shall never forget and I was on my way back to health. The only problem was that I was deaf! A side effect of the quinine distorted my hearing, so that the dogs barking sounded like Donald Duck in a rage and I completely lost the softer sounds, like birdsong. I was assured it was temporary and it was with great relief that I woke one morning a week later to the sounds of birds singing.

Stuart had given us permission to build ourselves a house, and we began to look in earnest for a house site. No problems with planning permission or building byelaws, we could just pick our spot and build if Stuart agreed on our choice. The choice, however, was endless. Brian was as enthusiastic as we were and took us around the farm showing us place after place that would be suitable, each one lovelier than the one before. The options were at last narrowed down by Stuart who felt that he would like a 'presence' on the far side of the farm in the woodland overlooking the area that Brian had regarded as the potential game park. At last we found a fairly flat area on the wooded hillside overlooking a long narrow valley. Here the natural contours would allow a driveway to be built and the tree spacing was such that we could build both driveway and house by felling just three trees.

I am sure that the Lord drew the plan for me! With no architectural knowledge whatsoever I sketched out an oval bungalow with a long lounge/diner which would be able to hold a large group of people for our bible studies, two bedrooms, shower and bathroom and a kitchen. Along the end wall of the lounge an open staircase led to a mezzanine floor which acted as office, spare bedroom and storeroom. It was built on stone foundations and the walls were of the traditional farm burnt bricks. Grass was gathered for the thatch from the surrounding area, and the roof was supported on a complicated series of gum pole trusses, put together by a specialist builder from the communal lands across the river. John supervised a team of about ten builders and it all came together beautifully. The floors were stone and with the high, unceilinged thatch it was cool and airy. Only the smaller brushwood was cleared from the surrounding area, and outside John built a high, round water tower with a storeroom beneath. The idea was that a reservoir would be built later on the top of the ridge to service the house, but in the meantime water was brought by bowser and tractor from the farm a couple of times a week and pumped up into the storage tank. It was then gravity fed to the house, and a line was diverted via a 'Rhodesian boiler' to provide us with piping hot water. The boiler was a common device used on most farms, and consisted of two empty oil drums in a brick cradle over a wood fire. To conserve heat and save on wood consumption John enclosed the drums in brickwork, using mud as mortar for one section to enable the drums to be changed easily when necessary. He also enclosed the fire with a heavy furnace door salvaged from the old disused tobacco barns on the farm. On the back of the furnace he built me an oven which was heated by the same fire as the boiler. It wasn't easy to fine tune, and the temperatures were judged by hand warm, hand hot and hand singed, but it cooked all meat and casseroles beautifully, and pastries and biscuits were also a success.

We moved in just before Christmas, two years after arriving at Bindura. Our first night was quite disturbed, the dogs had a pen a little distance from the house and barked at every new noise. Then we were awakened by the unmistakable sound of someone or something trying to get into the house. John went to investigate and half way across the lounge he got buzzed by a barn owl that obviously regarded us as the intruders. This happened quite regularly, and since all the windows were closed we were puzzled for quite some time. The Africans are very superstitious about owls, and obviously thought our visitations were of the supernatural variety, but then we found that it was determinedly getting in through a small hole left in the wall for a pipe.

With the house I also found myself with a cook. When the builders had been on site they had detailed one of their gang to cook the sadza and vegetables that they ate mid-day. One day John had jokingly suggested that when the house was finished he might like to cook for us. He was so overjoyed and excited by the suggestion that we didn't have the heart to explain that we hadn't been serious, so I found myself with a cook whose experience up to then had been mainly relevant to mixing concrete.

When you see, first hand, how adaptable and eager and quick to learn the African is, surely it must be a mystery why they are poor and not leading the world. The reason is, I believe, solely spiritual.

Within a few days Takesure had mastered simple meals, and went on to produce the lightest pastry and biscuits one could wish for. He also kept the house spotless and did the washing, wielding a charcoal iron with great expertise, and he still found time to sit on the steps in the sun and chat to Fredrikson who was busy building us chicken houses again.

I was worried about Fredrikson. Before leaving Juliasdale he had been ill and gone to hospital in Nyanga. When I went to see him he had already left, and Robert told me that he was staying with a woman nearby. We went to find him and I had been appalled to see the skin blisters and swellings that I now associated with AIDS. He had recovered well and his new 'wife' had moved with us to Bindura. She was a very thin, cross looking woman with a haranguing tongue. She also had two daughters, the second of which was fathered by a witch-doctor. I was quite sure that she was the source of Fredrikson's failing health, and knew in my heart it was AIDS. Here on the farm, with such a concentration of people, funerals were becoming almost a weekly event, and caused many ripples. Cathy had arranged 'peer educators' on all the surrounding farms as well as this one, who had been on specialised courses to teach and advise about the disease, but still the majority of people didn't take it seriously. One of the problems was that there is a stigma attached to the disease, and since people always died from AIDS-related problems, no-one wanted to admit the real reason. The funerals also caused financial hardship. The Shona are a very social people and it is an important cultural custom that all the women in the village or on the farm attend each funeral. The bereaved partner is taken offerings of food or money to help. This meant that whenever there was a funeral no women worked on the farm and there was a day's earnings lost to them and a day's work lost to the farm. In the communal lands the spirit-mediums also declared one day of the week 'chisi', which meant that on that particular day each week no-one would work on the land for fear of offending the ancestral spirits. They believed that if they did work on that day then the spirits would not send rain when they asked them and they could expect some kind of retribution such as lightning strike or a windstorm to destroy their property. So, given two funerals in any given week, plus the forbidden day, that left a two-day working week which was disastrous all round.

Work had started some time ago at the Christian Village site, and we had named it Famba mu Chiedza, which is Shona for 'Walk in the Light'. Anderson and his wife had arrived and were housed on the farm in a very pleasant bungalow until the time came for them to move to the site itself. He helped with the brick making part of the time and soon had a youth group started in the farm compound and spent much of his time chatting with the workforce and helping out where needed. Soon after his arrival we were called to the compound to see a 15 year old girl who thought she had been bewitched. Her legs had swollen dreadfully and she couldn't bear them to be touched. People from a local religious cult had tied strings around her to make her better and had made her sit in the blazing sun on the parched earth surrounding her hut. They had told her that if she went to hospital she would have both legs amputated and her brother, convinced she had been bewitched, came to us to arrange transport for her back to her home village where she would die. She was absolutely terrified, and there was no doubt that she would die if she did go home because she believed in the curse.

Anderson removed the strings and prayed with her. Next day the strings had been put back. He took them off again and talked to the brother and she was allowed to stay. Within a week she was walking and recovered completely.

Whilst waiting for the building to be done on the village site, we had planted dry-land maize on the adjoining land and reaped over 4.5t/ha which was twice the average for the land across the river under the same conditions. This gave us a saleable crop which financed our building programme. We had also been donated part of a container load of charity goods from Germany, which we sold very cheaply to the locals and then ploughed all the proceeds back into the project. Although we had the plan, and we had the site, and we had the finance, we found that development was painfully slow. We spent many hours in meetings and 'brain-storming' sessions and were trying to use our waiting time usefully in running Shona Alpha courses and Bible studies. Somehow our dynamic vision was becoming little more than a damp squib. It was frustrating for all of us and we knew we had lost impetus.

Looking back I can see now that the importance of the exercise was in the journey, not in the arrival. Working with the local people on a spiritual level we learned more about their beliefs and their fears, about the various cults and about the strength of the bondage which ensnares them. Just like the AIDS problem, where the truth was seen in action but denied to the point of physical death, so the truth of the Gospel could be agreed to by the lips but denied in the heart to the point of spiritual death. In both cases one seemed to meet a barrier, not the inability to understand, but the will not to. And the result was death. Even Harrison and Fredrikson were adamant that the ancestors could protect them, which was heartbreaking because we loved them both and knew that for Fredrikson in particular, time was short.

Each day when John retired for his siesta after lunch I would go out into the garden and have a quiet time of prayer. One day, with the problem of reaching the people surrounding us with the truth heavily upon my mind, I decided that if I was going to work for the Lord then the Lord must tell me how to set about it. So, sitting down under a shady tree I put my Bible by my side and told God, quite firmly, that I was going to sit there until He gave me an answer. Should we, I asked, aim at the women through Bible study? Should we aim at the children through Sunday school? How could we ever get through to the men? Then I leaned back comfortably against a tree and waited. There was no voice; no thought came into my mind. I listened to the birds singing and to the distant bark of baboons, but as Elijah found out (1 Kings 19.11-12) the Lord was not in them. Then I was suddenly conscious of another sound and looking up saw one of the dogs being sick on the grass. Wonderful! Here I am, listening for a word from God Himself and my dog pukes in front of me. After that, all that came into my mind was the Proverb (26.11) 'As a dog returns to his own vomit, so a fool repeats his folly'!

I tried to think about 'Heavenly' things, like sunlit flowers and tinkling crystal streams, but nothing blotted out the dog vomit. Well, I thought, who was I to give God an ultimatum anyway? I turned to pick up my Bible and noticed that one of the little tags that marked the beginning of each book was slightly torn. I opened the page to put the tag straight, and the words just jumped at me. 'A dog returns to his own vomit'! It was in 2 Peter 2. A little dazed I sat and read the chapter in front of me. There I saw them all, the spirit mediums who spoke false truths, the many who paid lip-service to Christianity and practised their cultural religion in private, those who gained the respect and privileges of position and salary through expounding the Gospel to their own people, and then abused those privileges and brought shame on the name of the Lord. I saw those thirsty for knowledge reaching out to the 'wells without water'. Every word was another colourful brushstroke creating a vivid picture of the world in which I lived. The innocent would be saved, I was assured, but those who preferred evil would be utterly destroyed. God knows the innocent. I didn't receive any directive, He said this is how they are and that He knows the problem only too well. In His own time and in His own way the problem would be dealt with, and His judgement, punishment and rewards would be just.

I learned something else that day. We shouldn't say ' This is the problem, I'm doing Your work so please help me sort it out'. My place is helping Him. Only the Holy Spirit can convict people of the truth, God would sort out the problem and He wouldn't necessarily involve me. My work began when the Lord called me to do it and I joined Him. From then on I stopped trying to see things as a whole and dealt with things that came across my path day by day, knowing that the seemingly unrelated incidents in my life, when dealt with prayerfully, were all minute parts of an infinite plan known only to the Lord.

CHAPTER TWENTY TWO

We would be so much more use to our Lord if we would ask. I once had an uncle who would tease me greatly when I was a small child.

"Them what ask don't get," he would tell me when I tried to get a sweet or a biscuit out of him.

Then, if I didn't ask but just looked hopeful I would be told,

"Them what don't ask don't want."

I couldn't win - but I usually got the sweets anyway!

It was drummed into me, however, that it was very wrong and bad manners to ask for anything, or even hint that I might want it. The only right way to get anything was to earn it. I expect that was quite a good yardstick to live by in human terms, but it doesn't work with God. There is no way we can earn anything from Him, but the whole Kingdom of Heaven is ours for the asking. Giving gives so much pleasure, we know that from our human experiences, so why are we so backward in letting God enjoy His children by giving to them? I expect there are many who feel, like I did, that anything I deserved I would get and if it didn't come my way I didn't deserve it. Or, I would ask if I knew I had a cast iron reason for asking, but not just because it would give me pleasure. I still felt that, in some way, I had to earn my blessings from God.

During my time at Chegutu, leading up to my baptism, I heard many people speaking in tongues. I always felt it would be a nice thing to be able to do, but as I couldn't see any reason for doing it I didn't really feel that was a good enough reason for asking for the gift. While at Bindura we went to an Alpha conference in Harare, together with Brian and Cath and others in the Fellowship It was held over several days and during that time we stayed in Brian's town flat. We enjoyed the conference, and you can imagine the singing with many hundreds of Africans all under one roof. At the end of each day we were invited to come forward for prayer, and after a talk about the gifts of the Spirit I decided to go forward. I had a great longing to be used in Healing, but when Maureen, who prayed for me, asked if I was drawn towards any particular gift I told her about the healing and then heard myself say, "and I would also like to receive the gift of tongues." I felt a bit guilty, because I didn't really have a good reason for asking, but Maureen was alrcady praying for me.

Next morning in the flat, waiting for my turn in the shower, I sat cross-legged on the bed and thought about the gifts. Maureen had said that to speak in tongues it was necessary to at least say something - the Holy Spirit needed to use my vocal chords as well as my tongue. I made a few experimental noises and suddenly had the strangest sensation, as if my tongue had taken on a life of its own. I was so excited. It was real, it was happening, it was true! What could I say? It isn't easy to say something that isn't a language. Then I hit on the phonetic alphabet and in doing that, of course, my first word was Abba. And away I went, sitting in sheer wonder listening to myself speaking this beautiful, beautiful and complicated language. It was just so wonderful and very quickly became just so natural. For a week or so, walking the dogs through the lovely countryside or sitting in the garden at my prayer time I prayed in this oh-so-special language every day. Then suddenly it stopped. I was heartbroken. In tears I prayed for my gift back again, I wept bitterly at the huge gap that had been left, and in a short time my gift was returned to me.

Maybe, because my request for the gift had been almost an afterthought, the Holy Spirit had shown me how much it really meant and how special it is. Many people call tongues the least of the gifts, but none of God's gifts can be measured. Paul says we should 'earnestly desire the best gifts' (1 Cor.12.31) and the Holy Spirit had shown me just how much I really did desire them.

John, Brian and Stuart all shared my joy, but the pastor of our Fellowship was a cessationist. He was quite sure that the gifts went out with the Apostles, and the Bible was now all that was necessary. He was so sure that he closely guarded his flock against the lies of Satan and would not hear any argument for the gifts. We had enjoyed a good and happy relationship with him since coming to the Fellowship and I could hardly wait to go and tell him it was true, the gifts are for now, I had been given one!

John and I went to see him in his little garden office and he listened quietly as we told him all that had happened. Well, he told us, as far as he was concerned it was demonic. I could not believe it. Did he really think that I had a demon? He obviously did! In fact he was so sure about it he got me worried. That evening I prayed hard to the Lord,

"Lord, if this beautiful gift is not from you, then please delivers me of it and let it be gone from me for ever."

I was very relieved to find that my gift was still there next day.

A little while later I had a dream. I was with our Pastor, sitting quite close to him, and he was clearly expounding some point or other. As he spoke I saw a film drop down over his eyes, then he would blink and the film was gone for a few seconds, only to drop down again as he continued to lecture. Next morning the dream was still crystal clear, as 'God-dreams' always are, and so was the meaning. In certain areas our Pastor wasn't seeing too clearly!

I mentioned the dream to Brian, who was a church elder, and suggested that he should tackle him on the whole issue and mention the dream. He didn't look at all taken with the idea, and I knew the matter would go no further. But the dream stayed with me and one morning, after church, I asked our Pastor for a few moments alone. I told him the dream in detail, sticking to the facts, and said that I felt it meant he wasn't seeing something clearly and that perhaps he should pray about it. He listened patiently and agreed that he would, then immediately ask why John and I hadn't 'officially' joined the Fellowship. Although we regularly attended all the services and all the house group meetings, we had felt unable to sign our agreement to a constitution that ruled out the gifts. So I told him just that. I was thrilled that he had asked, because it brought the problem immediately out into the open after talking about the dream and it was obvious that he saw the connection. It didn't change his mind, however, and later the church was to split over this same issue.

How often this seems to happen. And those against the gifts say ' You see? The Holy Spirit isn't divisive, if it was from Him the Church wouldn't split.' But it takes two sides to split. Is God on both sides? Either the Holy Spirit still honours our frail humanity with His supernatural power, or He doesn't. There is only one right answer. The problem is, of course, that Satan can supply counterfeit gifts, signs and wonders and many people, like our pastor, throw out the baby with the bathwater just to be sure! It is a fact that people of all denominations, all over the world, do speak in tongues, heal the sick, cast out demons, prophecy, speak words of wisdom and receive words of knowledge. Why is it easier to believe that this is the work of Satan rather than the Holy Spirit? Could it be because if all Christians allowed the Holy Spirit to empower them with His gifts for the work of the Lord, then Satan would have a very hard time of it? Who whispers to the Christian that these things are no longer available or necessary? Tongues is a wonderful, wonderful gift. I found it especially comforting when praying for my family, for they were five thousand miles away and all news when it came was at least seven days old. I knew that any prayer for them made by the Holy Spirit would be of that moment and exactly to the point. I also learned that we can ask for personal things.

We had been in Zimbabwe for eight years when we received the news that John's youngest son, Graham, was to marry Marinella his Italian girlfriend. The wedding was to be in Italy in the middle of May and the invitation was one that we knew we couldn't accept. It was made twice as sad because my daughter, Jo, was due to have her third baby a week before in England, and it would have been wonderful to be at both great occasions.

I felt I had a special share in this, our third grandchild. Six months previously I had a dream. It was about babies, and the clear message had been that it was just as beautiful and natural to have three as to have two. Well, unless I was to be another Sara I didn't think the dream was for me, I had two children and I certainly didn't expect a third, so I was puzzled - but not for long. That same afternoon I received a letter from Jo, both happy and sad. Jo loves children and wanted a third very much, but then on finding she was going to have her wish she suddenly felt guilty. Was she being selfish, she asked, she already had a boy and a girl. Would God be cross with her for being so self-centred? I had picked up the 'phone and made a rare and costly 'phone call. 'No,' I could tell her, ' God isn't cross with you. Three are just as beautiful and natural as two, He told me so!'

It was six weeks to the wedding. John's family would all be there, people he hadn't seen for eight years, people who didn't know him as a born again Christian and would doubtless notice the change in him. People I had been praying about every day, they would be there and it would have been good to talk to them again and tell them about what had been happening in our lives. Well then, the seed of a thought began to grow, would it be entirely selfish of us to want to go? I put it to John. If we asked according to God's will, how could it be wrong? It would cost Zim$ 26,000 for us both to get there, and then we would have hotel bills, transport the other end and all the unseen extras. Our total savings came to Zim$3,000. There would be no doubt as to whether it was God's will; if we were to go He was the only One who could arrange it!

Each morning John and I had a routine. John was always awake early, around 5.00 a.m. He would get up, make tea and bring the tray back to bed and then we would have a leisurely few cups of tea each and listen to the early radio news. Then we would get 'the book', whichever one we were studying. At that time it was Colin Urquhart's 'Listen and Live', which we were working our way through for the second time. After the bible passage, reading and general prayers for the day ahead we began to add one more.

'Lord, You know our hearts and You know we would love to go to the wedding and also see Jo's new baby. If it is Your will that we go Lord, please make the finances available.'

The days went by and Richard and his wife booked their air tickets and their hotel in Italy. The weeks went by and we went on with our routine. Finally the wedding was a week away, and we were called to an Outreach meeting on the preceding Saturday to meet a South African pastor who was visiting Zimbabwe and was interested in the work being done in rural communities. Mid-morning Cathy came in with the mail, which was collected sporadically from the nearest town, and a small brown envelope was given to me. It was dog-eared and had a badly typewritten address and I pushed it aside until later. At lunch time there was a lull and I opened the envelope. Inside was a cheque for Zim$26,000. It was drawn on the Christian Fellowship account, which made it anonymous. There were so many tears and smiles there should have been rainbows all around the room!

We had less than a week to organise everything, but we found that when the Lord makes the travel arrangements nothing is left to chance. The travel agents not only had two empty seats on the U.K. flight, they had a 'special' which gave one stop off in Europe from London free, which took care of the Italian leg of the journey. When Graham and Marinella heard that we were coming they telephoned to say they would collect us from Milan airport (no train journey) and we were to stay at a family flat (no hotel bills).

Jo had her baby at the beginning of the week and her husband, Brian, telephoned to say it was a girl and all was well, so I was able to say, ' Wonderful, we will see you at the week-end.'

An old friend offered to collect us from London. Everything was arranged and everything went so well. It was a wonderful three weeks, meeting our new grand-daughter at six days old and then a beautiful wedding and time to catch up with all the family.

It had been the Lord's will, and we still don't know those responsible for actually giving the money, but of one thing we can be sure, they have been blessed. For Jesus promises in Luke 6v38,

"Give and it will be given to you, good measure, pressed down, shaken together and running over will be poured into your bosom. For the same measure that you use, it will be measured back to you.'

We can never lose by giving. The world says hold on to what you have or you will finish up with nothing. The Lord says the more you give the more you will receive. How wonderful that we may take pleasure in doing both. Perhaps one reason that we give up on the Lord when we have asked for something, is because of His perfect timing. He has no reason to do things with time to spare, no reason to allow for accidents or unforeseen circumstances. We are the ones anxiously watching the calendar or, sometimes, even our watches. The Lord answers prayers on the dot, but in His perfect timing and according to His will. It's wrong to imagine that His will is always the same as our will, and we must accept His decisions because He knows the whole picture and often the piece of the puzzle we are holding isn't the same shape as we think it is. Either way the prayer will be answered. The Lord reads our hearts, not our diaries. He asks that we pray, believing in our heart that we have received, believing that the prayer has been granted. How often we come to the end of the time we have allocated Him and give up, no longer believing in our heart. It is a very hard lesson, but our faith is strengthened whilst living through God's promises. They are not always as easy to live through as our Italian trip.

As is often the case, we arrived home in high spirits only to have a bucket of cold water thrown over us to bring us down to earth again.

Whilst we had been away the maize crop on the Famba mu Chiedza lands, which was a special variety and potentially very important to the project, had matured and we had arranged for its harvesting and storage before we left. We found that a few days after we had flown to U.K. Stuart had stopped all work at the Village. Consequently the crop had been reduced substantially. Much had been stolen; the wild pigs and porcupines had taken their share and also the baboons and monkeys. The rest yielded less than a third of its potential. The building works had been stopped and the whole site had a dejected air about it. We were furious. Brian, busy with the main harvest, had no idea that it had happened or why.

The next Outreach meeting was very difficult, and the only answer we managed to get was that Stuart had changed his mind about the suitability of the site. As owner of the land, of course, he was quite within his rights but a more suitable site could hardly be imagined and we said so. Piece by piece we drew out the real reason.

Stuart's project had been a ' Green Belt' on the other side of the river on communal lands. Selected families had been invited to take part, and a long strip had been cleared parallel to the river to grow maize. It was quite a one sided partnership. Stuart would provide irrigation from the farm dam, the seed and fertiliser and the expertise, and they would do the clearing, planting, weeding and harvesting. Out of the profits they were to pay back only the price of the seed and fertiliser. It had never really worked. The weeds became so bad that the farm sent in helpers to weed, the communal cattle invaded the area so the farm put up a stock proof fence, and when the harvest was ready they came to the farm and demanded the use of a combine. Stuart had sent a tractor to help with the traditional hand reaping and a maize sheller which was little appreciated. The fence was 'broken' and the cattle got into it again, much was stolen and when the crop was eventually sold there was not enough to pay back the farm for the inputs.

Understandably, he was feeling very low about the whole thing and quite rightly blamed the collapse on the lack of Christian attitudes and the influence of the spirit-mediums. So what could be better than to build Famba mu Chiedza across the river and to have a totally Christian influence in their midst?

John and I could think of plenty. The most obvious thing was that the land didn't belong to anyone. It was communal land for the people, allocated by the local chiefs. We could never have a 'right' to be there, so when the site was developed and everything going nicely anyone could come along and take it over without the slightest qualm. It was also of paramount importance that the site should be free from satanic influence. If we had no say over who could live and work there we could have more witch doctors than pastors. The idea was a non-runner and we reached a brick wall. We were once again feeling frustrated and without direction. I had been so sure that the vision for a Christian village had been right and now we could do nothing and all our work seemed to have been to no avail. I continued at the office but found that relationships there were strained as I was secretary to the very cause of our frustration, and of course it was no easier for him and I knew that he would have been much happier without my being there.

Then 'flu hit the farm, most people in the office got it and although I escaped John came down with the symptoms. High fever, shivers, headaches and a general weakness. Parkinson symptoms become much worse under stress, so I wasn't too surprised to find that John needed support to get in and out of bed and since this was necessary day and night I soon became quite exhausted. The 'flu lasted about five days, but when John's five days were up he was looking worse and it was then that I called Ann, a friend and ex-nurse from the Fellowship, and asked her opinion. She came straight over, took one look and said

"'Get him to hospital. In fact get in my car, I'll take you!"

The rest of the farm had 'flu, my husband had malaria. By the time we reached Harare, two hours later, John was practically unconscious.

Brian was away on holiday in South Africa, but I had keys to use his town flat whenever I needed so I was able to stay there and be near to John. For four days he slid in and out of consciousness. Each morning I rang the hospital as early as I dared, knowing that he may not have made it through the night. Each day I spent by his bedside, rubbing him with ice-cubes to get the temperature down, massaging him to prevent sores and trying to be diplomatic with the nurses who insisted on trying to feed him hot soup. I was told in no uncertain tone by the African ward sister that I could stay if I didn't interfere, otherwise I could go. So I held my tongue and watched them spoon vegetable soup into my semi-conscious husband, who wasn't able to swallow it and eventually gagged and threw up all over the bed. After that they asked if I would like to give him his meals and a truce was reached. I prayed quietly all day as I sat holding his hand as he slept, receiving quinine through a drip. Each evening I returned alone to the flat and continued to pray. It was then, more than at any other time, that I thanked the Holy Spirit for my gift of tongues. I knew that by allowing the Holy Spirit to pray through me I was praying the best possible prayer. Paul tells us in 1.Cor.2 v 10, 11, that 'the Spirit searches all things, yes, the deep things of God', and that 'no-one knows the things of God, except the Spirit of God'. So, if I asked the Holy Spirit to pray to God for me, for John, I knew that no way could there be a better prayer prayed. I would wake several times during the night to the sound of music from the all night bars and the wailing of sirens and dogs barking, and before my eyes were open there would be a prayer on my lips.

In the mornings I would ring at 6:00 and then have a couple of hours to kill before they would let me into the hospital. I discovered, quite close to the flat, a Scripture Union bookshop with a huge selection of second-hand books from England. A few dollars brought a heap of books and then I would read myself to sleep each evening. One book was 'What happens when God answers' by Evelyn Christenson, and one of the first things I read there was that sometimes prayers don't get answered because we pray for the wrong things.

The Holy Spirit took that little comment and waved it about in front of me. That was, I knew, for me. But why? I had been praying for healing. My husband was desperately ill and I desperately didn't want him to die - why was it wrong to ask for healing? And then suddenly I knew. Some people have this glib little phrase ' Let go and let God'. I had to give John to the Lord and know that whatever He decided to do was right, and accept His decision. Maybe you have had to do that? When the person you love most in the world is slipping away and you are holding on to them with every prayer you can muster? To say, ' Lord, I give him to You, Your will be done'?

What if He took him? Well, I was reasonably reminded, God is God - how do you intend to stop Him? And so, amidst many, many tears I prayed the right prayer and instantly felt terribly alone.

"Please Lord," I asked, "Give me a word, a scripture, something?"

Into my mind came 'Amos'

I don't think I had ever read Amos. I turned the pages of my Bible and read the introduction. Amos was by profession a sheep breeder, perhaps a master shepherd. Like me, I thought. There were a few favourite verses listed and I looked them up. And there it was, the one for me, Amos 3.3. 'Can two walk together, unless they are agreed?'

Almighty God was asking me, ' Can two...' He and I, walk together if I wasn't in agreement with Him? How could I walk my life together with God if there wasn't absolute trust? Did I really think John was safer with me than with God? That night I slept, and the next day was Sunday.

I decided to go to Church on my way to the hospital, and as I was dressing I went over the Lord's message in my mind. It was just like Abraham and Isaac (Gen.22v9-12). Abraham had to be willing to give Isaac to God, just as I had to be willing to give John. I had also been struck by another verse in Amos, (9v13).

'Behold the days are coming,' says the Lord, 'When the plowman shall overtake the reaper....'

I realised what it meant in context, but somehow for me it seemed to mean that there was so much harvest to gather that there was a danger that some would be ploughed in before the reaper got there. Jesus needed people to take seriously the Great Commission (Matt.28 v 18-20).

That morning I joined worshippers at Avondale. The sermon was on Genesis 22 v 6-13, the story of Abraham and Isaac. It was followed by a reminder that the Lord needs workers for his Great Commission (Matt.28 v 18-20)

John slept all day and looked much better in the evening. On my way home I called in again at Avondale for the evening service, and the message was about refining fires followed by Holy Communion. A week later John was out of hospital.

Later he told me of his dream. While I had been giving him to the Lord, John had seen himself as if inside a huge skein of thread, and he knew that the thread he could see was his life line. A voice told him that his life was coming to an end, but if he wanted he could join on again and go back. John's answer was that there was still much for us to do together and so he would like to come back. From then on he was on his way to recovery.

On leaving hospital we were invited to go and stay for a week with Ken and Margaret, who owned the farm where John had been baptized. Margaret had been a nurse and they wouldn't hear of us going home as John was still very weak and on crutches and at home we had no neighbours, telephone or electricity. It was a wonderful week of relaxation and thanksgiving.

Towards the end of the week we heard that farm workers were going on strike so, as we were relying on Takesure to look after the dogs, Siwi and the chickens while we were away, we moved home. We found everything as we had left it and Takesure had secretly slipped away from the strikers, taking a short-cut through the bush, to feed and water our animals. We were very grateful, but knew that he had taken quite a risk as his actions could have been seen as siding with the opposition.

A few days later I was having breakfast when Takesure walked past going from the kitchen to the bedroom. I said something to him, but he didn't answer. I called him and got an answer, but he didn't come back so I went to investigate. He was lying on the bedroom floor with his eyes closed. Before we could get him to the car he was bathed in sweat and unconscious and an hour later he had been admitted to the Bindura African hospital. He had been poisoned, probably for being faithful to us during the strike. While he was recovering, a girl came from the village to help in the house and within two days she collapsed in the same way and we were rushing her to hospital too. There I was told by the African nurse that there was nothing physically wrong with her - she had been bewitched. I'm delighted to say that both made a complete recovery.

CHAPTER TWENTY THREE

I had made a lovely little place to sit and pray in the garden of our house. There were big, natural boulders among the trees, and next to one of them was a large horizontal slab with a shallow dip in it. Fredrikson had built up the end of it for me and we filled it with water to make a small pond. By the big rock, which had a flat top and made a good place to sit, I planted a buddleia which had taken well and was a mass of bloom. As I sat on the rock I would be surrounded by a cloud of butterflies attracted to the buddleia, and often tiny blue waxbills would come and drink from the water at my feet. Porgie would sit behind me and doze and it was just perfect.

Our circumstances, however, were far from perfect. Anderson was still working with the people in the compound, since the Christian village had come to a full stop he had nothing else to do. He had asked me if I would do a Bible study with some of the women who could speak English and whilst wondering what on earth I was going to talk about, I was given the idea of the Ten Commandments. After all it made sense. If their culture didn't take in God's moral laws then how could they follow them? But when I thought about the first commandment I was at a loss as to how to even start, for it came to me as

'You shall love the Lord your God with all your heart, with all your soul, and with all your mind.' (Matt.32 v 27)

How could I explain that sort of sentiment to a group of people whose native language doesn't contain a word for love? I looked up the Ten Commandments in Exodus 20 v 3, and saw

'You shall have no other gods before me.'

Well, that was easier. But, easier though it may have been I knew that it wasn't the one on which I should be meditating. In fact the more I thought about it the more I realised that it was me that the commandment was aimed at! I was to love God before anyone and anything. How many people did I know who thought that way! Certainly none of the Outreach team thought that way, there was always first the security of a job, a nice house, the family and the children's schooling to be considered. If God said "Go," how many people did I know who would just drop everything and go? Would I?

Oh, right! OK! Now I was beginning to get the picture. We were going to be on the move again, were we not? We had our first house for seventeen years that we could call our own, we had been in it just over a year, and we were going to have to leave it. And with the same certainty I knew that Brian was also going to have to leave his home of fourteen years. I didn't know why, but I knew. I remember driving through the beautifully farmed lands, the wheat golden ripe and stretching as far as the eye could see, and thinking ' I feel like Noah'. Somewhere amidst all that peace and prosperity a disaster was lurking and I was the only one who knew. Of course I talked to John about it, and he agreed that if that was what the Lord wanted then we must leave, but we would just carry on as usual until we got further guidance. I had no feeling that I should tell anyone else.

We had met, through Johnny and Mel, a lady who owned a Retreat Centre in Nyanga. She had often come to visit us in the Valley and brought friends to meet us and look around the various enterprises. Dorothy had been the one who had arranged for us to receive the donations from Germany to finance the Christian village, and she often sent us the Retreat newsletter. We had never been to the Retreat, but heard that it was very isolated and not easy to get to. Thus the newsletter meant little to us as we knew neither the place nor the people, but when the next one arrived in the post, I noticed that Dorothy had underlined part of it. The person running the place wanted to retire and they were looking for a couple to take her place. I pointed it out to John, but he didn't look wildly enthusiastic and neither was I. A little while later we had a letter from Dorothy saying that twice when she had been praying in the little Retreat chapel she had felt the Lord was telling her to ask us if we would run the Centre, and would we go for a weekend to visit. Put like that we could scarcely refuse.

We went for a weekend, and found a warm welcome with Dorothy and the present retiring warden, Elizabeth. We stayed in a little wooden cabin with beautiful views over the valleys and surrounding mountains. There was a main house with four small bedrooms, a large 'dormitory', a long dark kitchen, three bathrooms, lounge and dining room. A little way up the hill was a three roomed thatched cottage and down the hill a two bed roomed cottage which was still in the process of being built. There were staff quarters, a small bed-sitter where Elizabeth lived and a cottage inside the main entrance which was Dorothy's. The property was very large, but contained four mountains and a river boundary, so there was little arable land. Water came from the springs and the main house had solar lighting. We enjoyed our weekend and came away with something to think about, but no strong convictions.

Nothing had yet come to disrupt our life on the farm but we knew that we were again at one of the many crossroads in our life. Sitting on my rock amidst the butterflies I prayed for guidance in my prayer language, and as I listened to the Holy Spirit speaking the beautiful words through me the flow suddenly ceased, and one word came, repeated over and over again. "Om".

It was just a little word, just one syllable, but trembling with power and meaning. My spirit recognised the spiritual enormity of this tiny word and I knew somehow that the experience was very, very special.

We decided, eventually, to go to the Retreat Centre and soon after we had made the decision the Government published a list of farms that were designated to be taken over under the newly formed Land Acquisition Act. That part of the farm on which our house was built was designated, also the site of the Christian Village. Stuart decided, probably quite wisely, that as he owned several farms it would be best not to contest the acquisition of just one of them, and at the same time made it known that he would prefer the Outreach to be distanced from his farming operation. He gave Brian one of his farms nearer to Bindura to use as a base. He also felt that the time had come when he wanted to run the commercial farm himself, which meant that Brian and his family had to leave their home also.

The disaster had struck and at the next Outreach meeting we told the team that we would be leaving. Why else would the Lord have prepared us? He had provided us with a place to go and go we must. As always we had a choice, for the Lord never takes away our free will. The Outreach wanted us to stay, we knew we must go.

Having made the trip from Juliasdale to Bindura, we were now destined to return to a place only about 15 kilometres from the Valley. The whole horrendous journey stretched before us. We still had the horses, dogs and Siwi and the chickens. We still had Harrison and his family and Anderson who, although offered a very good position with the Outreach, decided that he would come with us as well. Kenneth and the others decided to stay as they had good jobs on the farm, and sadly AIDS had claimed Fredrikson and his wife, they had both died within five days of each other at Christmas.

A neighbour, also a member of the Fellowship, offered us the use of his cattle rig and trailer, and Stuart offered a driver and gave us two house cows as a going away present. Just when we felt that everything was settled we had a phone call from Dorothy. Before she had asked us to come to the Retreat Centre she had sent an email to all the churches, advertising the post of warden. Now she had a reply and the person who had applied was a very well know 'Christian businessman'. She was somewhat overwhelmed by his interest, as was Brian when I mentioned it. However, there was plenty to do Dorothy assured us, and no reason why we couldn't work together.

We were actually quite thrilled with the idea. It seemed that God was bringing a team together and we were to be part of it. We rang Lionel, the other applicant, and were invited to go to his house for the weekend and talk about things. We went happily, with open minds and high hopes. We were soon to be disillusioned. Lionel was a very busy person. He seemed to have many callers, 'coming to consult me on the state of the country', and would be off to Zambia early next morning (Sunday) on business. He had a map of the Retreat Centre and already had plans to build chalets for guests and live in the main house himself. He was going to re-route the access road - which was appalling, over three kilometres of deep ruts and erosion that played a major part in keeping the Centre remote! He thought a hydro-electric scheme on the spring would be an advantage. Since it was just a trickle which petered out into a wet sponge in summer I couldn't personally see how that would work, but I knew nothing about hydro-electrics. I did, however, recognise the startled look on my husband's face and guessed we were thinking the same. As he continued to unfold his plans I saw a picture in front of my eyes. It was a shaky tower built of playing cards, just floating above the ground.

At supper that evening he told us that it was his ambition to help hurting people. Then he suddenly put down his fork, stared intently at John and said,

"There's something wrong with you, isn't there! What is it?"

I just cringed with embarrassment. How could he be so thoughtless? John agreed quietly that yes, there was something wrong, he had Parkinsons. Satisfied, our host continued with his meal. So much for helping hurting people.

Changing the subject I asked Lionel what spiritual input he intended to give the centre. There was a silence and I noticed his wife give him a quick glance.

"None at all," was the answer.

We went to bed and in the early hours we heard our host depart.

His wife invited us to go to the church with her, which we did and enjoyed a very charismatic service. Their son, she told us, was a youth leader there, but would be much too busy to meet us. We left immediately after the service, speaking to no one. Alone in the kitchen I asked her if she thought the many ideas that Lionel had for the Centre were his own ideas or from the Lord.

"Knowing Lionel," she smiled, tiredly, "They will be his."

We also heard that they were bankrupt. Their bank account had been frozen and they were going to have to sell their very lovely house for 'long bucks'. Perhaps, I felt, the Retreat Centre would have been a good place to retire without losing face.

John and I were disturbed by our weekend. There was no way we could work with a person like Lionel. I liked his wife and felt very sorry for her, but we were wanting to do the Lord's work not work for Lionel. His idea seemed to be that he would run the Retreat and we could help him by running the farm for him. We rang Dorothy and told her; sorry, it was us or Lionel.

The next few weeks were very unsettling. We still had the option to stay with the Outreach team, but felt that moving to the Retreat was right and that we should stand our ground. We made a few discreet enquiries amongst those who would know and received ample confirmation that our conclusions had been right and partnership would be something from which to steer clear. Eventually we received a phone call from Dorothy asking that we should come and the whole task of packing up and moving began again.

NYANGA
1998 - 1999

'And the person who turns after mediums and familiar spirits, to prostitute himself with them, I will set My face against that person and cut him off from his people.'

(Leviticus 20 v 6)

' If you are reproached for the name of Christ, blessed are you, for the Spirit of glory and of God rests upon you. On their part He is blasphemed, but on your part He is glorified.'

(1 Peter 4 v 14)

CHAPTER TWENTY FOUR

Our final load this time amounted to six horses, two in-calf cows, fifty laying hens, the two dogs and the cat, plus two African families which included five children. We still had little furniture but brought with us the usual essentials such as chicken wire, feed troughs, metal drums for water containers, tools and bits of farm and self-sufficiency equipment. All this filled the 30 tonne open cattle rig and trailer, and was hauled down the infamous approach road at mid-night by a driver who had strict instructions not to!

John and I had seen everything loaded and then come ahead to prepare things the Nyanga end. We had arranged with Johnny that he would meet us at the top of the approach road with his tractor and trailer. There we could unload everything and take it down to the centre by stages, as the huge lorry would never negotiate the deep crevices and hair pin bends. We were going to walk the horses down and drive the cows, and all being well the driver could have a nap in his cab and then make the return journey in good time.

Well, we waited and Johnny waited, and at last he had to give up and go back to his farm. We drove down to the centre to see if there had been a phone message from the driver, and then rang the Bindura farm to see if any problems had been called in, but no-one knew anything. We waited an hour and then decided to back-track and see if we could find them. It had been dark for hours and there was a strong likelihood of us passing them on the road without seeing them, but we couldn't just sit. So at around eleven we started back up the road, not a journey I was looking forward to in the dark.

We had just reached the entrance gate to the Retreat when John pointed to lights at the top of the hill, which were moving. We thought it was a car and decided to wait at the bottom so that it could pass us. When I switched off the engine we could hear that it was something much heavier than a car. Lurching and swaying and changing up and down through the gears we heard our cattle rig making the decent. Horrified we watched the lights disappearing and re-appearing as Africa, the driver, negotiated the zig zag bends and deep ruts with all our precious animals on board. We sat and prayed.

From the cluster of African huts nearby came men, women and children, open-mouthed and chattering excitedly as this, the first big lorry to drive down into the valley, chugged steadily towards them. Just as I was beginning to breathe again there was a bang and a shout and the lights lurched. He had reached the stream crossing and the trailer was in danger of turning over. We drove up to meet him, and in the Suzi's headlights Africa unhitched the trailer, drove the horse and main rig to dry land, and then unhitched the horse and reversed up for the trailer. Trailer recovered he hitched everything up together again and headed for the last lap along the narrow track to the Centre. We drove ahead and then lit his way again as he reached the small concrete bridge which crossed a steam just inside the wire entrance gates. Lit by the headlights, long shadows thrown against the thorn bushes I watched Africa, like a weird dancer in a nightmare, arms outstretched for balance, pace his measurements heel to toe across the bridge and then go and do the same in front of his lorry. A quick thumbs up and he vaulted into his cab, revved up and came for it. To cross the bridge he was driving on the inside set of double wheels. His driving had been absolutely brilliant, but the bridge was at a slight angle to the road, and as he cleared it the front offside wheels hit a soft patch and he was stuck. The trailer holding the horses and cows was sitting right on the bridge, and since it was side unloading there was no way we could get them off. It was now well after mid-night, and we had no choice but to leave everything as it was until first light.

Chris arrived early next morning with Johnny's tractor and trailer again, cutting himself a new way in through the bush as the lorry was completely blocking the only entrance. Together John and Chris covered the trailer bed with sand, then jumped horses and cows down from the rig to the trailer and the trailer to the ground. It took three days to unstick the lorry. So began our new venture.

We soon found that our time at Bindura, the Christian values which had become a way of life with us, the insights we had received over the past three years into spiritual warfare and the problems of the cultural religion had been a very necessary part of our education. Although it had seemed on the surface that the Lord had taken us on a huge diversion, we couldn't possibly have been equipped spiritually to move straight from the Valley to the Centre just 15 kilometres away without living through the past three years.

We soon realised that it was a Retreat Centre, not a Christian Retreat Centre. Surrounded by small-scale farmers, practising their cultural ways of ancestral worship, the centre had been open to all in an 'inter-faith' venture, including Buddhism. The main house displayed amongst its ornaments, in all innocence, such things as sun-god images, and in the small library were books on spiritism and Buddhist meditation. The whole of Nyanga was renowned for being a witchcraft stronghold, and into this spiritual battlefield we walked, holding the banner of simple no-nonsense Christianity. Small wonder we upset the controlling spirits!

Once settled we began a physical and spiritual sort out. Physically we had fourteen years of accumulated rubbish to clear out. The answer to everything seemed to have been string, nails or a clothes peg. Kitchen shelves were rough planks piled into tiers on old undisguised paint tins. The one gas cooker smelt alarmingly of gas when turned on, and one had to blow on the grill every few minutes to distribute the flames. The ancient paraffin fridge and freezer worked well, once we had mastered filling them with paraffin and getting the tanks back into place without breaking the glass wick guards or letting the flame go out! It was a joint effort, needing my steady hand in place of John's shaky one and John's strength.

Turning our attention to the stores we found boxes of brown paper, discarded wick ends, broken crockery, bent candles and rusting baking trays. The linen cupboard was filled with good quality bed linen and blankets from the German sponsors, the beds had foam rubber sheets for mattresses and donated furniture filled every spare corner. The small, partly finished bungalow that we had hoped to occupy ourselves had no kitchen and no hot water or lights. The seemingly well stocked larder revealed ancient tins of vegetables, the contents of which were dried up and mouldy, and the jars of cereals and herbs were infested with weevils. Although we were a good two hour drive from a reasonable shopping centre there seemed to have been no attempt at self provision, not even a vegetable garden. So, after months and months of frustrated waiting to get on with our Outreach project at Bindura, suddenly we had a host of things to get our teeth into.

Anderson surprised us by admitting to being an experienced painter and decorator, and was soon at work brightening up the various bedrooms. Many of the rooms had nasty looking cracks in the walls, and the three roomed thatched bungalow had a crack which went down one end, along the floor inside and up the wall at the other end. We sent a letter to Lovemore, the builder who had been with us in the Valley and before long we were delighted to see his round figure and sunny smile as he plodded up the hill to the main house.

The cracks were stopped, tied in, replastered and painted, and then work began again on the chicken houses that seemed to be an indispensable part of our lives. John began fencing, as there were no paddocks on the place, cutting down and utilizing old gum trees that had been damaged by a bush fire. A vegetable garden was started, fencing it in with a tall grass fence and gate so that the baboons couldn't see what was in there. Then, our first guests were due.

A youth group from a Seventh Day Adventist Church arrived; they were booked in as self-catering and arrived with a truck load of ready prepared casseroles, boxes of fruit and vegetables and crates of soft drinks. Their leaders had appointed a rota for cooking, clearing up and washing up, and once they had mastered the old gas stove and the wood stove outside the kitchen door they were happy to be left to get on with things. The little stone and thatch chapel which stood apart from the main house was filled with the most beautiful music, and all without a single musical instrument other than the human voice. As a church, they didn't allow instruments, but sang joyfully in absolute harmony. We were invited to sit in during their service and on their last evening joined them for a delicious, completely vegetarian meal. They left, promising to be back again next year and we began the task of tidying up and getting ready for the next guests.

Our broiler house was finished and the time had come to collect our first new chicks. We were able to go back to our old suppliers in Rusape and were greeted with much warmth. Although the distance was about the same as when we had been in the Valley with Johnny and Mel, our little day olds had the additional stress of a very uncomfortable ride down the last three kilometres. John noticed an anti-stress medication in the Farmers Co-op to put in their drinking water so we decided it would be a good thing to try.

We filled their plastic drinkers with warm water so that the medication would dissolve properly, put the drinkers in place and carefully counted out the hundred chicks into their brand new home. They had survived the journey well and we left them to quietly settle in and went for lunch. An hour later I went back to see how they were and disaster had struck. Because chicks are attracted to warmth they had all chosen to gather around the warm water towers of the drinkers, instead of the warm lamp in the centre of the hut. Consequently at least a third of them had been pushed into the water and were now lying around with eyes closed and little fluffy feathers soaked, legs stretched out as if dead. As I picked up the bodies I thought I could feel just a tremor of life there and rushed to find a box to put them in. We had taken over the dormitory room in the main house as our personal quarters, and the sun was flooding through the windows as I carried my little tragic box in and began to unload the contents onto a towel spread on our bed in the sun. Without electricity I didn't know how I could warm them up. Then I remembered that when we were lambing in England I had often picked up a lamb in the same state as these chicks, and how the warm bath method usually worked. How can you bath a day old chick?

I fetched a pint jug from the kitchen and filled it with warm water. Taking a chick by the neck I carefully dunked it in the water and held it there. Within half a minute it stirred and abruptly brought its legs up to its chest and opened its eyes. I put it in the sun, blotted it dry with the towel and reached for the next one. Soon I had thirty chicks sun-bathing in rows across the bed, and the first ones were beginning to stir and sit up. They were probably the only chicks in Zimbabwe to have been prayed over! But they all survived and later that afternoon I was able to return them to their warm hut and they never looked back.

Our laying hens had taken the journey in their stride and continued to lay more eggs than we could use, so we began to meet more and more of the local people as they came to buy our surplus. The cows had also calved so we had milk to spare and, as in the Valley, people came to buy. I also found that it was easy to make butter and soft cheeses. There was a small orchard of peaches and plums that bore well if you could beat the baboons to them, and here Porgie and Bess became invaluable as they were great look-outs and barked at the first whiff of invader.

As I started to book in guests I began to offer full board rather than self-catering, preferring to be in control of the meagre little kitchen. It worried me that most of the African guests had never used a gas stove and the one we had was both unreliable and temperamental. Also, we were not really equipped with enough refrigerated storage for the supplies big groups brought with them, and stacking a dozen freshly killed and still bloody chicken in a small fridge which also held our milk and butter was a problem I could do without. Since we were now able to produce much of our own food we were able to keep the prices down to a very reasonable level, and most opted to have everything done for them during their stay.

We had a wide variety of guests who braved the approach road, ranging from the exuberant youth groups of many denominations to the quiet Franciscan friars who came on silent retreat. So as I cooked I could expect anything from two youngsters chasing a ball through the kitchen to a file of brown hooded friars drifting through on their way to the dining room. We had honeymoon couples, holidaying families who came to climb the surrounding hills and several 'regulars', mostly Franciscan, who came to recharge their batteries. It was a real pleasure to have these people, as they so appreciated both the family atmosphere we could provide and the home cooking. When you live in an institutional, all male environment it must make a welcome change. I well remember one such regular lingering in the kitchen doorway on a Sunday morning, and finally saying shyly,

"On Sundays I'm allowed a hug!"

So I found myself teaching pastry making to one and playing chess with another, and John found new skills in making apricot jam and making sandwiches as well as running our little farm.

Everything should have been happy, but it wasn't. The problem was that whatever we did we were unpopular with Dorothy. It is easy to see why. For fourteen years Dorothy and Elizabeth had run the centre in their own way, and now we had come in and changed everything. Dorothy had started the centre, she had worked hard and begged hard for the means and materials to build the cottages and restore the chapel, which had been all but demolished during the war. Having done all that, however, Dorothy spent little time at the Centre as she was a totally committed globe-trotter and her greatest love was climbing. It had been Elizabeth who had stayed there and run everything single handed, and she had done a wonderful job with the resources available to her. However, our attitude differed inasmuch as we believed wholeheartedly that the resources available to us were all the resources of God's Kingdom. We could not agree that running the Centre ruled by a spirit of poverty was in any way to the Glory of God. If we were willing to work He was willing to provide. So when we repainted a bathroom because it was a better colour and not because it was absolutely necessary, it went against the frugal approach that had previously been the norm. Previously the front of the house had been painted and not the back, because it wasn't so prominently on view. However, most of our guests used the back way once they got their bearings and so we painted that too!

It was just too much and every move we made came under severe criticism which was often delivered with pure fury. The Centre belonged to Dorothy, and as the owner we had to explain our actions to her, but that was almost impossible to do. The main way in which we differed was that we saw it belonging to the Lord. We had come because the Lord had prepared us way in advance for a move. We were not employed by Dorothy, we received no salary and were expected to provide for ourselves independently of the Centre. God had, we felt, spoken to Dorothy and suggested that she ask us to come, as she herself had believed. The problem was that now things were getting beyond her control she was unable to 'Let go and let God', but felt that she must have misheard the Lord in the first place! The fact that guests were booking up to come back and the guest book was full of happy and praising comments didn't seem to count. It was a more than difficult situation.

I believe that a huge majority of Satan's successes are chalked up to relationship problems. That was another thing, Dorothy refused to believe that Satan even existed and insisted that there was no such thing as evil spirits. We were also told that we mustn't tell the Africans that Jesus was the only way, as their cultural religion was their lifeline! So the spiritual attack was complete, physically, mentally and spiritually.

Whatever we did, we did it to make the place more attractive, more welcoming, more Christian. Our hearts were open to the Lord and we knew that we had done nothing that did not honour Him, but it took us into direct conflict with Dorothy. The greatest bone of contention was the little Chapel. Inside it was arrayed with candles, Stations of the Cross were pasted around the walls and a crucifix was tied to the wooden cross above the altar. As an interdenominational centre we felt that the Chapel should be simply Christian and strictly neutral. Each day, while John had his usual nap, I would go over and sit in the chapel and have my prayer time. As I sat I would look around at the Stations of the Cross, which completely surrounded me, and think 'where is the Glory and triumph?' Fourteen pictures of Jesus being arrested, beaten, humiliated, tortured and killed, and the very last one showing Him dead in the tomb. Where was the risen Lord? Where was His triumph over evil? According to the pictures He was there, dead in the tomb for ever. In fact there He was in front of me, still hanging on the crucifix above the altar. Where was the Gospel message that we were supposed to be bringing to these people?

What was wrong with a plain, empty cross and a vase of flowers that He had created and grown Himself?

Beyond the simple wire gate of the Centre lived half a dozen families in their traditional thatched houses. Most of the women came to the little church on Sundays and brought with them a legion of children. Anderson had taken over the services and although I sometimes sat in at the back it all went over my head. However, many of the women could speak English and were very friendly. They were also curious, as those in the Valley had been, about the way we raised the chickens and made bread, butter and the sorts of vegetables we had planted. So we developed a good relationship and soon they asked me if we could have a weekly Bible study. Time means nothing to the African, and they would gradually drift up the hill in twos and threes for our two o'clock meeting, finally gathering at around three thirty in the dining room.

I wanted to know just how much they did understand about the Gospel, so we started with the difference between Christianity and religious denominations. Each one declared fervently that she was 'Anglican'. Elizabeth had been a strong Anglican, and was also very drawn towards Catholicism, hence the furnishing of the little chapel. I wanted to find out how much of their professed religion was learned dogma and how much was heartfelt Christianity. It soon became apparent that the main objective was to be 'Anglican'. After much discussion they finally took me into their confidence.

"Amai Judy," a young woman ventured, nervously," We are really interdenominational, but it is necessary for me to be Anglican."

Her mother-in-law, Martha, took it a step further.

"I have eight children," she explained," where will they get an education if I am not an Anglican?"

And there we had it. The nearest good school was run by an Anglican mission. Both Dorothy and Elizabeth had been involved with this mission and so being faithful members of their little church and becoming 'Anglican' had been a big step in the right direction to obtaining good education for their children, which every African craves. Christianity didn't enter into it. That was why we never saw the men at church, the woman were the family representatives on a Sunday morning and the men got on with their own cultural religion unhindered.

That, however, left the women very hindered as far as being Christian was concerned. The man was head of the household, and therefore it was the duty of the woman to brew beer for the ancestors and to take her part in the various rituals and ceremonies associated with their way of worship. Thus we could have a church full of women singing lustily and praying long, worshipful prayers on a Sunday, and then listen to them banging drums and singing lustily to the opposition on Monday. The leaning towards Catholicism was also a problem, for how can one believe that it is quite alright to pray to Mary and the 'saints', who were human, but it is wrong to pray through your Grandfather, who was also human.

We enjoyed our Bible studies. For me it was a chance to be with other women who were not only friendly, but full of laughter and fun. I knew that all I could do was to pray for them and to point them to the parts of the Bible that they would need to know about most. We found a dozen Bible references where God explicitly and emphatically warns against consulting spirit-mediums and familiar spirits, and I could see that they understood and the message had hit home. We had trouble in explaining the Trinity, until I hit upon the idea of an egg. With an egg and three glasses I demonstrated that the egg was just one egg, as God is one God. But then that egg could be divided, I showed them carefully, into the yolk, the white and the shell. Each was different, each had its own function, but each was part of the whole egg. They were delighted and my demonstration got a round of applause, but I'm not sure how far the message got. As Martha pointed out,

"If you have to pray by the Spirit, through the Son to the Father, why can't I pray by the medium, through my grandfather to the Father?"

"Because Jesus is the Son of God and He says the only way to the Father is through Him. Which of your Grandfathers was a Son of God?"

"Ah," grinned Martha, mischievously, "Not many!"

CHAPTER TWENTY FIVE

Although it was clear that we were under quite a strong spiritual attack, we were always confident that we were in the right place and that the Lord was with us. One evening, after a particularly frustrating day in which we had been subjected once again to severe criticism and anger, I went to bed both physically and mentally exhausted. As I closed my eyes I saw in large letters the words 'ROMANS 12'. I had no idea what Romans 12 said, and although I knew that it was a message from the Lord I was just too tired to go and look for my Bible, so I was quickly asleep and looked it up first thing next morning.

The first part of its message to hit me was ' do not conform', and through that I received encouragement that we were right to be making the radical approach to the spiritual obligations of the centre that was causing us so much grief. The whole chapter was absolutely relevant to our position. 'Bless those who persecute you; bless and do not curse.' Well we certainly wouldn't curse anyone, but it wasn't too easy to bless them either. 'If it is possible, as much as depends on you, live peaceably with all men', well we were doing our best in as much as we soaked up the anger like blotting paper and responded quietly with simple truth. There the old worldly comment invariably held true, 'Be nice to your enemies, nothing annoys them more!' 'Beloved, do not avenge yourselves, but rather give place to wrath; ' we were allowed to feel anger as long as it was under control, and then followed the sobering assurance, 'Vengeance is Mine, I will repay,' says the Lord. And lastly further encouragement, ' Do not be overcome by evil, but overcome evil with good.'

So spiritually the Lord was with us and understood what we were going through. He also helped us physically. I had still lost my nerve with the horses. I rarely went riding, and was very nervous about walking through the paddocks to check them. I tried to overcome my fear, but experience had taught me that whenever I got within range something nasty would happen to me! I felt that we had been robbed of what had once been our greatest pleasure, and although I still loved the horses and longed for the wonderful freedom that we used to feel when we rode in the Valley, I just couldn't shake off the fear. Maybe I would have felt differently if we still had Tif, the little Arab stallion, but he had been 'borrowed' by his previous owners to sire some foals and had died whilst there. He had been, without doubt, a very special little horse. We had also lost Anzac at Bindura, when a particularly virulent strain of horse sickness bypassed all the vaccines and killed many horses in the area. So Gambler was now my mare, and John was riding Zebedee.

It was just before mid-night that Dorothy came banging on the door to say that the horses were out. They were only allowed in the one paddock, and the grass was much greener on the other side of the fence. It was a bright, moonlit night, and having to catch six young horses feeling full of themselves was my idea of a nightmare. I dutifully went with John, carrying the paraffin lamp and the spare head collars. We found the horses snorting and excited, trotting around the chapel and Harrison's house. Harrison, however, seemed to be very soundly asleep and was obviously not about to volunteer any help. John pointed quietly to Gambler,

"You lead her and I'll catch Zebs and then I think the rest might follow," he suggested.

I moved out reluctantly, from behind my tree. I didn't want the rest to follow. Leading an excited horse down a narrow path in the middle of the night, with the prospect of four others galloping up behind me, spooking her and running over me, was not attractive in my view. But I had to help John buckle up the head collar on Zebs, as his hands were shaky from the Parkinsons and Zebs wasn't in the mood to stand quietly. After that I found it relatively easy to catch Gambler, so praying that she would be good and that no-one would be hurt, I led her away towards their paddock.

And as I walked along that brightly moonlit track, between the tall blue-gums, with the mountains around us bathed in silver, my fear was just lifted away from me. Suddenly. One moment there - next moment gone. As if it had never been. I put Gambler in the field and went back for the next one. The five year old untrained colt followed me like a lamb. Next day I went to see them, walked into their field, through them and around them, patting and talking to each one. My fear had vanished and it was wonderful.

At last we could enjoy our horses again. Gambler was always alert, her walk was nearly a trot, her trot nearly a canter and her canter like a rocking horse. Sure footed and brave she was a lovely ride. Zebedee, now seven and silver grey, still had a mind of his own but went well with Gambler. We began to explore the countryside around the Centre, and immediately found relief in the freedom and change of atmosphere. But Satan never accepts defeat gracefully, and having been delivered of the spirit of fear that had dogged me for so long, he turned his attention to John.

One morning as we drank our early morning cup of tea, my husband was unusually quiet and then admitted that he had something on his mind.

"I woke a few weeks ago with this thought on my mind," he told me quietly, " I think I'm going to be killed, and Zebedee will be involved."

Well, you can imagine the thoughts that raced through my mind. Sell the horse, was the first one. We shall have to stop riding again, was the second. Pray about it was a late third.

Then a thought came into my mind. The Lord had taken away my fear of horses, suddenly and unasked, a gift of Grace. Now Satan was trying to get us back into that state of fear by putting negative thoughts into John's mind. It was a shabby, devious and despicable trick. John was determined not to stop riding. Over the next few weeks we enjoyed our horses, but I spent time in prayer before each ride, asking for our Lord's protection.

One morning we followed a troop of baboons. They led us up out of the valley, through the rocky outcrops and across mountain streams. The horses went well, and soon we found ourselves back on a track we knew would take us back to the Centre. We came out a little higher up than we expected and decided to follow the tarred road back to the turning for home. In the distance I saw a blue pick-up truck approaching. I was in front and watched Gambler's ears carefully for any sign of nervousness as we didn't meet many cars on our rides. She was unperturbed, but as the car passed me I heard a shout from John and turned to see Zebs on top of the high roadside bank and my husband on the ground. Zebs had jumped sideways and upwards and John had landed on the only rock in sight. He had hit his head, ribs and hip.

Zebs was wonderful. He stood while John carefully pulled himself upright and gingerly tested himself for broken bones. He had been wearing a riding hat, something he usually scorned, but without it his head would have come a poor second best to the rock. His hip was sore and he couldn't get back on his horse, but Zebs walked slowly as John leaned on him for support until we found a big felled tree to use as a mounting block. My husband couldn't lift his left leg off the ground, so had to mount from the wrong side and clamber painfully aboard. Zebs stood quietly and then walked steadily the remaining four kilomctrcs home. Once there John collapsed onto the ground and I fetched the car to get him from the paddock to the house, sitting him in the back of the Suzi with the door open as he couldn't get into the passenger seat.

In answer to a 'phone call our good friend Sue, who we had met through the local Christian Fellowship, and who was a physiotherapist, braved the road in her little low slung truck to have a look. She advised us that we would do more harm driving John up out of the valley than letting him lie flat. His hip was very sore and she suspected a hairline fracture. He spent three weeks in a lot of pain, moving around slowly with a pair of crutches and we rigged up a system of ropes to help get him into and out of bed. Six weeks later he was up on Zebedee again!

I believe that Satan's plan had been for John to be killed in that fall. We had prayed against it because the Lord had warned John, and in answer to our prayer Satan's purpose had been deflected. It was the first time the Lord saved John's life by a word of knowledge, the next time was to be far more dramatic.

My husband took to riding Zebs each morning around the fence line and out to see the work that was being done that day. I prayed for him as he disappeared through the blue gums and out across the steep paddocks. I had just nursed him back to health and didn't want to be back to square one. Sometimes he would come back with a broad grin of enjoyment, a ' two carrot' morning when Zebs had given him a wonderful ride and earned a good reward. Lately, however, the old sulky attitude had reappeared and rides were becoming hard work rather than enjoyable. I despaired over Zebs. Being home-bred we knew that he had always been well-handled and cared for. He had been carefully schooled as a five year old and was really a lovely ride, but he had this deep-down negative attitude and a quick temper that wasn't to be found in either Tif, his father or Rainbow, his mother. The other problem that had to be faced was that John's balance wasn't as good as it used to be before the Parkinsons had made itself known. Whereas, in the past, he had been a strong rider and would have taken no nonsense from Zebs, now he didn't have the confidence afforded by a good balance and a sure seat to stay with him through a clash of wills. It was then that I learned that I should choose my prayer and stick to it!

Seeing John's frustration, my first prayer was that a bonding should take place between Zebs and John, that they would enjoy each other's company and be friends, that Zebs would lose his sulks and begin to look forward to his daily outings. Well, I gave God three whole weeks and nothing changed - so I changed my mind. Why, I asked John, didn't he just sell Zebs and get a reliable horse he could enjoy? Eventually he agreed and we began to put out on the 'bush telegraph' that we had a horse for sale. Although I found him so infuriating, Zebs had a sweet and gentle side to his nature, so I prayed the Lord would find him a really lovely home.

Quite soon Pixie, a lady from the Fellowship, came to see us with her family. She was a very keen rider and horses were her life, and her three daughters were also horse mad and strong, capable riders. They immediately fell in love with Zebedee, who lapped up the attention and fell asleep with his head on a convenient and loving shoulder. It was clear that he would have a wonderful, knowledgeable home with other horses and I was delighted. Next morning John came back on Zebs and it had been two carrot ride. So it was the next day, and the next. A bond was beginning to form between them and suddenly John didn't want to sell Zebs. In my impatience I had prayed two opposing prayers and the Lord had answered them both. I could almost see the wide smile on His face! It was a lesson well learned and, as we were to discover later, the whole episode was to have a very important role to play in our future.

CHAPTER TWENTY SIX

When we had been in Bindura we had met Larry and Judy, and their children David and Jenny. We had all gone to the Fellowship, but they had left to join another church in the area as they felt they needed more Spiritual teaching and also Larry was a trained musician and he had the opportunity to lead the music ministry in the other church. We had often gone to the usual Fellowship service and then made a ten minute dash across town to join in their service. Although we were a generation apart we were just so completely in harmony in our outlook and beliefs they had become a very precious and important part of our lives. Frequently we had gone back after the service to their home on a farm outside Bindura, where a Sunday lunch would be waiting with a good bottle of wine. The rest of the day would be spent invariably debating and delving into the Bible to clear up some point or other. They were warm, happy, sunny times that we all missed, so when they were able to come and spend a week with us we were delighted.

They arrived in time for lunch, and within minutes it was as if we had never been apart. The ability to take up again where you left off six months ago is a mark of true friendship. It was so wonderful to be in the company of lovely, Spirit-filled, born again Christians. We had naively presumed that at a Christian Retreat Centre we would have been in such company all the time, but having them there with us only served to show the stark reality of our situation.

Together with Anderson we walked the whole of the perimeter fence, asking the Lord to bless the boundaries. We claimed the area inside for the Lord and asked Him to bless every person entering through the gateway, that their time spent with us would bring them closer to Him and be fruitful. Then we prayed in all the cottages and rooms, that His Spiritual presence would be there, throughout the centre. When we came to the chapel we were in a quandary. We all felt that the catholic symbolism should go, so go they did. We took down the pictures of evil triumphing over Good, untied the crucifix from the plain wooden cross, and asked the Lord for His blessing on all who prayed there.

During the rest of the week the main house was filled with music, as Larry played guitar, flute or piano and we all sang along. We had another house guest that week, a Franciscan friar whose retreat was fortunately not a silent one! He joined in with unexpected enthusiasm and Dorothy came to meet our friends and joined us for supper, together with some friends that she had staying. At one point our Franciscan friend, who was usually so very well controlled and sober, was doubled up with laughter and tears rolled down his wonderfully transformed face! Wonderful, deeply moving, Spirit-filled days, and when we sadly waved them goodbye retribution was swift. All hell seemed to break loose!

We had expected trouble over the chapel, and our expectations were amply fulfilled! We wanted to fill in the cracks and repaint the inside walls, so we were hoping that whilst we were doing this everyone would get used to the pictures being missing and it wouldn't be too much of a shock when they didn't reappear. It would have been too simple! In blind fury we were told that we had desecrated the chapel. In vain we tried to explain our point of view. We could not agree to go along with the Roman Catholic faith. We enjoyed the company of those of that faith who had come on retreat, and in no way would we ever attempt to change them. Our's was a simple faith, based on the Bible and without dogma or 'tradition', and it was there for all to see, it is for the Holy Spirit to open eyes and guide people in the truth. We were there to welcome, share and listen to anyone who needed a sympathetic ear, but we would not compromise and deny our own beliefs.

Dorothy was not a Roman Catholic. She had no denomination and described her faith simply as Christian, belonging to the same Fellowship that we had joined. I pleaded with her to read her Bible, not to just follow people. To use her head and see the discrepancies between the teachings of the Catholic church and the teachings of the Bible, they were plain for anyone to see. I pointed out that several non-Catholic guests had commented on the chapel, and had been as uncomfortable as we had been. We got no-where. It wasn't long before new photocopies of the original pictures were once again stuck around the walls, but we were happy to see that the cross remained empty.

Larry and Judy had really enjoyed their stay, so much so that they began seriously considering the possibility of coming to help us run the Centre. This, of course, would have been wonderful in other circumstances, but it seemed that they were tarred with the same brush as us and were far from welcome. The situation was very tense and uncomfortable to say the least. I prayed about it constantly, and knew that the Lord could see our hearts and understood. How could we honour Him and give people the teaching and encouragement that they needed if we had to follow very non-Christian rules? I didn't want to own the place; I just wanted us to be able to pray to the Lord for guidance and then be free to get on with His work!

I began to pray that we might have stewardship of the Centre. After all, Dorothy had admitted that if someone offered to buy it she would jump at the chance to sell it and she had no real love for the place. Her actions, I am sure, came from her strong loyalty to Elizabeth and her beliefs, and also to the previous owner who was an Anglican priest. There was no way we could afford to buy it, but we believed that it was the Lord's and if He wanted us there He could arrange it. It was less than a fortnight later when Dorothy called and said she wanted a meeting. The word 'meeting' still fills my heart with dread!

We made tea and took it into the lounge, and Dorothy came straight to the point,

"How would you like to lease the Centre? You can lease it, have complete control and I will be out of it."

How was that for a direct answer to prayer! A figure was mentioned that was far beyond anything that we could raise, but we accepted the offer. If the Lord could offer us the lease, I was quite sure He could pay for it.

For the next few weeks the pressure came off. We were busy with guests, getting up at four some mornings to make packed lunches before cooking breakfast for twenty on the temperamental old stove. Then, as relationships with the owner improved, we noticed a marked change in Anderson.

His wife had gone back to Chegutu a few weeks previously to see her family, and we thought that he was worried about her or that there was a problem between them. Everyone worked on the farm in the mornings and then in the afternoons Anderson was free to visit families in the area and make his own plans as we had complete faith in him and his attitude towards his work. On two afternoons a week he visited local schools and on Sundays he usually preached at the little Chapel. I did feel a little concerned that we had no idea where he actually went on the other four afternoons, but when I suggested he should plan his week and let us know where he would be he became very defensive. He got on well with Dorothy and wasn't under any of the pressures we experienced. So life just went on, day by day, with our Pastor becoming more and more withdrawn and brooding. Several times we suggested he should come and talk, but each time he refused saying he would come later.

We had an Assemblies of God, Pastor's conference for a long week-end and we were very busy, then on the Monday evening after dark Anderson came and knocked at the kitchen door. I was cooking supper and let him in, and he announced abruptly that 'things were not alright' and that he wanted to leave. Without waiting for a reply he began a long tirade of accusations and complaints, right out of the blue and, with the best will in the world, untrue and unfounded. John had joined me when he heard the raised voice and I saw him glance at me in utter disbelief in what we were hearing. Anderson wasn't just angry, he really wasn't himself. His hair had been cut in a different way, which may seem a strange thing to remark upon, but haircuts can be very significant in the African culture, and he had also been playing his radio loudly on the local stations, which was right out of character. It was as if he were either possessed or on drugs, both of which were quite possible. As he continued to rage we heard ourselves accused of being Satanists, and then finally,

"I am going to do God a favour and kill you both."

There was no doubt about it, he was quite capable of doing so, twenty years younger than us and very fit and strong. I remembered the time in Zambia, when in a similar situation John had kept our intruder talking.

"This is not a threat, it is a promise," Anderson was saying," You will see this face again. I will come back and I will kill you."

"Then what will you do?" I asked him, "And where will you go?"

"I will go to prison, that's where I will go. Call the police!"

Abruptly he turned and went outside. Calling the police would have been futile and he knew it, the police always lacked transport and had to be fetched.

While this was happening, Lovemore the builder was having a bath in the spare bathroom just off the kitchen. He had kept very quiet! Now he came out and joined us in the kitchen, as amazed and shaken as we were. Within seconds Anderson was back again.

"Lovemore, why are you with these people? Why are you associating yourself with them?"

Lovemore answered in Shona, quite truthfully, that he had been having a bath.

"No!" shouted Anderson, "You are associating with them. Now I have three to kill!"

He turned and disappeared into the hot dark night again. The crickets sang on unconcerned.

Lovemore seemed equally unconcerned, although his usual sunny smile was absent. He suggested that as Anderson had said that he wanted to leave, we should pay him whatever was due to him in wages so that he could go. Of course, we had no money. Wages were collected from town once a month, so John suggested I should 'phone Dorothy and see if we could have a loan until the next day. This I did, and Dorothy arrived a little later with the money. We were more than grateful, but I had to get a receipt signed by Anderson for it.

"Why?" stormed Anderson, when I offered the receipt for signature, " Never before a receipt, why now?"

"Because it is a final payment, you want to leave."

He gave me a very long and unpleasant look.

"I have not yet left. I will be back to finish our business."

Suddenly he threw the money on the ground.

"Keep you money, I will walk to Chegutu, I am strong."

He turned and was again swallowed up in the darkness.

Lovemore went back to his house and John and I did the English thing and made a pot of tea. Then we started to try and secure the house. There were burglar bars on the windows but very few doors had locks, and once when the lock on the back door had stuck I had seen Anderson open it with a knife quicker than I could turn a key. So we barricaded the kitchen door with a table, and brought the dogs inside for their own safety. The door to our room we locked and barricaded with heavy tool boxes, and John suggested that we move our bed to the centre of the room away from the windows. He didn't tell me at the time, but he had suddenly realised that out on the veranda there were all the materials necessary to make a petrol bomb! We spent a very uncomfortable night, taking turns to keep watch and not really sleeping in between.

Next morning, with the coming of daylight and with Harrison and Lovemore around, things seemed a little less tense but Anderson was still very sullen and brooding. He took the money I offered him and grudgingly signed the receipt. He then gave me instructions as to where I was to send his furniture, at which my patience nearly gave out. Later that morning I heard the dogs bark and saw him going off down the track with his rucksack. That morning I was due to attend a bible study in Nyanga. I hadn't slept and probably seemed a bit distracted, and as I explained the situation quietly to one of my friends who was sitting next to me, there was one of those sudden silences and the lady opposite heard a few snatches. Quite rightly she suggested that we needed prayer and asked me to share with them all that had happened. It was so good to have their support and understanding.

We didn't know where Anderson had gone, so with his threat still hanging in the air and evening approaching we rang Larry and Judy and asked for them to arrange a prayer chain for protection that night. Their church took a great interest in what we were doing and were always willing to pray for us. Soon afterwards the 'phone rang. It was Anderson. He apologised, asked for our forgiveness and sounded close to tears. I told him he was forgiven. Then I rang Judy back and told her what had happened.

"Wow," was her answer, "That was quick, but we'll keep on praying!"

We knew that he would be back to collect his things some time, but work at the centre had to go on. A week or so later John had taken all the farm staff up to our infamous approach road to mend the worst places. I was quite alone in the dining room, which also served as a library, sorting through the books. Behind me a quiet voice said, "Good Morning," and I recognised the voice as Anderson's.

I didn't have time to think. As I turned to face him the most incredible thing happened. It was as if love was being poured down over me, like a warm oil poured over my head and flowing over my whole body. I was completely enveloped in it. Without hesitation I walked over to him and took his hand in both of mine.

"How are you," I heard myself saying.

He smiled, the old familiar friendly smile.

"I'm O.K. I'm going to go back to the Bible school at Chegutu."

We talked for ten minutes and then he went up to his old house where his wife was waiting. Later she came and bought eggs and a chicken. Then came the demands.

He wanted the bicycle that went with his job and the sewing machine that I had loaned his wife. On and on it went and the situation turned black again. By this time John and the men were back, and as I remained firm we came to another grudging agreement. John stayed in the background, out of sight, as we talked. Later I found that he had been standing behind the door with a hammer ready to defend me!

Later that day Anderson's wife left, but as evening approached we saw Anderson, still brooding and thoughtful, walking aimlessly around the grounds. We rang friends down in the Valley and asked if we could come and stay for the night.

We arrived back early next morning, and faced a final haggling about money and property, on which we stood firm. At last he came to say he was ready to leave.

"I will go now," he announced," you don't want to be here with a murderer."

His face wore a strange smile, as if he knew something that we had thought secret.

"How do you mean?" I asked, "A murderer."

It was an unpleasant smile.

"God gave me a dream. I saw you surrounded by a circle of people praying for you, because you were here with a murderer."

Larry and Judy's prayer chain!

We didn't see him again. He telephoned many times, each time asking for forgiveness, each time asking if we were well and how things were going. Through all this he remained friends with Dorothy and I think he rang mainly to find out if we were still there. We heard later from the locals that he had been drinking and taking drugs, but many rumours fly around African villages as they do in English ones. Anderson had spent three years at Bible College, graduated with flying colours, worked with us for three years, and come nearer to doing Satan's work for him than anyone.

The centre was full for Christmas, and the old stove turned out a traditional Christmas dinner for twenty five people. Sue, our physiotherapist friend, came and joined us - the only other white face. Our guests were a joy to have, and insisted that after doing the cooking there was no way we were going to wash up. On Christmas morning they gave us chocolates, and as we had a pastor in the group we had a lovely service in the little chapel.

After Christmas Larry and Judy came again for ten days and we had our usual wonderful time. It was the rainy season. We sang, walked and got very wet, had barbecues on the veranda and generally relaxed and unwound.

A shower of blessings.

.

CHAPTER TWENTY SEVEN

It was the first week in February when John once again woke with 'something on his mind'.

"I have a really strong feeling," he told me thoughtfully," that we should be in the U.K. by March."

It wasn't a feeling I wanted to go along with. In April we were due to take over the lease of the centre. We had people booked in for that month, we were beginning to see the light at the end of what had been a long, dark tunnel, and I didn't want to leave Zimbabwe.

"Maybe you have to be in U.K. by March," I suggested.

Over the next few days the thought became stronger, and John was more convinced that we should go.

"Something is going to happen to me," he told me seriously, "And I must get you back to your family."

It was a double blow. Of course I didn't want anything to happen to my husband, and also I knew that if we were to leave we could only do so by giving up everything that we had been working for.

"You realise," I told him, in tears," That we will have to get rid of the dogs and the cat, the horses and all the other things that are part of us."

He nodded, but he was sure. I rang Sue and told her.

"I don't feel the Lord is saying anything to me," I explained.

"I'll pray about it," promised Sue.

A couple of days later she 'phoned me back.

"The message I got," she told me, with a smile in her voice," was that when God told Abraham to move He didn't tell Sara"

Well, that had put me in my place!

So, I began to think seriously about the idea. We had three weeks to March. We had six horses, two cows with calves, fifty chickens, one cat and two dogs. We had an African family who had faithfully followed us for nine years. We had collected a heap of tools and equipment, some furniture and had our Suzuki jeep. We had no money. To go to the U.K. we would have to sell everything and the Zimbabwean dollar was worth very little. On top of that the things we had were not really the sort of things people would want to buy. So, as usual we gave it all to the Lord.

"Lord, if You want us to be in U.K. by March, then please will You sort it."

Then we began to get confirmation that we should go.

Harrison came to us and said he had decided to get his own piece of land and wanted to leave after the rains, in March. We had a letter from our daughter Jo, in England, asking for the first time in nine years if we wouldn't please consider going back to the U.K. We had been given an expense account to run the Centre on the understanding that it would be returned in its entirety when we took over the lease in April. Two guests sent us thank you letters with donations which made up the account to that precise amount, both cheques clearing in March.

The final confirmation came from Dorothy. She had re-thought her decision and had decided not only to withdraw the offer of the lease but asked us to leave. That seemed a pretty final confirmation!

However, the Lord rarely takes away our free will and we immediately received an offer from Sue who wanted to start a retreat on her farm higher up in the mountains. She said she had been waiting for all the wheels to drop off before she asked us! Sue had the perfect answer. We could move all our belongings to her place and then go and keep our 'Divine Appointment' in the U.K. in March. It would all be waiting for us when we returned, together with a new house that she was building. It was tempting, and we knew that if it was the Lord's will for us to do it that way then He would provide the air fares, but we both knew that it wasn't His will. We told the Fellowship that we were leaving and then waited on the Lord.

Nothing happened for a week and March was coming nearer. Then Pixie, who had come to see Zebedee earlier in the year, telephoned us at 6:00 a.m. on the Monday.

"I want to come at 8.00 this morning and collect all your horses," she told me, "we can sell them much more easily from my place, it's more accessible".

So after breakfast we set off with the horses, leading them up the track to the tarred road. Pixie had a two horse trailer and none of our horses had been in such a small box, but they just walked in and backed out at Pixie's home, no problems. Two by two she ferried them, an hour's round trip each load.

Later that evening a neighbour phoned about one of the cows.

"What breed is it?" she asked.

"Half Jersey,"

"And the other half?"

"I haven't a clue," I told her truthfully.

"Wonderful," she laughed," Just what we wanted."

Another lady 'phoned and bought the second cow, unseen. When she came to collect her she asked if we could go and see the horses and bought two.

John went to get petrol early the next morning and whilst he was waiting for the pump attendant a lady drove up in a car that was well past its best. She told John she needed a car like the Suzuki. John told her it was for sale and the next day she bought it.

We gave our chickens to Dennis and Doreen, our friends in the Valley who had so kindly taken us in that night whilst Anderson was on the prowl. We delivered them in the Suzuki, which her new owner had agreed we could keep until we actually left the centre, and whilst we were gone a stranger arrived on a motor bike saying that he needed tools for a training centre. Harrison showed him what we had and he left a note to say he was interested. Next day he bought them all for cash.

Sue bought the furniture as she was going to be building chalets, and a friend of a friend bought bits of veterinary equipment and the oddments we had left, paying twice the price that we asked.

Larry and Judy's daughter, Jenny, was thrilled to have Bess and Porgie went together with Siwi to one of Pixie's friends.

Within ten days everything we had was gone and we had enough dollars to convert into two single air tickets and a very few travellers cheques. Larry came to collect us and we spent our last week with them.

We arrived in London on the 18th March

ENGLAND

1999 - the Lord only knows!

' And the prayer of faith will save the sick, and the Lord will raise him up.'
(James 5 v 15)

'Blessed is the man who perseveres under trial, because when he has stood the test, he will receive the crown of life that God has promised to those who love him'.
(James 1 v 12)

CHAPTER TWENTY EIGHT

We arrived at Gatwick with three suitcases, a battered well travelled holdall loaned us by Larry, and the beginnings of 'flu.

Our last week spent with Larry and Judy had been a bitter-sweet time with a sprinkling of tears all round and sadness at our parting, but sweet because we knew that we were all in God's hands.

Graham and Marinella were now living in Surrey, and Graham had made a very early start for Graham, to meet us from the night flight. We stayed overnight with them and then travelled to Jo and Brian's farm next day. Jo had made a wonderful job of re-arranging their three bedroomed bungalow to sleep a total of eight people and still maintain privacy.

The following day was Sunday and we were whisked along to the local Christian Fellowship to which Brian and Jo belonged and then on to lunch with one of the Elders and his wife. We immediately felt at home, enjoying a welcome into this new Christian family, which was so much like the Fellowship we had left behind. And it wasn't just a verbal welcome, for within no time we had offers of furniture and anonymous gifts of money.

Before we left the Centre the Lord had given me a dream. I was standing in front of an empty cross holding my very familiar handbag and it was half full of my tears. I watched myself walk up to the Cross and pour the tears on it. I told Sue about the dream, and remarked that it would have been a much more poetic dream if I had been holding my tears in a bowl, not my handbag! Then I thought, well, my handbag is a symbol of our financial state, which had usually been the source of our problems. In pouring those troubled tears onto the Cross I had given it to the Lord and now he would deal with any financial problems. I was sure that this was the meaning, and it proved to be so.

We had been so sad to leave our horses behind, but in the stable at the farm was a three year old filly waiting to be introduced to a little work. John decided we would put her in harness to muscle her up and to get her quiet and biddable so she would be ready to back when a bit older. Within a few days Brian had located an exercise cart and a set of harness and then, true to English tradition, the snow began to fall.

The 'flu, meanwhile, had really taken a hold on us both, although none of the family caught it. I had such high temperatures and shivers that it was horribly reminiscent of malaria. Eventually both John and I went for a blood test, just to be on the safe side. Results showed that we were anaemic, but there was no malaria. The 'flu, however, got worse and was accompanied by a racking cough which kept us both from sleeping and lasted for weeks.

Thursday, 21st April was Jo and Brian's wedding anniversary, and the 22nd was Jo's birthday. So, with a double celebration in mind John and I set off in their car to get a few things for the farm, a present for Jo and a bottle of wine. The previous day John had been determined to get a small paddock ready for the pony. He had come back in the late afternoon having knocked in all the posts and strung up the electric tape as far as it would go. Now we would get more tape and finish it on the morrow.

We drove along slushy grey roads to town, the wipers pushing aside the soft, wet snowflakes. We went to a big agricultural supplier and found all that we needed under one roof. Jo had admired John's warm, quilted waistcoat, so we found one for her birthday present. Then, with the car piled high with chicken food, electric tape and various farm bits for Brian, plus the precious bottle of wine, we drove home.

Well, does anything ever go to plan? As the steak went under the grill Jo had to dash off to collect children from somewhere, Brian was late with the milking and the small house-group which met there on

Thursdays was due to come at 8.00 p.m. The chances of us all sitting down together gradually dissipated with the last of the snow as it trickled and pooled and slid off the window cills. We ate in relays, draining the last of the wine as the first group members rang the doorbell. It was a good meeting, sitting around the wood burner in Jo and Brian's cosy lounge and we made our way to bed around 10.30 p.m.

Soon after getting into bed John began to shake, his whole body trembling uncontrollably. Gradually he began to calm down and after about two hours he was able to sleep. Next day he was tired and sat around not feeling like doing anything. It was Jo's birthday and she came to our room to get her present, but John stayed in bed. For several days he just moved from bed to chair and chair to bed, and at last agreed to see the doctor. After several days of house visits, chest soundings and antibiotics he worsened and the doctor had him whisked into hospital by ambulance. An X-ray showed pneumonia. Ten days later after an intensive course of antibiotics he was eating a good three meals a day, and walking on swollen ankles with the aid of crutches he came home. We were all delighted, but day by day he went downhill again, until four days later he was eating and drinking next to nothing and his legs had swollen to the knees. We arranged a doctor's visit for Friday morning, but during Thursday he said he felt he wanted to see the doctor that day. At 6.30 that evening the duty doctor arrived and decided John would be better off in hospital, called for an ambulance and left. Half an hour later we could hear the liquid in John's chest bubbling in his throat and he began coughing blood. As the ambulance arrived he collapsed.

The paramedics were wonderful. Calm, confident and brisk they had the oxygen mask on and a needle in the vein within minutes. Soon John was giving them the thumbs up sign and off we went again on a blue-light ambulance ride. This time, as we reached casualty, I was expertly fielded into the little room you always see on T.V. where the doctor sympathetically meets the relatives to tell them the worst. I was joined by a nurse and an abrupt, tired looking, Asian doctor who started with,

"Well, you've seen him!"

I agreed I had seen him. I didn't add that we had been inseparable for twenty years and that I had been sitting by him almost constantly for the last two weeks.

"There are four classes of heart failure," he continued, "he has class 4. The heart is practically not working at all. If it stops we can resuscitate, but there may be permanent disability. What I need you to tell me is if you want the resuscitation."

I knew more sympathetic vets! I sat a few seconds and looked at this tired, hopeless man. What did he have? Certainly no faith, no hope and very little patience as he waited for the reaction he expected. The nurse glanced from one to the other and tried to soften the situation.

"I think a short resuscitation is always worth a try," she suggested, "Especially if he's active usually."

"You know," I told them, "We have talked about this."

I was so calm, no fear, no sadness.

"We are both strong Christians, John's not afraid of dying and I'm not afraid of him dying - although I want him to be with me, of course. We will just pray, and give it to the Lord."

The nurse smiled at me, the doctor walked out.

I followed them to find John. Jo had arrived and together we went with him up to the Emergency Medical Unit where he had been admitted two weeks previously, and were immediately greeted like old friends by the staff who remembered him. By then it was 3.00 a.m. and having seen him fitted up with a high pressure oxygen mask and got the thumbs up sign again, Jo and I prayed with John and with a feeling of absolute peace went home for a couple of hours sleep.

Next morning I rang at 6.30 and found he was comfortable and stable and the nurse said she would see if there was a message. In a few seconds she was back,

"Message is ' I love you'," she reported, and I could hear the smile down the 'phone.

I had to catch the bus into town that morning, and the early one took me the scenic route round all the little villages of stone cottages and narrow lanes. Bluebells were brilliant beneath the beech trees, which were just coming out in a haze of new leaf. On one side as we travelled down a narrow lane, a hill rose steeply absolutely covered with cowslips, and everywhere ewes and lambs enjoyed the warm spring sunshine. Bluebell time had always been special for John and I. I prayed as the bus meandered onwards and gave John to the Lord as He had taught me I should just a few years before. Unbelievably I was still perfectly calm.

That morning, at the hospital, I spoke to the consultant who had seen John previously. He was also less than optimistic and asked if I could remember when the electrocardiogram had been taken before

John's recent discharge. I could tell him there hadn't been one - which accounted for the fact, as he pointed out grimly to his staff, that no-one could find one. The machine was duly brought to John's bedside, there was a hurried conference and another doctor approached us. John had a leaking and infected aortic valve and needed an immediate heart operation. He was to be taken to Southampton by ambulance and would be operated upon straight away.

Again there was the peace and the calm.

To make the journey as stress free as possible John was to be heavily sedated and accompanied by an anaesthetist. Jo had joined us and we saw him sleeping peacefully before we left and drove back to the farm to fetch an overnight bag for me. My mother lived about ten miles from Southampton, so I would go there. We had bought an old, but hopefully reliable car, and Jo had collected it for me that morning - the Lord's timing again - so I had my own transport. I rang the hospital as soon as I reached my mother's house.

"Come right in," I was told, so I literally just passed through the house and arrived at the hospital to meet a young surgeon, who again stressed the seriousness of the situation, but with a surgeon's optimism!

A place had been found for Jo and I to stay overnight, so I rang my mother to say 'see you sometime', and went over to the hospital house for relatives. John went into theatre at 11.00 p.m. and came out again at 2.30 a.m. The operation, to them, was routine and successful - the problem remaining was the infection that had been on his heart and the pneumonia.

Jo and I sat next to him that morning in intensive care, talking to the nurse and holding John's hands. He was still unconscious and on a breathing machine, but the surgeons were happy. Jo and I continued to pray. Suddenly, the young nurse asked if we would leave for a few minutes, and we could see the concern beneath the outward calm. John's blood pressure had suddenly plummeted. When we were allowed back there were more people in the room, doctors and surgeons, all looking worried. Jo held my hand.

"Thy will be done," I prayed silently, over and over, "Thy will be done."

At mid-day my husband stabilised and began a long climb to recovery.

John was in intensive care for seven days. Free and luxurious accommodation was found for me in 'Heartbeat House', a beautifully appointed house a stone's throw from the hospital that had been set up for relatives of seriously ill heart patients. I had my own room and an added blessing was that everyone staying there had the same sort of problems and anxieties and we were able to help one another. It was a perfect time to witness about the Lord's love and provision for us, for when we are faced with death our own courage evaporates very quickly and reassurance is craved. We were quite a cross section of people. There was the young son of a very tough, volatile and voluble ex-SAS officer, who looked after his dad with all the tenderness and care of a mother looking after a fractious child. His father, a huge man with a bald head, tattoos and gold chains was to become a very good friend of ours during the next few weeks and for all his outward appearance he had a soft centre and kept pet chipmunks.

"Don't mind me askin', Missus," said his son shyly one evening, "but was you one of them flower children?"

For some reason I was very flattered.

Another guest was an elderly Yorkshire man, tough and outspoken, who told me, as we ate a quiet breakfast alone one morning, of how desperately worried he was about his wife. She was in her eighties and about to have an exploratory heart operation. He couldn't live without her he said, tears in his eyes.

"You must pray," I told him.

"Hmm. Well, I don't do much of that."

"Never too late," I told him gently, "Don't just worry – pray."

I think he did. His two daughters visited daily and from the odd glances that came my way I guessed he had told them of my attitude. I prayed for them and his wife, who was a few beds down from John in Intensive Care.

She went for her op. and during the night the telephone rang. I guess we all lay in our beds waiting for that knock on the door that would summon us to the bedside of our loved one. For me the knock didn't come, but the next morning the old man greeted me with tears. He had been called. His wife's heart had stopped and all support had been switched off, except for the monitor. He had stood by the bedside, quietly talking to the doctors and nurses. Four minutes went by and then suddenly one of the nurses exclaimed,

"Look at that!"

On the screen the heart monitor light began to blip, and 'all by itself' his wife's heart began to beat again. He had stayed with her until the early hours and left her sitting up in bed drinking a cup of tea. She went on to have a successful operation and left hospital in record time.

I spent my days with John. It was one to one nursing in large glass sided cubicles and as John was still kept below the level of consciousness I had long chats with the various nurses caring for him. Invariably they asked where we were from. The answer 'Zimbabwe' was also invariably followed by 'Why did you leave?' which, of course, was an open invitation to tell the whole story of the Lord's word to John about something happening to him and getting back to U.K. I was never disappointed with the reaction! The only time I hesitated was when asked by a male nurse, who sported a spiky haircut and wore an earring, but I plunged ahead anyway. I was rewarded by an understanding nod and the guarded admission that he was a believer and his dad was something very high up in the Anglican Church! Never go by outward appearances. He also went on to tell me of events that he himself had witnessed. There was the man admitted with a large brain tumour. The surgeons had given a routine injection into the tumour, which is done to reduce the size and cause minimal trauma during the operation. The tumour rapidly reduced and disappeared completely to the absolute disbelief of the surgeons. Another patient, a Christian, had been terminally ill and his life support was going to be switched off. His family and church came and prayed for him and sang praises to the Lord in the waiting room. Then his pastor, 'an insignificant little guy in an anorak', had gone to the bedside, put a hand on the sick man and prayed simply, " Lord, please give us our Jim back," and walked away. My nursing friend had been called away for a few minutes but when he came back he passed all the friends and relatives in tears. Instead of a body in the bed, however, it was empty. The sick man had suddenly sat up, pulled the breathing tube from his mouth and said apologetically, "Sorry, I really need to go to the loo!" And he rushed away to do just that.

As the days passed John was allowed to come up out of his sedation until at last he could hear me again and communicate in sign language, as the breathing tube prevented him from talking. So thumbs up, thumbs down, a wink for a nod and both eyes closed for a 'no', we became adept at reading his needs. As in Harare, when he had been so sick with malaria, I was able to sponge him down to lower temperature and massage his feet and legs. The first sign that he was really better was when he gestured by a throw away motion that he wanted the breathing tube out. When permission was refused a very defiant tongue suddenly appeared next to the tube. The nurse got the giggles and next day it came out.

The next eight weeks were a slow climb back to near normality with physiotherapy for the last traces of pneumonia and slowly adjusting to walking again – first with a Zimmer frame and then with crutches. I got permission to take John out in a wheelchair, and the first time he reached down with his feet and touched the grass he burst into tears. After that they couldn't keep us in. May was hot and sunny and at the end was my birthday. I had a sudden craving for chocolate and so I treated myself to a large bar of dairy milk and took it up to the ward. John was still not really eating well, but I broke two pieces off and put one on his bedside table. To my surprise it disappeared. So did the next one and the next. Together we ate the whole bar. After that he began to forge ahead until he was at last ready to be discharged.

Then John turned yellow. First a very becoming, bronzed tan effect, and then eyeballs the colour of free-range egg yolk. More blood tests and scans and eventually instead of coming home we moved wards. John apparently had an obstruction in the bile duct which was probably a gallstone. Off he went for a thorough examination and came back with a stent (tube) in his bile duct. Very quickly his normal colour returned. His doctor, a very tall, attractive brunette, had become quite a friend over the weeks and we always enjoyed seeing her. That day she came to the bedside, drew the curtains around and sat on the bed.

"We've found the cause of the pressure on your bile duct, and I'm afraid it looks as if it's cancer."

She got up quickly and made to go, the pen she was holding snapped in her hands and she turned her face away,

"Dear God, at times I hate this job."

Left together John just seemed to crumple. Pneumonia, open heart surgery, eight weeks climbing back to health and now cancer. We just hugged each other for a while, crying quietly. When we could talk we made up our minds. John was in no state to take more surgery so that wasn't an option. We would pray about it and give it to the Lord. The doctors were more than a little relieved that we had decided to just wait and see what developed and within days John was discharged. Fifty kilos, incredibly fragile and just itching to get back to horses.

All the time I had kept in touch, by letter, with Larry and Judy and with Sue. Their replies had been identical.

"How wonderful that you were both obedient to the Lord! If you had stayed John would never have survived."

CHAPTER TWENTY NINE

We both missed Zimbabwe. We missed our friends there and we sorely missed our animals, but we knew that God understands and that if it was His will then we should have animals in our lives again. Our dream was still to own our small farm and it would be wonderful if we could also make this a retreat for those in need. That was our dream, but I know now that unless it's also God's purpose for us, then finding our dream would still have been an under-achievement. With the Lord we can expect the ultimate.

Soon John's home country, Zimbabwe, was again in turmoil and the lives of our many farmer friends and neighbours turned upside down. As the Government followed its cultural traditions and asked advice from the 'ancestors', the result was there for the world to see. Death, beatings, hunger, poverty, cruelty, AIDS, a people and a country in the throes of death. A beautiful country, a warm and friendly people. Shall we cry for the country or shall we cry for the people? Neither will help, unless they cry for Jesus.

On our arrival in UK we had filled in the usual sheaf of forms and applied for accommodation with the local Housing Association. We knew that these things took time. Looking back I remembered how John would sometimes say, as we climbed the treacherous road out of the Retreat Centre,

"What on earth are we doing living in a place like this!"

And I would look back at the lovely mountains and the gentle slopes clad in the rainbow colours of the m'sasa trees and retort,

"Well, we could always go back to England and live in a council house!"

And now the Lord had arranged just that. John came out of hospital at the end of June and at the beginning of July we received a letter from the Housing Association offering us a two bedroomed bungalow in a small village six miles away from Jo and Brian. Jo took us to see it and as we reached the village my optimism returned. An old, old village with stone houses and dry stone walls. A stream running parallel to the one main street, with ducks and weeping willows, and the gardens all ablaze with colour. As we turned into the little cul-de-sac where our bungalow should be we passed green lawns and flowering shrubs, clipped hedges, window boxes and vibrant hanging baskets. I peered excitedly ahead to glimpse our new home. Number 18 stood dejectedly in a large patch of bare earth littered with stones and half bricks. A few blades of grass poked above a haze of dying brown groundsel and a rusty wire on leaning fence posts marked the boundary.

Inside it was almost like a new house. The kitchen was full of brand new units, the bathroom recently refurbished and the whole place freshly decorated throughout. A little shed was built into the back of the house – and ideal workshop for John – and our garden was clearly the largest and backed onto a private green lane. In John's weakened state it was more than a challenge. By the end of July we had moved in and for a very modest sum had the whole garden rotovated. Brian came and planted the lawns, the Christian Fellowship supplied second hand furniture and essentials and soon the little house was full. We bought fruit trees and planted a little orchard and as John regained his strength the back garden took shape and became productive. We gathered heaps of blackberries and made wine, stocked up on logs and settled down to our first winter in UK for ten years. Gradually John put back the weight he had lost and our walks lengthened until we could do 6 kilometres at a stretch.

We still missed our animals. Suddenly there was nothing to get up for. No plan, nothing needed feeding, the days stretched aimlessly before us. This was a recuperation period, we told ourselves. God knew the sort of life we had always lived and what made us tick. When the time was right we were sure He had a job for us but we just had to be patient.

A year later we were still being patient and John was not quite so well. Then came the 'phone call from John's sister, Judy, in Australia. For her birthday she wanted us to go and stay, all expenses paid including the airfare. We were overwhelmed. We really had just one more dream apart from the ongoing one of owning our own farm. We wanted to go to Australia and ride a camel! And so we did.

John was reunited with his three sisters for the first time in 24 years. We had seven wonderful weeks of sunshine, sundowners on the beach (sampling the local wines) and just catching up with all the family again. We climbed up into the treetops in the Karri Forest where the treetop walkway took us 40 metres up. We strolled along empty, white sandy beaches and splashed in a warm crystal clear sea. We relaxed in the garden and watched parrots lining up at the bird table, and on our last day we rode that camel.

The flight home, with a 24 hour stop over in Singapore, was incredibly long and John was exhausted but happy – it had been a wonderful holiday.

The exhaustion didn't really go away. Little by little we walked less, gardened less. Late mornings followed by afternoon naps and early nights began to form the pattern of our lives and eventually as John began to lose weight we realised that we were facing the cancer that we had put to the back of our minds two years ago.

In the September of our second year, just a few days after his birthday, my lovely, lovely husband slipped away to be with his Lord. The 'something' had happened. Because of John's obedience in leaving the country he loved I was back with my family, surrounded by friends, old and new, and in a home of my own full of memories and all the little things we had chosen together.

The day before John died the Lord gave me the same text in our daily reading that He had given me before,

'Can two walk together, lest they be agreed?'

So, what now? I have no idea, but I know the Lord knows. Right now I feel He wants me to write this book, not because I am anyone special but especially because I'm not. I know that many people are struggling in this world with sin and misfortune because they have no idea what it means to have the Lord as their personal friend. Many don't believe it is possible, or they feel that direct contact with God is reserved for 'great men of God'. Many think, as I did, that because we were christened as children we are automatically Christians and will automatically go to Heaven when we die. A few evenings ago I watched a police thriller on T.V., where a kindly detective assured his partner that the person he had just shot and who, in turn, had shot and killed several people including her father, was now 'at peace' ! Very far from the truth, but believed in all the innocence of ignorance along with thousands of others. Being a Christian necessitates a positive step from us, a lot of learning and a great deal of commitment, for to survive as a Christian in a Satan centred world needs survival skills that have to become as natural to us as breathing. The Bible is the manual, the Holy Spirit our teacher and good Christian fellowship our encouragement. The established churches, in many cases, actively discourage the idea that the gifts of the Holy Spirit are for today. It is 'politically incorrect' to suggest that Christianity is in any way ' more right' than the many other world religions. But England was a Christian country, thousands of English people have been martyred for their faith, the Monarch is still head of the Church of England, although I hear that Prince Charles would prefer to be Defender of Faith, not the Faith, should he become King. We are told ' we all worship one God '. We don't! The God of the Bible describes Himself clearly in Exodus 3 v 15 :

' Moreover God said to Moses, "Thus you shall say to the children of Israel: 'The Lord God of your fathers, the God of Abraham, the God of Isaac and the God of Jacob, has sent me to you. This is My name forever, and this is My memorial to all generations'.'

It is 'politically correct' to pretend that we all worship one God. Our African neighbours in Zimbabwe believed that they worshipped the same God, but by ignoring the words of Jesus,

'I am the way, the truth and the life. No one comes to the Father except through Me.' (John 14v6)

they tried to reach the Father through their ancestors and found Satan.

If the politically correct Church leaders really believe those things written in the Bible and, of course, many of them don't, then they must believe that Jesus is the Son of God, and that the only way to the Father is through Him. It is all very well to be 'understanding' of other viewpoints, but if we profess to be Christians then we are not being obedient to Him, or effective, if we don't follow His instructions.

'And He said to them, "Go into all the world and preach the gospel to every creature. He who believes and is baptized will be saved; but he who does not believe will be condemned." (Mark 15 v 15-16)

Should Church leaders allow people to be condemned for the sake of peace? Should they be 'understanding' or should they be standing up for God's Word?

So that leaves the ordinary person like me, and perhaps like you, so confused that it is much easier to just get on with our lives and not bother about 'God and stuff' ! And yet, there is a tremendous surge towards all things 'spiritual'. Man is made of mind, body and spirit, anything less makes us incomplete, so we all need help to find the kind of spirituality for which we were created.

Ideally this would be the job of the Church, but here again we are encouraged to believe that the 'Church' means the Anglican Church or the Roman Catholic Church, or any other of the established Churches. In today's language, Church means an establishment, bishops, candles, richly decorated clothes, cold, musty smelling and daunting buildings, non-user-friendly prayer books where it is embarrassingly difficult to find the right page, sleep-inducing lectures and dogma. Jesus's church means people.

His people. People who follow Jesus Christ. Christians. It is so simple. The world hates simplicity! And Satan hates simplicity, there is very little for him to hide behind.

The 'great men of God' in the Bible heard Him because they were simple people. Shepherds, fishermen, even tax-collectors! The people who followed Jesus were not even good people. Prostitutes, cheats, swindlers. But by the power of the Holy Spirit they became the people God intended them to be. They became brave, unswerving followers of Jesus, preaching the message of the Gospel. God still uses people like you and me today. Simple people. People who are willing to follow His guidance and listen to that small voice within, which guides us into His ways.

He graciously followed me throughout that part of my life when I didn't follow Him, and did not let me go. Without going to 'Church' or reading the Bible, the Holy Spirit led me into the right ways, with that quiet inner conviction that disturbs a soul not right with God and brings inner peace when we return to Him. We all have that. For me, the Bible and the need for Christian fellowship was a natural progression. The emptier we are the fuller we can be of the Spirit. The fuller we are of ourselves the less room there is for Him.

We can fill ourselves with many things, not just sin. We can fill our minds and hearts with desire for all that the world has to offer, but nothing worldly will satisfy. There is always something even bigger and better to strive for, the ultimate always moves away to present the penultimate. The ultimate is God. He has no penultimate and to reach Him we don't have to strive.

In seeking bigger and better experiences the addict moves from glue sniffing to heroin and beyond. Satan is the ruler of this world (John 12 v 31) and is always there to offer more thrills, more wonderful experiences, more money, and more possessions. Only God can give inner peace, only Jesus can give salvation and eternal life. God created us all, whatever viewpoint we choose to take or whichever religion we choose to follow. Mark's gospel tells us, "preach the gospel to every creature..." (Mark 15 v 15). 'Creature' doesn't just mean an animal, it means 'that which is created', and that means all of us.

Again, many church leaders go along with the majority of the world and dismiss Creation in favour of evolution, a theory in which even Darwin lost faith. Personally, I would prefer to be lovingly fashioned by Almighty God, my Heavenly Father, as the Bible tells me I am, than to being the freak offspring of a monkey.

Inside all of us is the longing for something better, for the something that is missing, for spirituality. Satan is right there too, offering spiritist 'churches', séances, and many other occult practices. I heard just the other day of a 'Christian Spiritist Church', where one sings to Jesus and then gets teaching from a Medium. Just like our neighbours in Africa. Satan offers lies, God's promises are true. Peace and salvation come only through Jesus.

If Jesus isn't your personal friend, then you only have to ask Him. He says,

'Behold, I stand at the door and knock...' (Rev. 3v20)

He has made the first move by dying for us, the second is ours. It is personal.

'Can two walk together unless they agree?' God asks. Two. You and Jesus.

He wants to walk with us, and if we ask Him He guides us to people who will help us understand Him better. Our lives here on earth take us through a spiritual minefield, no-one can expect to survive such a journey without help, but help is there in the guidance of the Holy Spirit, in the companionship of true Christian brothers and sisters, in the promises of the Bible.

Nothing brings you nearer to God than living through His promises.

QUESTIONS ?
HAPPY TO CHAT -- Judy.
01258 861926
07580853478

Printed in Dunstable, United Kingdom